D1011220

*f*P

ALSO BY DINESH D'SOUZA

Illiberal Education:
The Politics of Race and Sex on Campus (1991)

The End of Racism (1995)

RONALD REAGAN

How an Ordinary Man Became

an Extraordinary Leader

Dinesh D'Souza

THE FREE PRESS

New York London Toronto Sydney Singapore

PUYALLUP PUBLIC LIBRARY

973.927
D'Souza

THE FREE PRESS
A Division of Simon & Schuster Inc.
1230 Avenue of the Americas
New York, NY 10020

Copyright © 1997 by Dinesh D'Souza
All rights reserved,
including the right of reproduction
in whole or in part in any form.

THE FREE PRESS and colophon are trademarks
of Simon & Schuster Inc.

Design by Kim Llewellyn

Manufactured in the United States of America

10 9 8 7 6 5 4 3

Library of Congress Cataloging-in-Publication Data
D'Souza, Dinesh, 1961–
    Ronald Reagan : how an ordinary man became
an extraordinary leader / Dinesh D'Souza.
        p.   cm.
    1. Reagan, Ronald.   2. United States—Politics
and government—1981–1989.   I. Title.
E876.D83   1997
973.927'092—dc21   97-31396
                                                    CIP

ISBN 0-684-84428-1

For my grandparents,

Joe and Irene D'Souza

What can the young give back,

But love and gratitude

Contents

—

Acknowledgments

———

This book is based not only on the published record of the Reagan era but also on more than a hundred interviews with people who participated in Reagan's life and in the major events of his presidency. In addition, I draw on my experience as a domestic policy analyst in the Reagan White House in order to make personal observations about the man. My research assistant, Nita Parekh, was indispensable to this study, helping with all facets of the book from setting up interviews to checking facts and offering valuable suggestions at every stage. I also appreciate the help of my intern, Doug Robertson. The staff at the Reagan Library in Simi Valley, California, where I conducted some of my research, was unfailingly courteous and helpful. I can only partially list the people I interviewed or whose advice I solicited, but I especially wish to thank: Elliot Abrams, Kenneth Adelman, Richard Allen, Brian Anderson, Martin Anderson, Hadley Arkes, Leon Aron, Michael Barone, Jeffrey Bell, Walter Berns, Tom Bethell, Morton Blackwell, Lou Cannon, Kenneth Cribb, Paul Dietrich, Paula Dobriansky, Sam Donaldson, Gregory Fossedal, Hillel Fradkin, David Frum, Michael Fumento, Jeff Gedmin, David Gergen, David Gerson, George Gilder, Josh Gilder, Mikhail Gorbachev, Rachael Hammer, Peter Hannaford, Owen Harries, Václav Havel, Charles Heatherly, Ed Hoffman, David Horowitz, Jim Johnston,

Father Michael K. Jones, Clark Judge, Charles Kesler, Mark Kielb, Jeane Kirkpatrick, William Kristol, Paul Laxalt, Michael Ledeen, Lawrence Lindsey, Fang Lizhi, Dan Mahoney, Harvey Mansfield, Edwin Meese, Allan Meltzer, Adam Meyerson, Stephen Moore, Joshua Muravchik, David Murray, Peggy Noonan, Grover Norquist, Michael Novak, Pavel Palazhchenko, Thomas Pangle, Ranna Parekh, Richard Perle, James Piereson, Burton Pines, Richard Pipes, Wladyslaw Pleszczynski, John Podhoretz, Ramesh Ponnuru, Jonathan Rauch, Robert Rector, Robert Reilly, Amy Ridenour, William Schneider, George Shultz, Steven Silverman, Joseph Sobran, Christina Sommers, Matthew Spalding, Herbert Stein, Irwin Stelzer, Donald Sutherland, Michael Uhlmann, Scott Walter, Ben Wattenberg, Paul Weyrich, Faith Whittlesey, George Will, James Q. Wilson, Richard Wirthlin, and Fareed Zakaria.

I am immensely grateful to the American Enterprise Institute, which allows me the freedom to undertake my research projects, and to its president, Christopher DeMuth, for his leads and suggestions. I am pleased to acknowledge that the John Olin Foundation has provided me with research support for several years. As with my previous books, Adam Bellow's editorial guidance has proved invaluable. My agent, Raphael Sagalyn, helped shape the concept for this book and managed my business affairs. My wife, Dixie, whom I first met at the Reagan White House in 1987, has been a constant source of love and encouragement, and a vital source of advice and constructive criticism. As for little Danielle, her presence has greatly strengthened my optimistic outlook toward life, a contribution that Reagan would have understood and approved.

Self-portrait, 1981

Prologue

The Wise Men and the Dummy

SOMETIMES IT REALLY HELPS to be a dummy. Consider the dinner that took place in mid-1985 at Republican grande dame Clare Boothe Luce's apartment in Washington, D.C. Conservative luminaries George Will and Michael Novak were there, and they were taken aback when their president, Ronald Reagan, who was scheduled to meet in Geneva with the new Soviet leader, Mikhail Gorbachev, revealed his naiveté to them in the following way. "I only wish that I could get in a helicopter with Gorbachev," Reagan said, "and fly over the United States. I would ask him to point to people's homes, and we could stop at some of them. Then he would see how Americans live, in clean and lovely homes, with a second car or a boat in the driveway. If I can just get through to him about the difference between our two systems, I really think we could see big changes in the Soviet Union." At this point, Novak recalled, his glance met Will's across the table, and both of them rolled their eyes and sighed.

"Our view," Novak recently told me, "was that it was foolish bordering on suicidal to think that the Soviet leaders would respond to personal initiatives. We thought in terms of a totalitarian system. The particular leader of the Soviet Union didn't matter, because it was the system that dictated policy. It was a bit of a shock, and an unpleasant one, to see that Reagan didn't share our view at all." Novak permitted himself a nervous chuckle. "It really makes you wonder, doesn't it? What did he know that we didn't?"

Wise men from the fields of politics, economics, and divinity issued Solomonic pronouncements about the Soviet Union throughout the 1980s that now make for informative reading. Here is the Reverend Billy Graham, commenting on material conditions on returning from a 1982 trip to the Soviet Union: "The meals I had are among the finest I have ever eaten. In the United States you have to be a millionaire to have caviar, but I have had caviar with almost every meal."[1]

Perhaps this eminent clergyman, possessed by a religious afflatus, was misled by his Russian hosts, so let us consult a more objective source. In 1982, the learned Sovietologist Seweryn Bialer of Columbia University wrote in *Foreign Affairs,* "The Soviet Union is not now, nor will it be during the next decade, in the throes of a true systemic crisis, for it boasts enormous unused reserves of political and social stability."[2] This view was seconded that same year by historian and *eminence grise* Arthur Schlesinger, Jr., who observed that "those in the United States who think the Soviet Union is on the verge of economic and social collapse [are] wishful thinkers" who are only "kidding themselves."[3]

John Kenneth Galbraith, the distinguished Harvard economist, wrote in 1984: "That the Soviet system has made great material progress in recent years is evident both from the statistics and from the general urban scene.... One sees it in the appearance of well-being of the people on the streets . . . and the general aspect of restaurants, theaters, and shops. . . . Partly, the Russian system succeeds because, in contrast with the Western industrial economies, it makes full use of its manpower."[4]

Equally imaginative was the assessment of Paul Samuelson of the Massachusetts Institute of Technology, a Nobel laureate in economics, writing in the 1985 edition of his widely used textbook: "What counts is results, and there can be no doubt that the Soviet planning system has been a powerful engine for economic growth. . . . The Soviet model has surely demonstrated that a command economy is capable of mobilizing resources for rapid growth."[5]

James Reston, the renowned columnist of the *New York Times,* in June 1985 revealed his capacity for sophisticated evenhandedness when he dismissed the possibility of the collapse of communism on the grounds that Soviet problems were no different from those of the United States: "It's clear that the ideologies of Communism, socialism and capitalism are all in trouble."[6]

But the genius award undoubtedly goes to Lester Thurow, economist and well-known author, who, as late as 1989, wrote, "Can economic command significantly . . . accelerate the growth process? The remarkable performance of the Soviet Union suggests that it can. . . . Today it is a country whose economic achievements bear comparison with those of the United States."[7]

Wise men tend to be impatient with dummies, and thus we can understand the tone of indignation with which Strobe Talbott, a senior correspondent at *Time* and later an official in the Clinton State Department, faulted officials in the Reagan administration for espousing "the early fifties goal of rolling back Soviet domination of Eastern Europe," an objective he considered misguided and unrealistic. "Reagan is counting on American technological and economic predominance to prevail in the end," Talbott scoffed, adding that if the Soviet economy was in a crisis of any kind, "it is a permanent, institutionalized crisis with which the U.S.S.R. has learned to live."[8]

Equally scornful was Sovietologist Stephen Cohen of Princeton University, who wrote in 1983: "All evidence indicates that the Reagan administration has abandoned both containment and détente for a very different objective: destroying the Soviet Union as a world power and possibly even its Communist system."[9]

Finally, a wise man gets something right. But then he spoils it by condemning Reagan for pursuing a wrongheaded and suicidal objective, one that revealed that the president was suffering from "a potentially fatal form of Sovietophobia . . . a pathological rather than a healthy response to the Soviet Union."[10]

Perhaps one should not be too hard on the wise men. After all, explains Arthur Schlesinger, Jr., in the aftermath of the Soviet collapse: "History has an abiding capacity to outwit our certitudes." The wise men may have been wrong, Schlesinger concedes, but then *"no one foresaw these changes."*[11]

But here is the problem with this view. *The dummy foresaw them!* Consider what he said long before the wise men issued their pronouncements. In June 1980, Ronald Reagan met with a group of editors at the *Washington Post*. As reporter Lou Cannon, who arranged the meeting, recalled the incident to me, his colleagues expressed grave concerns that Reagan was escalating the arms race. Reagan told them not to worry: "The Soviets can't compete with us." Everyone around the table was astonished, because no one shared Reagan's presumption of Soviet economic vulnerability. Yet Reagan assured them, "I'll get the Soviets to the negotiating table." Cannon recalls, "When he said that, nobody believed him."

In 1981, Reagan told the students and faculty at the University of Notre Dame, "The West won't contain Communism. It will transcend Communism. It will dismiss it as some bizarre chapter in human history whose last pages are even now being written."[12] He repeated this theme, in almost exactly the same words, in a subsequent speech in Orlando before the National Association of Evangelicals.[13]

How dumb can you get? From the wise men's point of view, Reagan's rhetoric was too inane and outlandish to take seriously. But Reagan wouldn't stop. In 1982, he addressed the British Parliament in London. "In an ironic sense," Reagan said, "Karl Marx was right. We are witnessing today a great revolutionary crisis. . . . But the crisis is happening not in the free, non-Marxist West, but in the home of Marxism-Leninism, the Soviet Union." Reagan added that "it is the Soviet Union that runs against the tide of history by denying freedom and human dignity to its citizens," and he predicted that if the Western alliance remained strong, it would produce a "march of freedom and democracy which will leave Marxism-Leninism on the ash-heap of history."[14]

The wise men could hardly contain their derision: Give the man a brain transplant. In 1987, Reagan spoke at the Brandenburg Gate in West Berlin. "In the Communist world," he said, "we see failure, technological backwardness, declining standards. . . . Even today, the Soviet Union cannot feed itself." Thus the "inescapable conclusion" in his view was that "freedom is the victor." Then Reagan said, "General Secretary Gorbachev. . . . Come here to this gate. Mr. Gorbachev, open this gate. Mr. Gorbachev, tear down this wall."[15]

Not long after this, the wall did come tumbling down, and Reagan's prophecies all came true. The most powerful empire in human history imploded. These were not just results Reagan predicted. He intended the outcome. He advocated policies that were aimed at producing it. He was denounced for those policies. Yet in the end, his objective was achieved.

If Reagan was such a fool, what does that make the wise men? What does that make us?

Chapter One

Why Reagan
Gets No Respect

RONALD REAGAN DID MORE than any other single man in the second half of the twentieth century to shape our world, yet his presidency and his character remain little understood and often grossly misunderstood. Any intelligent examination of Reagan must begin with the recognition that he was a mystery personally and politically. Most people find this difficult to believe, because during his two terms in office Reagan established an intimate television rapport with us. Whether we approve or disapprove of his policies, we think that we know him. Yet we forget that he was an actor.

Lou Cannon, who has covered Reagan journalistically since the 1960s and written three books about him, told me, "I regard Reagan as a puzzle. I am still trying to understand the man." Virtually everyone who knew Reagan well or observed him closely would agree. They are familiar with the public Reagan, but their efforts to discover the individual behind the mask have proved frustratingly elusive. Historian Edmund Morris, Reagan's official biographer, confesses that from a personal or human point of view, Reagan is the most incomprehensible figure he has ever encountered.[1] Reagan's chief of staff, Donald Regan, who felt an Irish affinity with the president, writes that despite his best efforts, he couldn't figure out his boss at all.[2]

Even Reagan's family found him enigmatic and impenetrable. His four children confess that, in many ways, he was a stranger to them. "I never knew who he was, I could never get through to him," remarked Patti Davis.[3] "You get just so far, and then the curtain drops," Ron Reagan told a reporter.[4] "He doesn't like to open himself up, even with us," Maureen Reagan wrote in her autobiography.[5] Reagan's adopted son, Michael Reagan, revealingly titled his book about his relationship with his father, *On the Outside Looking In.* The conventional view is that Reagan had such a close relationship with his wife that even the children felt excluded. Yet Nancy Reagan also felt that there was a part of Reagan that was inaccessible to her. "There's a wall around him," she writes. "He lets me come closer than anyone else, but there are times when even I feel that barrier."[6]

Peggy Noonan, a shrewd observer of Reagan and one of his star speechwriters, told me that his life was "paradox all the way down." Here was a man who had the most important job in the world, yet he seemed relaxed, even casual, about the way he went about it. He seemed determined to transform the size and role of the federal government, but he seemed curiously detached from its everyday operations. Even though he was the most ideological man to occupy the White House in half a century, he was the furthest thing from an intellectual. Indeed, he provoked the derision of the intelligentsia and many in the press; even his own aides condescended to him; yet he laughed it all off and didn't seem to mind the scorn. He was comfortable consorting with aristocrats and playing golf with millionaires, who considered him one of them, yet he was equally at home with miners and construction workers, who were convinced that he shared their values and had their interests at heart. Few other presidents have enjoyed greater public accolades and affection, yet none of it appeared to satisfy a deep emotional need in him; he was far too self-contained for that. He was gregarious and liked people, yet he allowed virtually no one to get close to him. As president, he often spoke of God and championed a restoration of spiritual values in American life and politics, but he didn't go to church. He was an avid exponent of "family values," yet he was divorced, had strained relationships with his children, and rarely saw his grandchildren.

The political mystery surrounding Reagan was well expressed by his national security adviser, Robert McFarlane, in a conversation with Secretary of State George Shultz. "He knows so little," McFarlane said, "and accomplishes so much."[7] Richard Nixon made the same point at the opening ceremonies for the Reagan Library in 1991. Earlier, Nixon had visited Reagan in the White House and tried to engage him in a discussion of Marxist ideas and Soviet strategy, but Reagan simply wasn't interested; instead, he regaled Nixon with jokes about Soviet farmers who had no incentive to produce under the communist system. Nixon was troubled to hear such flippancy from the leader of the Western world. He wrote books during the 1980s criticizing Reagan's lack of "realism" and warning that "the Soviet system will not collapse" so "the most we can do is learn to live with our differences" through a policy of "hard headed détente."[8] Yet two and a half years after Reagan left office, Nixon admitted that he was wrong and Reagan was right: "Ronald Reagan has been justified by what has happened. History has justified his leadership."[9]

The American electorate did not regard Reagan as an enigma. During his two terms in office, he was a beloved and popular man who was also seen as an effective leader. In evaluating Reagan's leadership, most people used a simple "before and after" rule that seems to apply to all presidents: What was the world like when he came to office? What was it like when he left? For better or worse, a president is held responsible for the things that happen during his tenure. Most people considered Reagan a successful president because the world seemed a better place in 1989 than it did in 1981. For practical people who don't follow politics closely, this fact was decisive. Reagan himself endorsed this crude standard when in 1980 he posed the question, "Are you better off now than you were four years ago?"

Reagan won the affection of the American people because he seemed like a "regular guy," and they identified with him. Young people thought of him as a national father figure. Even those who disagreed with his policies were quick to concede that he brought dignity and aplomb to the presidency and that he had a twinkle in his eye and laughed a lot. How could you dislike a man who was asked whether he was too old to run for reelection at the age of seventy-three and replied, "What the devil would a young fellow like me do if I quit the job?"

People understood that Reagan wasn't an intellectual, but this only confirmed his identification with the average person. Sure, he made mistakes, but that showed he was normal.

Yet this public understanding of Reagan as a good-natured typical American, which predominated throughout the 1980s, solves neither the personal nor the political mystery of the man. Here was the son of the town drunk who grew up poor in the Midwest. Without any connections, he made his way to Hollywood and survived its cutthroat culture to become a major star. He ran as a right-wing conservative and was elected governor of California, the largest and one of the most progressive states in the country. He challenged the incumbent president, Gerald Ford, for the Republican nomination in 1976 and almost beat him. In 1980 he defeated Jimmy Carter to win the presidency in a landslide. He was reelected in 1984 by one of the largest margins in history, losing only his opponent's home state of Minnesota and winning 525 electoral votes to Walter Mondale's 13. For eight consecutive years, the Gallup Poll pronounced him the most admired man in the country. When he left office, his approval rating was around 70 percent, the highest of any president in the modern era—higher than that of Eisenhower or Kennedy.[10] He was one of the few presidents in this century to bequeath the office to a hand-picked successor, George Bush, who was elected president in 1988 largely on the strength of Reagan's success. With the election of many of Reagan's ideological offspring to a new Republican majority in both houses of Congress in 1994—one of the most stunning developments in modern political history—one may say (as political pundit William Kristol put it) that Reagan won his fourth term. Television reporter Sam Donaldson, who sparred with Reagan throughout his presidency, recently told me that if not for constitutional limitations and his physical condition, Reagan could have been president for life. Moreover, Reagan was more than a mere occupant of the White House. Throughout the world, his name was identified with a coherent philosophy and outlook that people called "Reaganism." He thereby defined a whole era; the 1980s would be inconceivable without him. He changed both his country and the rest of the world, and his legacy continues to loom large over the landscape of contemporary politics, dwarfing politicians of both parties.

How many ordinary fellows have accomplished all of that?

To the intellectual elite—the pundits, political scientists, and historians—all of this speculation about the mystery of Reagan's success is sheer nonsense. To the degree that Reagan accomplished anything, the wise men attribute it to "incredible luck," in the words of economist and Nobel laureate James Tobin.[11] Overall, however, the wise men do not believe they have to resort to blind fate to account for Reagan's success. Many of these professionals argue that, taken as a whole, Reagan's record is one of embarrassing failure. They contend that his short-term gains are greatly outweighed by the long-term liabilities with which he burdened the country. Even accomplishments directly attributable to his administration, they charge, are not his work but those of his aides, who handed him a script and stage-managed his performance.

In this view, Reagan was a thoroughly inadequate and inept chief executive. Like Peter Sellers's character Chauncey Gardiner in the film *Being There,* Reagan was a cheerful simpleton who had no idea of what was really going on, but happened to be in the right place at the right time and somehow managed to convince everyone that he was in charge. But even his critics grant Reagan one skill: he was a master illusionist, the Great Communicator, whose theatrical and oratorical skills kept his countrymen spellbound and cheering through the 1980s, after which the curtain went down, the lights came on, and most of us, at least the smart ones, realized that it was all an act.

This view may seem unduly harsh, but the cognoscenti mean it to be duly harsh. Many intellectuals are convinced that future generations will remember Ronald Reagan in precisely this way. History, the editors of the *New York Times Magazine* declare, is the "ultimate approval rating." In December 1996 the magazine asked historian Arthur Schlesinger, Jr., who served in the Kennedy administration and helped establish the Camelot myth, to recruit several of his colleagues for a collective verdict on how history is likely to judge American presidents. Schlesinger's list included historians who have apotheosized the New Deal, such as Doris Kearns Goodwin and James MacGregor Burns; Robert Dallek, a Lyndon Johnson enthusiast; the Marxist scholar Eric Foner; and two liberal Democratic politicians, former New York governor Mario Cuomo and former Illinois senator Paul Simon. Not surprisingly, these historians ranked Reagan in the bottom half of the "average" category. They scored Reagan even below his successor, George Bush, and placed him in the undistinguished company of Jimmy Carter, Chester Arthur, and Benjamin Harrison.[12] Other surveys of American social scientists have produced similar results.[13]

"There they go again," Ronald Reagan might have said. It is easy to laugh off such surveys, which tell us more about the pundits being polled than they do about the subjects under consideration. Most adults have lived through the tenure of several presidents. They know and remember too much to have their views altered by scholarly evaluations that can hardly be termed objective or balanced. Yet we now have a new generation of young people with no alternative source of information about Reagan. All they hear is the perspective of their teachers and the media. It is hard for them to detect even transparent bias under those circumstances.

Here is another example of how young minds are being shaped. When Adam Meyerson, editor of *Policy Review,* consulted the 1992 edition of *Bartlett's Quotations,* he found thirty-five entries from Franklin Roosevelt, twenty-eight from John F. Kennedy, and only three from Reagan. Even Carter had twice as many as the man whom critics called the Great Communicator. Moreover, the quotations from Reagan were hardly memorable; indeed, they were selected to make him look inane. For example, Reagan is quoted as saying that there is no shortage of food in America. Meyerson contacted Justin Kaplan, the editor of *Bartlett's,* who said he had made his selections quite deliberately. He added, "I'm not going to disguise the fact that I despise Ronald Reagan."[14]

Even with its excesses, the critique of Reagan is worth examining because it reveals such hostility on the part of the cognoscenti. The degree of animus requires an explanation. Why was this man whom so many people held in such high regard viewed by elites with such fierce derision? Moreover, stated in its most defensible form, the Revised Standard Version (RSV) of the critique is based on facts that we know about Reagan; thus there is a ring of truth to it. Consequently the RSV has made its way into the body politic in one form or another. It is no longer just the enlightened people's view of Reagan, as it was in the

1980s. It seems to have sunk in more broadly. Even some people who like Reagan and voted for him now partly embrace the RSV, and many who don't are unsure how to resist it. So let us face, as candidly as possible, the critique of the Reagan era.

First: those awful Reagan deficits. The RSV blames Reagan for attempting the impossible—cut taxes, increase defense spending, and balance the budget at the same time. Obviously, the critics said, that cannot be done; the numbers don't add up. So Reagan must be held responsible for what his budget director, David Stockman, termed "two hundred billion dollar deficits as far as the eye could see." The national debt tripled during his eight years in office. The Reagan years added $1.5 trillion (measured in 1990 dollars) to the national debt, more than was accumulated in the entire prior history of the United States. Our children and grandchildren, we are constantly reminded, are going to have to pay it off.

The RSV acknowledges that there was prosperity in the 1980s but insists all the good stuff was purchased on credit. "It was an age of illusions," writes Haynes Johnson of the *Washington Post,* "when America lived on borrowed time."[15] Social critic Barbara Ehrenreich is ashamed of the selfishness unleashed during what she terms a "decade of greed." She titled her account of that period, *The Worst Years of Our Lives.*[16] Who can deny in retrospect that the 1980s were a "me decade" in which many people went on a kind of national spending binge? This was the age of Michael Milken and Ivan Boesky, of junk bonds, corporate takeovers, and insider trading. The Reverend Jim Bakker installed gold-plated fixtures in his bathroom and an air-conditioned doghouse for his favorite pet. *Dynasty* was a top-rated television show, and Madonna made her reputation as the "material girl." Then there were those selfish yuppies in their BMWs, speaking animatedly into their car phones. These were all unattractive symbols of the Reagan era.

The end of the cold war? Well, okay. The RSV holds that Reagan deserves praise for signing an arms control treaty with an adversary he once called the "evil empire." But does it really make sense, his critics ask, to credit Reagan with bringing down the Soviet Union? No. The Soviet Union collapsed for internal reasons. There was an economic crisis, the RSV affirms, and finally the old men in the Kremlin had to face it. They appointed a younger man, Mikhail Gorbachev, and he dismantled the Soviet empire and ended communism. Gorbachev deserves the credit for ending the cold war. No wonder that *Time* in January 1990 named Gorbachev and not Reagan as Man of the Decade.[17] Reagan's critics insist that it would be wrong to give him credit for events he merely witnessed but did not control. In this view, Reagan was like Peter Sellers once again: when the processes of *glasnost* and *perestroika* got under way, he just happened to be there.

So much for Reagan's record. What about the man? According to the RSV, Reagan cannot be regarded as an effective leader because, let's face it, he just wasn't that smart, and he had a penchant for kooky ideas. He was, in diplomat Clark Clifford's view, an "amiable dunce."[18] Columnist Michael Kinsley charged that Reagan was "not terribly bright" and therefore "not up to the most important job in the world."[19] Robert Wright of the *New Republic* pronounced him "virtually brain dead."[20] Frances FitzGerald wrote that "he knew not much more than what was written on the three-by-five cards his advisers handed him."[21] Writing in *Harper's*, Nicholas von Hoffman confessed that it was "humiliating to think of this unlettered, self-assured bumpkin being our president."[22]

These observations will strike Reagan supporters as cruel, but it is not difficult to see how some could reach these judgments. Reagan graduated with a C average from Eureka College, which isn't exactly Harvard. At various points in his career, he was quoted as saying that trees cause pollution, and if you've seen one redwood, you've seen them all. Environmentalists were not amused. Later, when he was president, Reagan outraged scientists by confessing doubts about the theory of evolution. He expressed interest in the use of biblical prophecy as a guide to future events, especially the last days of the world, raising fears of what he might do to bring about Armageddon. He made a statement implying that intercontinental nuclear missiles, once fired from their silos, could be recalled. Tip O'Neill, Democratic Speaker of the House, who worked with Reagan, said "he knows less than any president I've ever known."[23] Reagan's aides seemed to be constantly trying to protect him from gaffes or issuing "clarifications" correcting his misstatements. Indeed there is an entire book of such gaffes, titled *Reagan's Reign of Error.*[24]

More broadly, it must be conceded that whatever Reagan's strengths, he was not an intellectual. He didn't have the historical learning of Woodrow Wilson or the encyclopedic knowledge of Teddy Roosevelt. He lacked the two characteristics of the liberally educated person: self-consciousness and open-mindedness. Even Reagan's defenders say this. Peggy Noonan writes that Reagan's life is proof that "the unexamined life is worth living."[25] He had a famous stubbornness to him that is the hallmark of dogmatism. As governor, Reagan liked to quip that he considered all proposals for government action with an open mind before voting no. Ever since he first ran for political office, it is hard to think of a single major point on which he changed his mind.

A second major element of the critique of the RSV is that Reagan was too uninterested and detached from the process of government to function effectively. Reporter Carl Bernstein, of Watergate fame, charged that Reagan was "remote" and "disengaged" in the White House.[26] Authors Jane Mayer and Doyle McManus dubbed Reagan's governing approach as a "no-hands presidency."[27] Anthony Lewis, a columnist for the *New York Times,* faulted Reagan for being "a president with a seven minute attention span."[28] He was said to nap at cabinet meetings. Author Gail Sheehy worried about the state of the nation while its chief executive went about his business "half asleep."[29]

In a 1986 article on Reagan's preparation for the Iceland summit with Gorbachev, *Time* portrayed a president who spent most of his time on photo opportunities while aides made major decisions. Reagan was "less the originator of policy than the chief marketer of it."[30] The critics' view of Reagan's disengagement was reinforced when he announced in November 1994 that he had Alzheimer's disease. The wise men winked at each other and exchanged meaningful looks. Publicly they were more reserved, but they knew that this latest medical information carried with it a subtle implication that, even as president, Reagan might not have been "all there."

There is no factual basis for the Alzheimer's accusation. Reagan was frequently examined by doctors during his presidency, and there were no traces of mental decline apart from the natural aging process. Aides who visited him in California during the early 1990s testify that he was in full possession of his faculties. When his illness was diagnosed, it was found to be in an early stage. Still, the broader point of the critique seems to be confirmed by Reagan's obvious lack of interest in the minutiae of government. He seems to have been outside the loop when major decisions were made. Nothing illustrates this better than the Iran-contra affair, which seems to have been transacted in the White House without Reagan's knowledge or approval. Reagan obviously didn't have Jimmy Carter's attention to the detail of administration or Bill Clinton's interest in policy implementation.

An incident at the very end of Carter's presidential term appears to illustrate Reagan's blithe indifference to the complexity of executive responsibility. Reagan had just been elected, and Carter felt it was important to brief him on some of the major issues that the new president would have to face. Carter went down his list, discussing various treaties and secret agreements the United States had with other countries. Reagan listened politely but did not write anything down or ask any questions. The information was "quite complex," Carter writes, "and I did not see how he could possibly retain all of it merely by listening." Yet when Carter asked him if he wanted to take notes, Reagan said no. Carter was understandably nervous about turning over presidential authority to a man like Reagan.[31]

By all accounts, Reagan persisted with this approach while in office. At a meeting of big-city mayors early in his administration, Reagan didn't even recognize Sam Pierce, his secretary of housing; he addressed him as "Mr. Mayor." At the beginning of his second term, Treasury Secretary Donald Regan and chief of staff James Baker decided to switch jobs. They made the decision to do this on their own. Reagan's attitude seemed to be that of the bored teenager: Whatever.

Conservative commentator Patrick Buchanan remembers a meeting in the White House where a furious debate over the issue of grain exports erupted between budget director David Stockman and Secretary of Agriculture John Block. Others got into the fray, and tempers were heating up. Buchanan looked over at Reagan, who seemed to have removed himself from the argument. He reached toward the middle of the table and pulled over the jar of jelly beans. Then he fastidiously began to pick out his favorite colors. Buchanan was amazed. What in heaven's name was wrong with the guy?

Finally there is the issue that Reagan's critics could never get over: he was an actor. Reagan's Hollywood background was seen not only as an unworthy springboard for an American president, but, according to the RSV, Reagan could not distinguish the fictional universe of moviemaking from the real world of public policy. Lou Cannon writes that for Reagan, "the heroic world of make-believe and the real world coalesced. . . . The man who lived in both of them could not always distinguish one from the other, and he came to believe in many things that weren't true."[32]

When Reagan announced his Strategic Defense Initiative, his critics quickly nicknamed it "Star Wars" after the popular motion picture of that name. Some even suggested that, in a case of life imitating art, Reagan probably derived the very idea of missile defense from the 1940 film *Murder in the Air,* in which he played U.S. intelligence agent Brass Bancroft, whose mission was to recover a secret weapon developed by America that would paralyze the forces of the enemy. Critics traced a number of Reagan's presidential ideas to old movie plots.[33]

The elites found in Reagan's movie background an important clue as to why he was so popular and why their disdain for the man was not shared by the American public during the 1980s. Many pundits argue that Reagan was an "acting president" who converted politics into show business.[34] His was a celluloid presidency in which aide Michael Deaver supplied the lighting and stage directions. Reagan's critics allege that he used his acting skills to bedazzle the people. Columnist Anthony Lewis called the president a "master magician."[35] Social critic Garry Wills wrote that Reagan "cast a spell," drawing Americans into a "vast communal exercise in make-believe."[36]

The wise men do not take a benign view of Reagan's theatrics. Rather, they charge that he was able to deploy his rhetorical skills to mesmerize the voters, distracting them and preventing them from seeing the world as it really was. For some, Reagan's title of Great Communicator was not intended entirely as a compliment; it was a veiled insult, as one Democratic party strategist made clear when he observed that a more accurate description would be Great Manipulator. Writing in the *Atlantic Monthly,* James Nathan Miller alleged that Reagan made "skillful use of the manipulative techniques of Hollywood" to con the American people into adopting his destructive policies.[37]

Critics complained that Reagan had a peculiar knack for deflecting criticism; Congresswoman Patricia Schroeder dubbed him the Teflon president, because nothing negative seemed to stick to him. Revisionist critics believe the reason was that the country was enraptured by "Hollywood on the Potomac." Reagan is said to have played his part so well that he really had the people going, at least for a while. During the 1980s we were, in journalist Haynes Johnson's view, "sleepwalking through history."[38] The Reagan era constituted, in author Sidney Blumenthal's phrase, a "long national daydream."[39] Then we woke up.

Perhaps it is not surprising that the pundits and intellectuals were so critical of Reagan. They accused him of being outside the mainstream of enlightened thinking about issues—and they were right. Reagan represented a challenge to their entire worldview. Moreover, accustomed as they were to calling the shots, they had come to see their perspective not as one view among many but as an objective account of reality itself. Thus they considered Reagan's challenge to their orthodoxy to be not only wrong but rude. Right when they were busy sorting out the world's problems, along came this corny Californian with no credentials or experience, armed with nothing but his own wacky ideas. He was able to oppose them successfully because he enjoyed a rapport with the American public that the elites never really understood.

Since many of these pundits disapproved of Reagan's views from the outset, regarding his policies as wrongheaded and destructive, we cannot expect them to applaud his success in enacting his agenda. It is human nature to judge the effectiveness of a leader based on whether we approve of what he put into effect. Incredible resources have been invested by Reagan's opponents since the 1980s to discredit his record, which in a way is a tribute to his legacy.

What is surprising is that since he left office, Reagan has not had more defenders from among his aides and from political conservatives in general. One might expect these former lieutenants and their ideological allies to mount a ferocious counteroffensive for the Gipper. No such luck. While his enemies have been excoriating him, his aides and allies have responded for the most part with a deafening silence. Their failure to defend Reagan naturally reinforces the liberal critique. Why the reticence? It turns out that many intellectuals and pundits on the right were, even during Reagan's tenure, ambivalent about the man and no less mystified than the liberal elite as to the source of his appeal. Even now, they cannot bring themselves to credit the remarkable events of the 1980s to a man of Reagan's unusual background, unscholarly intellect, and whimsical style. In truth, they do not rush to defend Reagan because they are a little embarrassed by him.

A reluctance to defend Reagan is one thing; outright hostility is another. No other president seems to have inspired less loyalty among his aides. There are a few exceptions—Attorney General Edwin Meese and domestic adviser Martin Anderson come to mind—but by and large, the memoirs penned by senior officials who served in his administration have been antagonistic and demeaning to Reagan. Even the legendary loyalist, George Bush, broke ranks with Reagan in his last year of office. How can Bush's 1988 promise of a "kinder, gentler America" be interpreted other than as an implicit criticism of Reagan? Bush was too much of a gentleman to put down Reagan himself, but officials in the Bush administration made no effort to defend the Reagan record, and sometimes they expressed undisguised scorn for the man. They seemed resolved to get beyond what they regarded as Reagan's amateur, simplistic approach and finally do things like true experienced professionals.

Reagan's other aides were no different. To judge them by their comments when he left the White House, Reagan was surrounded by ingrates and apostates. The memoirs of several Reagan aides are characterized by an almost defiant disloyalty. David Stockman, Reagan's budget director, presents his former boss as a tragically confused figure who "accepted but never grasped" the political consequences of his policies and who allowed himself to become the puppet of supply-side fanatics and hard-liners in the Defense Department.[40] In his 1987 memoir, Michael Deaver, a senior White House aide, portrayed the president as a kind of detached figurehead, whose statements and actions had to be carefully managed so he didn't embarrass himself. Deaver also disclosed that Nancy Reagan played an active role in many aspects of personnel and policy, lobbying her husband on issues from the homeless to Star Wars.[41] This portrait was reinforced by Donald Regan, Reagan's chief of staff, who confirmed the first lady's machinations and revealed that some of her actions on the president's behalf were based on her consultations with an astrologer. Regan depicted the administration as utterly lacking direction from the top and perennially prone to blunders. Indeed in 1986 he told the *New York Times* that "some of us are like a shovel brigade" following the circus elephant, cleaning up his droppings along the parade.[42]

Political conservatives are more appreciative of Reagan and view him as a successful leader. Robert Bartley, editor of the *Wall Street Journal*, published an unapologetic defense of supply-side economics, and right-wing magazines like *National Review* and *Policy Review* have consistently defended Reagan against his liberal critics.[43] A committee of conservative historians, recently assembled by the Intercollegiate Studies Institute to counterbalance Arthur Schlesinger's liberal group, rated Reagan in the top tier of American presidents.[44] Yet, although Reagan is fondly remembered at GOP conventions, his style and approach have had few self-conscious political imitators in the Republican leadership. Moreover, right-wing pundits like John O'Sullivan, editor of *National Review*, have expressed their doubts that the "Reagan model" is a useful one for conservatives to adopt now.

Speak to leading thinkers on the right, and here is what many of them will say: We like Ronald Reagan. We think he did an outstanding job, especially on foreign policy. His policies played an important role in bringing down the Soviet Union. His tax cuts ignited the economic recovery, but he should have worked harder to cut spending. His failure to shrink the size of government contributed to those large deficits. Reagan deserves credit for reviving patriotic sentiments after an era of national self-doubt, but he put off dealing with the social issues, with the result that he left American culture in worse shape. Still, let's not be too hard on Reagan. Yes, he was a simple man, but that helped him to communicate with the American people. He had only a few ideas, but they were the right ones. When you consider the performance of his successors, Reagan looks better all the time.

It does not take too much insight to see an element of condescension even in this generally favorable assessment. Yet the patronizing tone of some contemporary conservatives toward Reagan should not be entirely surprising, coming from people who were often dubious and in some cases dismissive of him even when he was in office. Toward the end of Reagan's first term, *Policy Review,* the flagship magazine of the Heritage Foundation, polled leading conservative politicians, intellectuals, and activists to ask them how the President was doing. Eight out of eleven were highly critical. The wise men of the right portrayed Reagan as a conventional Republican whose lackadaisical governing approach could not be expected to fulfill his promise to change fundamentally the landscape of American politics.[45]

Throughout the 1980s, many right-wingers expressed suspicion of Reagan's governing strategy. Conservatives perceived that there was a battle for the president's mind between the ideological "true believers" and the more moderate "pragmatists." From the perspective of the right, most of Reagan's deviations from the straight path were attributable to the influence of pragmatists like James Baker and George Shultz. During Reagan's second term, some conservatives grimly joked, "None of this would have happened if Ronald Reagan were still president." The right kept demanding that Reagan fire those nefarious pragmatists, but he wouldn't do it. Many conservatives privately complained that Reagan was a kindly old bumbler. They saw him as a malleable figurehead who could be easily controlled by his wife and pragmatist advisers.

I was one of those conservatives. In early 1987, at the age of twenty-six, I joined the Reagan White House as a senior domestic policy analyst. What could be more exciting? We were a generation of young conservatives who came to Washington in the 1980s inspired by Reagan and the idea of America that he espoused and embodied. The world was changing, and we wanted to be instruments of that change. Reagan was a septuagenarian with a youthful heart. He hired people like me because he wanted fresh faces and new ideas in the White House. Full of vigor and determination, we rallied to his cause.

But on joining the Reagan team, I found an administration paralyzed by the Iran-contra scandal and torn by internecine conflict. Far from altering the course of history, we seemed to spend most of our time on political damage control. No one—not even the president— seemed to be in charge. Everyone was concerned about perks and titles, but it was hard to figure out who had real power. Like many other Americans, I liked Reagan as a person, but like many other conservatives, I worried that he lacked the intellectual temperament and administrative skills to give new direction to the country.

When Reagan left office and his critics resumed their attack on his record, many of us on the right fell awkwardly silent. Meanwhile, the grand old warrior was spending the last part of his life in California. Recall the melancholy lines from Robert Burns: "The white moon is setting behind the white wave, and Time is setting with me, O!" He came out of the wilderness and then he returned, in many ways as much an outsider as when he first arrived. He was the lion in winter. What did he make of all this unpleasantness? Most people would be upset if their supposed friends, no less than their critics, spoke of them in such a demeaning tone. What was Reagan's own view?

One of his former aides who understood Reagan's isolation, Jeffrey Bell, recalled for me a conversation he had with Reagan on the telephone in 1989, in which Bell commented about how lonely it must have been for Reagan in the White House, given the way that many of his own people regarded him. Reagan expressed surprise. He said he hadn't felt that way at all; he didn't know what Bell was talking about. In 1994, Peggy Noonan wrote Reagan a letter, asking how he felt about the attacks on his reputation. Reagan replied that he wasn't going to "lose sleep" over them. When biographer Edmund Morris was asked in a C-Span profile whether Reagan was happy to see him for interviews, Morris replied: yes, but he would have been equally happy to spend the time with anyone else.[46] Here was a famous historian charged with establishing Reagan's place in history; yet, incredibly, Reagan showed no particular interest in Morris's final conclusions about him.

This book reevaluates the leadership of Ronald Reagan with the benefit of hindsight and greater detachment. It is customary for such accounts to begin with expectant idealism and end with mature disenchantment. When I look back at Reagan, however, I am struck by the degree to which I underestimated him. In rejecting the prejudices of the liberal elite, I adopted those of the conservative elite.

"No man is a hero to his valet," the old maxim goes. This is thought to be true because the valet is close enough to observe the defects of the master. Yet the deeper truth is that the valet's low opinion of his master arises mainly because he does not understand the ingredients of the master's success. The valet is the toughest guy to convince that there are good reasons that he is the valet and his master is in charge.

Even when Reagan proved us wrong and showed how effective a president he was, many of us in his ideological camp nevertheless failed to understand the secret of his success. We could not fathom how he conceived and realized his grand objectives, effortlessly overcame his powerful adversaries, and won the support of the American people. Many who worked closely with him are still bewildered. This study seeks to solve the mystery. In the process, I have turned my early impression of Reagan on its head. Previously I admired the man but had doubts about his leadership. Now I see that he had his faults as an individual but was an outstanding statesman and leader.

Reagan was not merely a successful president who belongs in the impressive corner of Woodrow Wilson, Harry Truman, and Dwight Eisenhower. Reagan was truly a great president whose achievement rivals that of Franklin Roosevelt. Only the two nation builders, Washington and Lincoln, occupy a more elevated place in the presidential pantheon. Reagan dominates American politics in the second half of the twentieth century in much the way that FDR dominates the first. On the world stage, he was the supreme statesmen of his era, a leader of the caliber of Charles de Gaulle and Winston Churchill.

Clare Boothe Luce once said that history, which has no room for clutter, will remember each president by a single line: "Lincoln freed the slaves," for example, or "FDR won the war and brought the country out of the depression." Thomas Jefferson wanted his gravestone to record three achievements for posterity—his authorship of the Declaration of Independence and the Virginia statute on religious liberty, and his founding of the University of Virginia. But he is mostly remembered for just one: writing the Declaration. Margaret Thatcher came close to composing Reagan's epitaph when she said, "Ronald Reagan won the cold war without firing a shot." Yet he did more than that. Most likely, Reagan will be remembered in the following way: "He won the cold war, revived the American spirit, and made the world safe for capitalism and democracy." No American president other than Washington, Lincoln, and FDR can claim a legacy of comparable distinction.

The impressiveness of Reagan's achievement is obscured by an irony inherent in historical greatness: great leaders are not always appreciated in their time. The British people revered Churchill during World War II, but in 1945 they ungratefully voted him out of office. As Churchill's example reveals, truly great leaders are sometimes shortchanged by their contemporaries because they abolish the very problems that tested their greatness. Today we recall, but we cannot keenly feel, the scourge of inflation or the dangers of the cold war, because after Reagan, those problems disappeared.

A second obstacle to understanding great leaders is that we live in an era that is cynical about greatness. There are grounds for our suspicion. We have become accustomed to seeing the high and mighty routinely pulled down and discredited. Yet democratic societies, which have always been accused of elevating the mediocre, have shown that they are capable of producing outstanding leaders like Washington and Lincoln or, in our own era, FDR and Churchill. These men were great despite their all-too-human flaws, which historical scholarship has excavated.

A further problem in assessing greatness in leadership is that those who study the subject frequently apply biased, self-interested, or arbitrary criteria that render their evaluations incomplete or suspect. Intellectuals, for example, sometimes demand that a great leader be an intellectual, even though highly analytical men like Nixon and Carter failed miserably. Moreover, as strong supporters of the New Deal and the Great Society, many wise men have tended to judge presidents who expanded the role of government as vigorous and successful leaders, while they consider those who slowed this trend, like Coolidge and Reagan, as lethargic, do-nothing presidents.

Conservatives, by contrast, tend to place a greater emphasis on character. Some of their animus toward Bill Clinton, for example, is surely driven by outrage over his acknowledged personal weaknesses. But who says that these traits, any more than scholarship and book learning, are crucial for leadership? History records many examples of exemplary individuals, such as Jimmy Carter and George Bush, who were poor leaders, while presidents with obvious character flaws, like John Kennedy and Clinton, have clearly been more successful.

A final obstacle to a clear perception of greatness is that historians and others tend to apply anachronistic standards in their evaluation of a leader. They assume a posture of superior understanding toward their subjects that is usually based on nothing more than the clarity of hindsight. Yet even the finest statesman cannot be expected to make decisions relying on information that only comes into existence many years later. As Churchill noted in his panoramic history of World War II, his criticism of his country's leaders for appeasing Hitler was based solely on the knowledge that was available to them at the time. It is now possible to read columns by pundits who insist that because the Soviet Union collapsed in the late 1980s and early 1990s, it was obviously destined to do so, and therefore anyone who regarded the Soviet threat seriously was a paranoid alarmist. Let us try to rise above this kind of reasoning.

Reagan's legacy must be judged against the conditions that he faced at the time. By any measure, his record is astonishing. When he came to office in early 1981, America was on a downward spiral in economic well-being and global influence. The most serious domestic problem was inflation, which had been accelerating since the 1960s and reached double digits in the 1970s. At the 12 percent rate of 1979–1980, inflation promised in the space of a few years to double the prices of basic goods and cut in half the value of savings accounts and pension plans. Prices changed so fast that a single piece of merchandise often carried several price stickers, and in a grocery store it was a common sight to see an elderly shopper on a fixed income reaching to the back of the shelf to find items still marked with the price of three months ago. When the currency is debased in this way, it is discouraging to save, and very difficult to plan, for the future.

Another serious problem for the Carter administration was the energy crisis, symbolized by rising gasoline prices and fuel shortages. Gas prices had soared from around 35 cents a gallon in 1970 to more than $1.50 in 1980, and politicians like Senator Edward Kennedy called for a nationwide system of gasoline rationing. In the election year of 1980, interest rates peaked at 21 percent, the highest since the Civil War, making it difficult for many families to buy homes. Hardest hit were those who didn't have jobs at all. Unemployment and poverty rates were high. Productivity was down. Economic growth had ground to a halt. Consumer confidence was at a low ebb. It was the greatest economic crisis since the Great Depression.

When Reagan left office, inflation was no longer a problem. The inflation rate plummeted during his first term, averaged 3 percent during his second term, and remained low under his successors. Interest rates fell to single digits. Housing starts were up. Gas prices dropped steeply, and the oil crisis ended. After the recession of 1982, the economy went into a seven-year period of growth, the largest expansion in American peacetime history. Nearly 20 million new jobs were created between 1983 and 1989. At a growth rate of 3.5 percent, the gross national product increased by nearly a third. The stock market more than doubled in value. Both poverty and unemployment rates declined. The United States reaffirmed its position as the world's preeminent economy. It became the vanguard of technology at a time of breathtaking progress.

In his 1976 campaign against President Ford, Jimmy Carter had developed a concept called the "misery index," the sum of the inflation and unemployment rate, to show the depth of economic hardship. The failure of the Carter presidency is encapsulated in a single statistic: the misery index rose from around 13 percent under Ford to more than 20 percent under Carter. By contrast, the misery index fell by more than half, to under 10 percent, during Reagan's tenure. In 1992, economist Robert Barro issued an economic report card for presidents, based on who did the most to boost economic growth and reduce inflation, unemployment, and interest rates. Of eleven presidents from Truman to Bush, Reagan ranked both first (for his first term) and second (for his second term).[47] Objectively, Reagan's record on this score is the best of all the postwar presidents, including Clinton.

Abroad, the turnaround produced under Reagan is even more startling. When Reagan was elected, capitalism and democracy were on the retreat in much of the world, and the Soviet model appeared to be in the vanguard of history. Khrushchev's boast that the Soviets would bury the West seemed a real possibility. Most of the Third World seemed to be opting for some form of socialism or Marxism. In Latin America, the United States's own backyard, guerrilla revolutions fueled by popular discontent against the old dictatorships apparently presaged a socialist future for the region. For the first time, in the 1970s, the Soviet nuclear arsenal surpassed that of the United States. The Soviets deployed hundreds of long-range SS-18 missiles, each carrying multiple warheads targeted at the United States, as well as a new generation of intermediate-range missiles, the SS-20s, targeted at Western Europe. Between 1974 and 1980, while the United States wallowed in post-Vietnam angst, nine countries fell into the Soviet orbit—South Vietnam, Cambodia, Laos, South Yemen, Angola, Mozambique, Ethiopia, Grenada, and Nicaragua—topped off in 1979 by the Soviet invasion of Afghanistan.

During the Reagan administration, all this changed. No more nations fell into the clutches of the Soviet bear. Capitalism and democracy began to advance around the world. On Reagan's watch, dictatorships collapsed in Chile, Haiti, and Panama, and nine more countries moved toward democracy: Bolivia (1982), Honduras (1982), Argentina (1983), Grenada (1983), El Salvador (1984), Uruguay (1984), Brazil (1985), Guatemala (1985), and the Philippines (1986). Fewer than one-third of the countries in Latin America were democratic in 1981; more than 90 percent of the region was democratic by 1989. In Nicaragua, shortly after Reagan's second term ended, free elections were held, and the Sandinista government was ousted from power. Apartheid ended in South Africa, and a black-majority government was elected. All these changes occurred relatively peacefully.

In addition, as part of the Intermediate Range Nuclear Forces (INF) Treaty of 1987, the Soviet Union agreed to dismantle and destroy its SS-20 missiles. A year later, Moscow agreed to pull its troops out of Afghanistan, the first time that the Soviet Union voluntarily withdrew from a puppet regime. The revolution soon penetrated into the Soviet bloc. Poland held free elections, and Lech Walesa became president. Suddenly all of Eastern and Central Europe was free, and the Berlin Wall came down.

There was more to come. In 1991 the Soviet Union abolished itself, and power passed into the hands of Boris Yeltsin, who became the first freely elected president of Russia. An era of friendship between the United States and Russia became possible as a consequence of the diminished nuclear rivalry between the two nations. So in the dawn of the twenty-first century the United States found itself the world's sole superpower, and its political traditions of democratic capitalism came to embody the aspirations of peoples everywhere. The century-old debate between capitalism and socialism was resolved.

These developments, both domestic and international, were no accident. Reagan was the prime mover; he brought them about. He was the architect of his own success. This is not to say that he transformed the world single-handedly. He had help—from Margaret Thatcher, Pope John Paul II, Václav Havel, and Lech Walesa. Though it is often exaggerated, Gorbachev also played a crucial role. Yet none of these things would have happened when they did, and in the way that they did, without Reagan. He was the decisive agent of change. This study explores how a seemingly ordinary man became an extraordinary leader.

Let me briefly summarize my conclusions. Reagan's greatness derives in large part from the fact that he was a visionary—a conceptualizer who was able to see the world differently from the way it was. While others were obsessed and bewildered by the problems of the present, Reagan was focused on the future. This orientation gave Reagan an otherworldly quality that is often characteristic of great men.

The source of Reagan's vision was his possession of what Edmund Burke termed moral imagination. He saw the world through the clear lens of right and wrong. This kind of knowledge came not from books but from within himself. Moreover, Reagan firmly believed that however prolonged the struggle, good eventually would prevail over evil. He was an apostle not so much of blind optimism as of hope. His hope had a religious root. Reagan was not a conventionally religious man, but he had a providential understanding of destiny—both his own and that of his country.

It wasn't Reagan's philosophy or his ideas that were novel. They were grand ideas, but they were not uniquely his own. He derived them from lived experience of the founding principles of freedom and self-government. Reagan valued ideas to the degree that they were anchored in the firm tether of experience. He understood the moral power of the American ideal and saw how it could be realized most effectively in his time.

To say, as even his allies do, that Reagan had "a few good ideas" is like calling Abraham Lincoln a single-issue politician. It is true that Lincoln focused both his presidential campaigns on one question, slavery, but great leaders view the entire landscape of events and detect which issues among many are absolutely decisive, and lay bare the fundamental question of what it means to be an American, which in every period of American history is always the most important question. Like Lincoln, Reagan had an unerring capacity to separate the things that mattered from the things that were peripheral.

Reagan understood Soviet communism with the same moral clarity that Lincoln had in understanding slavery. Both men were fundamentally motivated not by political calculation but by a basic sense of right and wrong. They approached evil with a pure childlike simplicity that sophisticated people take pride in having outgrown. Like Jimmy Stewart in the film *Mr. Smith Goes to Washington,* Reagan never lost his innocence or his capacity to be outraged. Although his country-boy style was often seen as revealing Reagan's naiveté, in fact he had a shrewd understanding of human nature, as well as a sharp political antenna, and he exploited the fact that he was consistently underrated by his adversaries.

Unlike Jimmy Carter, who forgot his priorities by immersing himself in a morass of detail, Reagan kept his sights on the road ahead. He understood the importance of the big picture and would not be distracted by petty detail. He was wrong not to recognize Sam Pierce, but the reason for his oversight was that he had no interest in the Department of Housing and Urban Development, which he saw as a rat hole of public policy. He knew that if he went in, he might never come out. By and large, he was right.

He was an intensely ambitious and even opportunistic man, but he was ambitious mainly for the triumph of his ideas. He didn't care about power for its own sake. Unlike many who seek the highest office in the land, he wanted to be president for one reason only: to realize his principles and improve his country and the rest of the world. He had a Churchillian tenacity about his moral and political beliefs; no matter what anybody said, he would never give in. On the fundamental questions, no pollster in the world could have changed his mind. In this sense, he was closed-minded.

He was extremely strange among politicians in that he was incorruptible and cared nothing for personal glory. Reagan had a sign on his desk at the White House: "There is no limit to what a man can do or where he can go if he doesn't mind who gets the credit." He courted the affection of the American people, in part so he could build support for his policies. But when it came to a point of principle, he was impervious to personal attacks. People in the elite media, the universities, and even his own party sneered at him and called him the most hurtful things imaginable. He laughed it all off. He didn't care what the soi-disant intellectuals at the Aspen Institute or the *New York Times* editorial page thought of him. He was truly rare in this respect.

Although Reagan was resolute in principle, he was creative and flexible about putting his ideas into practice. Those who called him an extremist and a dogmatist never understood that he was an intensely practical man, which is odd for a visionary. Yet Reagan's attachment to ideas was not purely theoretical; he wanted to see them implemented. He was patient and willing to compromise; if he could not get 100 percent, he would accept half. Yet he was a superb negotiator who usually got 75 percent: he drove an extremely hard bargain.

Like most other successful leaders, Reagan used his rhetoric and his acting skills as part of his governing strategy. If you think he was effective because he was a "mere actor," just try to imagine whether the same results could be obtained by, say, Susan Sarandon or Ed Asner in the White House. Reagan understood that leaders in a democratic society have to play a variety of public roles. He used his theatrical talents to establish his public persona and had a keen sense of how people expect their president to act. Although he never served in combat, as commander in chief Reagan proved more popular with the armed forces than his successor, George Bush, who was an authentic war hero.

Reagan was not an orator in the conventional sense. An ancient writer commented that when people heard Cicero speak, they said, "What a clever man is Cicero." But when Demosthenes spoke, the people said, "Let us march against Philip." Reagan was more like Demosthenes; he deployed his famous skills not to display his own eloquence but to generate support for his ideas. Once Reagan had won people over to his side, he would urge them to pressure their congressional representatives; then he would cut a deal that was very favorable to his policy priorities. His strategy in this respect was the classical one: he spoke in poetry and governed in prose.

Yet he rarely talked to the American people about the specific details of policy; instead, he talked about principles. He knew that a democratic leader must embody the aspirations of the people. Reagan did not merely follow the path of public opinion, however. Like a true leader, he worked hard to shape it, so that he could point out the best way for his country to achieve its ideals. He was a Great Communicator because he forcefully articulated the principles of liberty and equality that are at the core of what it means to be an American.

Good leaders understand that they often have to work with people who don't share their vision. Unlike his conservative critics, Reagan recognized the value of pragmatists in the White House; despite their disagreements with him, they helped him get his agenda through. He could not have done it without them. But while he valued the talent of his aides, they did not always value his. They thought they could do better. Yet, without Reagan's vision to guide their pragmatic skills most of them have done very little since he left and they went out on their own. More than one who served in the Bush administration had an undistinguished subsequent record.

Reagan was uniformly fair-minded and pleasant with aides but did not get close to them personally. He saw them as instruments to achieve his goals. People would work for him for a decade; then they would leave, and he would not associate with them—not even a phone call. Thus the conventional wisdom must be turned on its head: he wasn't their pawn; they were his. Eventually many of them came to recognize this, and it angered and frustrated them. His aides all wanted to be part of the inner circle, and they fought their way up the ranks until they finally realized that there was no inner circle—just Reagan.

Eventually his aides came to see how dispensable they were. They were not the source of Reagan's ideas, from the Strategic Defense Initiative to the Reagan doctrine of aid to anticommunist guerrillas. On the issues that he cared about, they didn't make any of the major decisions; he did, and often over their strong objections. Reagan went through four White House chiefs of staff, six national security advisers, and numerous cabinet members, but he forged on with his agenda. Speechwriters came and left, yet Reagan's message remained the same. He won his elections no matter who his campaign managers or political consultants were.

Reagan had lots of acquaintances but no real friends. This fact was hard for most people to recognize because Reagan had such a genial public exterior. He did like people in general but was indifferent to Tom, Dick, and Harry. People who wanted to be his close pal, like Donald Regan, found themselves gently but firmly rebuffed. It is in his relationships, not in his decision making, that Reagan can rightly be said to be detached. This must be recognized as a flaw in his character, but it may have helped him as a leader to endure vicious attacks with equanimity.

The problem of detachment extended even to Reagan's family. He seemed incapable of genuine intimacy. His first wife, Jane Wyman, realized this and left him. Reagan grieved but moved on. He was always helpful and decent with family members, yet even his children felt the icy blast of his emotional withdrawal. If he was close to anyone in his life, it was to his mother, Nelle, and his second wife, Nancy.

This is not to say that Nancy Reagan ran the White House. On the contrary, she was a socialite who didn't care about politics. She cared deeply about her husband. He usually listened to her on personnel matters. Reagan hated to deal with the low and conniving side of people, but he knew it existed. He trusted Nancy because she had lower expectations than he did, and she was willing to take tough measures to protect him from those who she felt were undermining him. When she wanted to get rid of someone, that person usually was gone. But when she attempted to change his position on substantive issues like strategic defense or support for the contras, he generally ignored her advice and maintained his course.

The portrait of Reagan that emerges from this book is one of a highly complex man, hardly the transparent or one-dimensional figure that both his admirers and critics are used to. He was a distinctive personality, not without flaws, but nevertheless larger than life. There is much about leadership that we can learn from him today. Our world is the one that he made, and our challenge now is to fulfill his vision for America. Whatever we do, the effects of his revolution are enduring. As he put it, "We meant to change a nation, and instead we changed the world."[48]

Chapter 2

The Education of an Actor

IN 1980, AMERICA WAS IN need of a new kind of leader. The problem was not just that the economy was in a mess or that the United States was losing its dominant position in the world. The problem was that in the face of these crises, no one seemed to know what to do. Two years earlier, Michael Blumenthal, President Carter's secretary of the treasury, conveyed the bewilderment of the experts when he noted that "inflation is caused by a number of factors that act together and interact in strange and mysterious ways." Economist Lester Thurow wrote that "to get a significant improvement in the inflation rate, the U.S. needs some good luck." In a confession of helplessness, President Carter himself told Congress that, at current consumption rates, the United States and other countries "could use up all the proven reserves of oil in the entire world by the end of the next decade."[1]

Carter was an honorable man who will be remembered in history for brokering the Camp David Accords that brought an enduring peace between Egypt and Israel. His philanthropic ventures in recent years, including his humanitarian service with Habitat for Humanity, may have vitiated public memories of his lackluster record in office. Yet there is no denying that Carter was a weak and indecisive president. Bewildered and frustrated over his own failures of leadership, he decided that the nation's problem was a kind of psychological disorder on the part of the people. Americans, Carter famously declared, were suffering from a national malaise, reflected in "a crisis of confidence . . . that strikes at the very heart and soul and spirit of our national will . . . threatening to destroy the social and political fabric of America." Carter worried that people had taken for granted that they would live better than their parents and that America would be the world's leader. These expectations, Carter suggested, needed to be modified. Americans, he emphasized, would have to learn to live with less. The new era would be an era of limits.[2]

Carter's invertebrate leadership was dramatized by the hostage crisis of 1979. On November 4, a mob of Iranian extremists invaded the U.S. embassy in Tehran, seized fifty-two American hostages, and held them captive. President Carter tried freezing Iranian assets in the United States and appealing to the United Nations, but none of his economic and diplomatic initiatives worked. For more than a year, Americans were treated to lurid images of mullahs, led by the Ayatollah Khomeini, who denounced the United States as a collective "great Satan." Every day people turned on their television sets to see throngs of men and women burning American flags in the streets of Iran and chanting "Death to America."

Finally Carter ended his vacillation and hastily approved a rescue attempt, which failed miserably in the desert southeast of Tehran. One helicopter flew into a sandstorm and lost the use of its gyroscope, two others malfunctioned, and a fourth crashed into a transport plane carrying Delta Force commandos and blew up. Because the gas fires were likely to alert the Iranians, the mission was aborted. For many Americans, the sight of dead U.S. soldiers surrounded by dancing Iranian militants symbolized the humiliation of the nation, the dysfunctional condition of its military equipment, and the impotence of its leadership in the election year of 1980.

In this time of ignominy and crisis, when the very issue of national identity was at stake, Americans needed a leader of unusual vision and determination. The country required a statesman who would not accept his country's decline as an inevitable fate. Such a leader would need to find creative solutions to domestic and international problems that had eluded the most sophisticated minds and were the source of national demoralization. Even more important, he had to have the skills to navigate the treacherous currents of politics, in order to win legislative victories and put his programs into effect. Since even the best remedies take time, he would require tremendous resources of patience and tenacity, so as not to be distracted from his goals. Moreover, in a democratic society like the United States, such a leader required the ability to win the support of a large majority. The nation's woes called for nothing less than a man who could turn the tide of history and renew the American spirit.

In California, there was such a man.

When Reagan was first elected in 1980, the reaction from most intellectuals and elite media was one of disbelief. They didn't just consider him unqualified or "nowhere near presidential," as journalist Hedley Donovan wrote.[3] They considered him a howling idiot, a reactionary kook, a dangerous warmonger. Columnist William Greider summed up the sentiment of many reporters: "My God, they've elected this guy who nine months ago we thought was a hopeless clown. There's something going on here that we don't understand."[4]

In the period leading up to Reagan's election, many pundits were candid in expressing what they really thought about him. "Ronald Reagan is an ignoramus," opined John Osborne in the *New Republic* in June 1980.[5] He was seen as a man of another era, a curious relic. "Reagan seems to be a nostalgic figure whose time has passed," Richard Reeves wrote in *Esquire* in May 1979.[6] Others were genuinely frightened because they considered Reagan's views reactionary. "He is the most dangerous person ever to come this close to the presidency," warned the *Nation* on November 1, 1980. "He is a menace to the human race."[7] Economist Robert Lekachman considered him a "fascist."[8]

Even many in the Republican party viewed him with sneering condescension. During the 1980 Republican primaries, candidate George Bush called Reagan's supply-side ideas "voodoo economics." Another Republican contender, Congressman John Anderson, quipped that "smoke and mirrors" were required to make sense of Reagan's policies.

This disdain, which was far more harshly expressed in private, betrayed a broader sentiment within the GOP establishment that Reagan was a hopeless amateur among seasoned professionals, a witch doctor in a field of competent surgeons.

Before Reagan was elected, it was customary among those who considered themselves well educated to ridicule him. Senator Paul Laxalt, a close ally of Reagan since the 1960s, remembers accompanying Reagan to places like the Bohemian Grove, an elite gathering of political bigwigs and business tycoons. The guests would look at the list of speakers, Laxalt told me, "and when they came to his name they would groan and say: Oh, no, you mean we have to listen to that same old crap again?" This attitude was pervasive on campuses as well. The late political scientist Aaron Wildavsky, who wrote about presidential leadership, recalled a typical incident in which he was asked at a conference, "What kind of man is Ronald Reagan?" And immediately, Wildavsky said, faculty and students broke into disdainful chuckles and giggles. They simply could not bring themselves to take Reagan seriously.[9]

Yet this magnitude of scorn, which would have produced a profound crisis of self-confidence in most people, seems to have had no effect on Reagan. He remained personally effervescent and confident about his prospects for election to the presidency. His core convictions remained solid despite the turbulent currents of criticism. Moreover, even in a time of hardship and confusion, he was irrepressibly optimistic about his country's future. He was a real-life Gatsby, of whom Fitzgerald wrote, "He had an extraordinary gift for hope."

At first, the American people did not share Reagan's optimism. The late Lee Atwater, one of the Republican Party's top strategists, once told me that Americans were undecided about Reagan until the final week of the 1980 campaign. I recently checked, and Atwater was right: polls shortly before the election showed Reagan and Carter running very close. Yet in the silence of the booth, the American people, ignoring the harsh denunciations and stern warnings of their elites, repudiated Carter and voted Reagan into the highest office in a landslide. Reagan won forty-four states to Jimmy Carter's six and gathered 489 electoral votes—ten times the number of Carter's. Riding on Reagan's coattails, his party also gained control of the Senate for the first time since 1952. Prominent liberal Democrats like Frank Church, Birch Bayh, and

George McGovern were swept out of office. Not since Herbert Hoover and the debacle of the early 1930s was an incumbent president and a party in power so thoroughly repudiated.

Reagan's stunning rise to power over the objections of the wise men of his day raises two related questions: Where did he get his firm convictions and the optimism with which to press them despite adversity? Moreover, on the question of whether Reagan was qualified to lead the country, who was right: the intellectuals or the American people? By tracing Reagan's life from his midwestern origins and Hollywood years to his tenure as governor of California, we can seek the origins of Reagan's principles and the distinguishing features of his character that were to prove so endearing to the voters and so exasperating to the pundits. By exploring Reagan's background, we can witness the formation of a leader and understand better how this complete outsider transformed the Republican party into his own image and then rode his way into the White House, where he would change the landscape of the nation and the rest of the world.

"My optimism," Reagan observed in 1991, "comes not just from my strong faith in God but from my strong and enduring faith in man."[10] The roots of Reagan's optimism go back to his early childhood, a period that he remembered as "the happiest time of my life."[11] His daughter Maureen recalls that he loved to narrate stories from his boyhood days to anyone who would listen: "It only takes the slightest impulse to take Dad back to the wonders of his youth." When she accompanied the president at a parade in front of the White House, Reagan's eyes filled with tears when he spotted his old high school marching band.[12] I heard the same account of his dad from Michael Reagan.

Yet by conventional standards, Ronald Reagan had a difficult childhood: his family was poor, and his father was an alcoholic. This paradox has prompted a good deal of amateur psychoanalysis among Reagan's critics, who are quick to detect in him early warning signs of emotional "repression" and "denial."[13] Children of alcoholic parents survive by learning to "deny reality" or by "creating their own reality," declares Haynes Johnson of the *Washington Post*. "Something similar seems to have happened with Reagan."[14] More broadly, social critic Garry Wills charges that Reagan's ideas about America evoke an invented past, "a heritage that never existed" except in fables and Mark Twain novels.[15]

Ronald Reagan was born on February 6, 1911, in Tampico, Illinois, in a little apartment above the bank building. "We didn't have any other contact with the bank than that," he later joked. The Reagans were poor and came close to being ruined during the Great Depression. Recalling his childhood, Reagan acknowledged their precarious economic status but said he never thought of himself as poor because lots of people lived the same way; moreover, his family was always helping others less fortunate.

Reagan's father, Jack, was a canny shoe salesman with charm and the ability to tell a good yarn. He nicknamed Reagan "Dutch" because he thought he resembled "a fat Dutchman," and he called Reagan's brother "Moon" after a comic strip character. As an Irish Catholic, Jack Reagan was sensitive to ethnic prejudice and taught his children the evils of bigotry from an early age. Reagan says that his father taught him ambition, a belief in the rights of the individual, a suspicion of established authority, and "maybe a little something about telling a story."[16]

Jack Reagan suffered from what his sons called the Irish disease; he drank so heavily that he would rant incomprehensibly and sometimes pass out in the front yard. Reagan confesses that there were times he had to drag his dad, virtually comatose, into the house. He is reticent about describing his reaction to the scene, which must have been traumatic for him. Nancy Reagan in her memoirs speculates that Reagan, like other children in the same circumstance, reacted to his father's alcoholism by withdrawing into himself. Reagan recalled that in his moments of solitude, "I lived in a world of pretend."

Reagan seems to have derived his emotional security from his mother, Nelle, a petite woman with auburn hair who convinced him that his father's drunken ravings did not represent his true nature; rather, they were symptoms of an illness. She was a deeply religious Protestant whose favorite saying was, "The Lord will provide." Possessed of a theatrical bent, Nelle Reagan read stories and poems aloud that became part of her children's moral education. She told her sons that everything that happened in life was for a purpose and that they had tremendous inner resources with which to surmount obstacles. She tended to see the best in people not because she rejected the reality of sin, but because she accepted the more powerful reality of redemption.

Thus it was from his mother that Reagan seems to have derived some of his most striking personal traits, notably his optimism and what George Will terms "a talent for happiness."[17] She taught him the capacity for maintaining a positive outlook even when receiving bad news and for believing in noble ideals and in people even when experience and reality inevitably fell short of his expectations. From her, Reagan seems to have learned the value of cheerfulness, not so much as a way of denying hardship as of overcoming it. She showed him the importance of never letting real-life problems destroy his ideals. Rather, the ideal supplies a standard of hope and of measurement to which he should always aspire.

His self-confidence and optimism were strengthened by his spiritual outlook, also shaped by Nelle Reagan. "Looking back," Reagan recalled in 1981, his mother's stories as well as his early reading left in him "an abiding belief in the triumph of good over evil."[18] In his early years, Reagan developed a self-confidence that derived from the awareness that the most important knowledge concerns right and wrong, and it is obtained not by consulting outside sources but by an interior examination of one's conscience. Even though in adult life Reagan was an infrequent churchgoer, he retained and frequently echoed his mother's religious outlook and her providential theology: "I've always believed that we were, each of us, put here for a reason, that there is a plan, a divine plan, for all of us."[19]

The family moved around a lot in his early years, another source, according to Nancy Reagan, of Reagan's later emotional detachment. She speculates that he learned not to become attached to any single place or any particular group of people. The Reagans finally settled in Dixon, Illinois, a town of 10,000 people, ninety miles from Chicago. Dixon was small-town America, a Norman Rockwell setting where people borrowed sugar from their neighbors and policemen stopped in for apple pie.

In some respects, life then was difficult: infant mortality was much higher, and life expectancy much lower, than it is today. Yet the murder rate was a fraction of what it is now. Hardly anyone was rich, but people did get to know their neighbors, and there was a sense of community.

America is a much more urban-oriented and homogeneous place today, and many of those small communities, with their distinctive cultural accents, are gone. There are not many areas in America today where you don't have to lock your door at night. But later in life Reagan would never be convinced by his critics that these places never existed. He saw them; he was there.

Reagan's fondness for his childhood years was deepened by his memories of good times at Dixon Northside High School. Reagan grew to nearly six feet and played on the football team, which gave him the experience of camaraderie with his teammates and competition against rival teams. In 1981 Reagan told *Inside Sports* that football "is the last thing left in civilization where men can literally fling themselves bodily at one another in combat and not be at war."[20] His popularity in high school is suggested by the fact that in his senior year, he was elected student body president. When school was out, Reagan worked as a lifeguard at Lowell Park, a local recreation center. Reagan enjoyed this job so much that he returned to it for seven summers, and reputedly saved seventy-seven people from drowning. At the age of seventeen, he published a poem in his high school yearbook, *The Dixonian,* which conveys a jaunty optimism that would stay with him through the years:

> I wonder what it's all about, and why
> We suffer so, when little things go wrong?
> We make our life a struggle
> When life should be a song.

In 1928, Reagan enrolled at Eureka College, a few miles east of Peoria. Eureka, a school run by the Disciples of Christ, gets its name from the Greek word meaning, "I have found it." What Reagan discovered at Eureka was largely outside the classroom. "My favorite subject," he confessed, "was football." Reagan majored in sociology and economics, but even at this academically undistinguished college, he was a mediocre student.

Yet the poor grades that his critics would seize on to suggest a lack of intelligence never troubled him. He was never apologetic about his college performance, and indeed routinely made light of his academic record. The great advantage of being president of the United States, he once told a group of students, was that you could have your grades classified as top secret. Speaking before Eureka students during his first term, he credited the political theme of his 1980 campaign to a question that the Eureka College president allegedly asked him on his graduation day, when he received his diploma: "Are you better off today than you were four years ago?" Ruminating further upon his undergraduate grade point average, President Reagan told the Eureka community, "Even now I wonder what I might have accomplished if I had studied harder."[21]

Reagan's insouciance about his mediocre academic performance probably derived from his conviction that the most important truths are moral, not intellectual. They are part of our nature, and accessible through the experience of life. Reagan seems to have been unconvinced that Eureka could add very much to this core knowledge. Moreover, he was confident that his college grades didn't reflect his true potential. Reagan says that he consulted his textbooks only right before tests and worked just enough to maintain the C average required for eligibility in the extracurricular activities that constituted his real interest. Several of Reagan's former teachers over the years have confirmed this to journalists. They said he had a photographic memory and was capable of doing much better academically, but that wasn't one of his top priorities.

Reagan did distinguish himself as a varsity football player and swimmer, editor of the yearbook, and head of the student council. He became active in the drama club and enjoyed his stardom so much that he resolved to pursue a career in acting and communications. In an early sign of ambition, he told his classmates, "If I'm not making five thousand dollars a year when I'm five years out of college, I'll consider these four years here were wasted." His colleagues were pleasantly skeptical; in those days an annual income of $5,000 was a great deal of money.[22]

Reagan's steady girlfriend at Eureka was Margaret Cleaver, a shy beauty from his hometown who was the daughter of a minister. Yet strikingly Reagan seems to have formed no lasting male friendships, in either high school or college. In all his nostalgic reveries about those years, he doesn't mention any close pals. Even on the field and in the huddle, a part of him remained aloof.

When Reagan graduated from Eureka in 1932, America was in the throes of the Great Depression. His father had lost his job, and his mother supported the family as a seamstress. But Reagan was not deterred; confident that he would be able to find a job, he borrowed his father's Oldsmobile and set out for all the local radio stations within driving distance of his hometown. His first stop was station WOC in Davenport, Iowa, where there was an opening for a sports announcer. Reagan had never called a game before, but he was given a tryout and produced such a convincing rendition of the previous year's Eureka–Western Illinois game that the station manager offered him the job. Soon he was transferred to WOC's sister station, WHO in Des Moines, Iowa, where his sports broadcasts reached much of the Midwest.

Reagan was gifted with a mellifluous voice. He had a natural dramatic flair, so that even though he was getting his information from the wire, he could give listeners the feeling that they were actually at the game. He also had an inventive imagination, which came in handy during one broadcast when the wire went dead and Reagan kept going, maintaining the suspense of the audience until the connection was restored. Yet Reagan may have acquired, from this period, a bad habit that he retained in political life: embroidering news accounts by adding details for effect. A more desirable trait that Reagan developed was the capacity to read fluently from a script. He recognized early on how difficult this is, so through painful rehearsal, he cultivated a style that sounded spontaneous and natural even though it was the product of careful preparation and training.

Although Reagan became a regional celebrity as a radio personality, his real ambition was to become a successful Hollywood actor. He lobbied his station managers to send him to cover the Chicago Cubs' training season in Catalina, and finally they did. In 1937, Reagan made the trip to California where he met Joy Hodges, a Des Moines native who was a Hollywood singer and actress, and confessed his aspirations to her. She told him that if he would discard his horn-rimmed glasses, she would introduce him to her agent, Bill Meiklejohn, who represented Robert Taylor and Betty Grable. Meiklejohn, impressed by Reagan's all-American good looks and his nonregional accent, called Warner Brothers to declare, "I have another Robert Taylor sitting in my office." Reagan did a screen test and then returned to Des Moines, where there was a telegram from his agent waiting for him: "Warner offers contract seven years . . . starting at $200 a week. What shall I do?" Reagan wired back, "Sign before they change their minds."[23]

The glib young loner from Dixon, Illinois, headed off to a career in the movies. It was an American story. Reagan was born poor, but lots of people were born poor in those days. He was lucky, but luck is an American trait. And who could deny that Reagan had, to some extent, created his opportunities and seized them when they came? Given how his early years turned out, Reagan seems justified in seeing his early life as a successful odyssey—a triumph of hope and effort over deprivation and difficulty. He didn't repress the hardships of his childhood but rather learned to transcend and overcome them. It is not difficult to see why, from those times, Reagan's optimism was strengthened and he faced the future with a romantic sense of possibility.

———

Reagan's tenure in Hollywood haunted him for his entire political career. Even though he made his last feature film in 1957, many of his critics and election rivals for the next two and a half decades accused him of being a B-movie actor and thus unsuited for public office. Typical was the charge of California governor Pat Brown, who said in 1966 that while he was running the state, his opponent Ronald Reagan "was off making such film epics as *Bedtime for Bonzo* and *Tugboat Annie Sails Again.*"[24] The implication of the charge was that actors are role-players. They pretend to be something they are not, deceiving people through appearances. They are inauthentic. They may amuse us, but they cannot be taken seriously.

This was not Reagan's view of acting at all. He never minded the label of actor, although he was sensitive to being called a mediocre actor. During one of his political campaigns, he happily signed for a reporter a picture of himself in bed with a chimpanzee from *Bedtime for Bonzo,* writing across the bottom, "I'm the one with the watch." Reagan never defended himself against the accusation of being an actor, because he came to realize that the charge helped rather than hurt him politically. He was even convinced that this acting background enabled him to govern more effectively. Edwin Meese, who served as Reagan's attorney general and counselor to the president, told me that Reagan frequently said to him, "Ed, I don't know how I could do this job if I were not an actor."

The most important political lesson Reagan learned from his Hollywood years was the difference between the endorsement of the critics and success at the box office. If you have the second, you don't need the first. Reagan made fifty-two full-length films during his Hollywood career. "They don't want them good," he once said, "they want them Thursday." In his first movie, *Love Is on the Air,* released in 1937, Reagan was cast in the familiar role of a radio announcer. He essentially played himself. Many of his films were like that. As with the late Jimmy Stewart, his clean-cut, likable nature typically translated into clean-cut, likable parts. His roles were rarely very demanding, in the sense that he was usually playing a character not very different from Ronald Reagan. The critics faulted him for not being more versatile, but Reagan knew that as long as people kept coming to see his films, he would be assured of a successful career. In his subsequent political career, Reagan never forgot the difference between appealing to the pundits and winning the votes of the general public.

In Hollywood in the 1930s and 1940s, the way to win popularity at the box office was to appeal to a universal audience. It was the age of the big studios, which sought to cater their films to the widest possible constituency. (Woody Allen's movies about the neurotic obsessions of Manhattan's Upper East Side would not have passed muster.) It was also an era before television in which movies were a form of shared entertainment for the country. If you wanted to be a star, you had to get rid of that Brooklyn accent, which would be useful only as an object of satire. Reagan's Hollywood was a distillation of traditional values and mainstream aspirations. So as an actor and later as a politician, Reagan learned how to transcend regional and provincial identity and appeal to a mass audience.

Undoubtedly Reagan's most memorable role was that of star football player George Gipp in the 1940 film *Knute Rockne, All American.* After Gipp died of pneumonia, the legendary Notre Dame coach asked his team to go out and "win one for the Gipper." Reagan used this phrase as a trademark in subsequent political battles because he had learned from Hollywood the tremendous visual and emotional power of embodying heroic archetypes. Hollywood specialized in the evocation of great American mythic heroes: the lone sheriff arriving to rescue a frontier town, the pioneer exploring new frontiers in search of a dream, the citizen-crusader taking on the corrupt establishment, the battle-weary soldier relinquishing his life to save his comrades. During World War II, Reagan, whose nearsightedness kept him from active combat, made training films for the military, which were praised by military personnel as inspirational and realistic preparations for battle.

Reagan saw actors not as fakers but as people who were capable of conveying noble ideals. He understood that these ideals could be communicated all the more effectively if they were not abstract but personalized and visualized. In this context, Reagan's own hero was John Wayne, who became one of his political supporters. Social critics would later deride Wayne as a hypocrite whose real life bore no resemblance to his famous characters. Yet this criticism missed the point. What astonished Reagan about Wayne was that he was an ordinary fellow, Marion Morrison, who *became* John Wayne. Once he had established his public persona, Wayne indignantly refused roles that departed from his mythic character who defined the ideal of American manhood in that era.

Reagan himself learned to project a public image so that, for the rest of his life, he always seemed to be "on camera." One of his favorite sayings was that "you can't lie to the camera." What he meant is not that the camera will always unmask the actor standing before it but that only an actor who truly believes his lines can produce a convincing performance before the lens. Great acting is the product of deep conviction. Far more shrewdly than those who considered him a "mere actor," Reagan came to appreciate the political appeal of embodying on the public stage mythical ideals in which he believed. As president, White House aide David Gergen told me, "Reagan understood, better than anyone since de Gaulle, the dramatic and theatrical demands of national leadership." Statecraft involves an element of stagecraft.

Another lesson that Reagan learned in Hollywood was the art of negotiating and being part of a team. For many successful actors, Hollywood is a kind of dream universe that revolves around themselves. Reagan was never a big enough star to permit himself such consuming narcissism. He appreciated the magic of filmmaking but also adopted the realistic view that films are a profit-making industry. He spoke of "the picture business" and approached it that way, always showing up on time for shootings, memorizing his lines so that he could recite them effortlessly, and learning to take direction without being difficult. Later, when many actors were too fastidious to be seen on television, regarding it as inferior to film, Reagan obligingly switched to the new medium, thus guaranteeing himself more parts.

Reagan recognized that actors were handsomely paid—his standard contract was for forty weeks a year and paid around $3,500 a week— but he also knew that even well-known stars are at the mercy of the vicissitudes of public taste. He was especially appalled that actors who made several films a year found themselves paying marginal tax rates that consumed the bulk of their extra income, so it was uneconomical for them to make more than three or four films a year. Reagan liked to tell the story of William Holden, who moved to Switzerland to avoid paying confiscatory tax rates in the United States. "Bill sat down with the Swiss tax people and negotiated how much he would pay—he made a deal which was good as long as he continued to reside officially in Switzerland," Reagan recalled. "Now that's a great system!"[25]

Reagan also knew that the way for an actor to seek some professional security in a rough and uncertain business is to join a union and take part in collective bargaining, so he became a member of the Screen Actors Guild in 1938. There he met big stars like Cary Grant, Robert Montgomery, and James Cagney, but he also got to know the stagehands and extras. He was familiar with the "other Hollywood"—the tens of thousands of people who, like him, came to California aspiring to make their fortune in the world of entertainment. Many of them worked as cooks and waitresses in local restaurants, waiting and hoping.

Reagan's leadership skills were soon apparent to the members of the Screen Actors Guild, who elected him president in 1947. He was reelected four times and was brought back in 1959 to lead the first successful strike against the movie producers. It was in this role that Reagan seems to have developed his intuitive interpersonal skills into a superb negotiating style. Charlton Heston told me during the mid-1980s that Reagan was one of the toughest and shrewdest bargainers that the guild ever produced. Heston said, "Even actors who disagreed with his politics would concede that." Reagan dealt with some of the toughest movie bosses that Hollywood has produced; he later commented that they prepared him for his subsequent negotiations with the Soviet Union. "After the studios," Reagan said in 1988, "Gorbachev was a snap."[26]

One of the mistakes the studio bosses routinely made, and that would also characterize Reagan's political opponents in the future, is that they mistook his good-natured style for naiveté. Reagan discovered that his genuine affability was a valuable negotiating asset and used it to the fullest. In his autobiography *An American Life,* Reagan writes that he learned from union negotiations that the best way to work out a problem is to shut the door and talk it over in private, that you will do better if you don't issue ultimatums but rather leave your adversary room to maneuver, and that you are unlikely to get everything you want.[27]

"I have never believed in jumping off the cliff with the flag flying," Reagan told journalist Laurence Barrett in 1982.[28] Reagan often said that when confronted by the choice of getting most of what he wanted or nothing, he always took the deal. His approach was to develop three lists: the things that his membership absolutely must have, the things they would like to have, and a few other items thrown in as bargaining chips. It is a measure of Reagan's skill that he was frequently down to the third list before he shook hands on an agreement.

With this arsenal of skills, Reagan was ready for politics. He got his first sampling of it in Hollywood, where he came into conflict with the communists at the Screen Actors Guild. In his later years, Reagan was certain that there were communist front organizations in Hollywood because he had belonged to at least one, the Hollywood Independent Committee of Arts, Sciences and Professions, and possibly a second, the American Veterans' Committee. Yet he joined these and many other groups out of idealism, not knowing of their communist affiliations and thinking that they espoused liberal causes to "save the world," as he put it. He quit the communist front groups immediately upon discovering their objectives.[29]

These objectives were, quite explicitly, to advance communist influence in the film industry, which was rightly perceived as influential in shaping the beliefs of the American public. Contemporary critics who fault Reagan for his cooperation with the House Un-American Activities Committee (HUAC) do not deny this fact, but they choose to downplay it.[30] They champion the targets of HUAC as victims of a witch-hunt and chastise Reagan for his role in blacklisting, yet Reagan knew that there were two blacklists: one kept by the politicians in Washington, who were investigating communist influence in the film industry, and the other kept by the communist activists in Hollywood, who sought to destroy the careers of those who opposed them.

Reagan had firsthand knowledge of the latter: when he worked to reduce communist influence in the union movement, his life was threatened, and he was forced to travel with a gun. Longtime aide Peter Hannaford told me that through his dealings with the communists in Hollywood Reagan saw firsthand that they were not inhibited by traditional moral constraints and were willing to practice deceit and even violence to further their ideological cause. Reagan, however, refused to use the same tactics in opposing the communists. He defended the rights of union members who were wrongly accused of communist affiliations. Later he would say of Joseph McCarthy that he "used a shotgun when a rifle was needed, injuring the innocent along with the guilty." He also refused to provide any names of alleged communists to the HUAC committee and testified in 1947 that he opposed government legislation from Washington that would make membership in communist groups or the espousal of communist views illegal. In a statement that all good liberals will agree with, Reagan said that, in dealing with communism, "I never as a citizen want to see our country . . . compromise with any of our democratic principles."[31]

It was Reagan's obsession with union politics that his first wife, the actress Jane Wyman, blamed for destroying their marriage. She met him in 1939 on the set of the film *Brother Rat*. They were married the next year and raised two children, Maureen and Michael. The gossip writers considered theirs an ideal marriage, yet there were problems from the outset. Some writers have speculated that these derived from the fact that Reagan's career was going down while Wyman's was going up.[32] This was not the case. Wyman did go on to win an Academy Award and become a big star, but this was after her marriage with Reagan had ended.

Wyman stated during her divorce proceeding in 1948 that she had become increasingly frustrated with Reagan's emotional detachment until "finally there was nothing in common between us."[33] Over the years she had told the Hollywood papers that she found him to be a very good-natured and considerate husband. Neither she nor the gossip columnists ever charged him with marital infidelity. But she seems to have encountered an insurmountable barrier—something about him that was somewhere else. She attributed the emptiness in their relationship to Reagan's extensive involvement with the Screen Actors Guild, but lots of people have busy careers and still remain close to their spouse. It seems that Jane Wyman left Ronald Reagan after their eight-year marriage because she, like so many other people after her, encountered The Wall. Reagan was, by all accounts, shaken by his divorce—"Maybe I should have let someone else save the world, and saved my own home," he ruefully remarked—yet once Jane Wyman walked out of his life, he seems to have erased her from his mind.

It was through his involvement in the Screen Actors Guild that Reagan met his second wife, Nancy. Nancy Davis was an aspiring young actress who had a fragile, delicate beauty. In 1951, she read an article in a Hollywood newspaper listing her as a communist sympathizer. It turns out to have been another woman of the same name. Troubled that her career would be affected, she called her agent, who called the president of the Screen Actors Guild, Ronald Reagan. His solution to her problem was simple: ask the publicity department at the studio for a new name. Reagan was under the impression that she was using a stage name, but she informed him that Nancy Davis was her real name and she was determined to keep it. Eventually, however, he persuaded her to marry him, thus neatly solving the problem.

She was attracted, she says, by the fact that "he was less like an actor than anyone I had known." Why was this important to her? She was born Anne Frances Robbins and nicknamed Nancy, a name she liked and used for herself. Her mother, Edith Luckett, was a stage actress who traveled most of the year, performing in plays and on radio soap operas, including the old *Amos 'n' Andy* show, in which white actors played black characters. Her father, Kenneth Robbins, was a car salesman.

Nancy's parents were divorced soon after she was born, and her mother had to take her on the road or leave her with relatives.

Her life became stable only when Edith Luckett was remarried to a Chicago neurosurgeon, Loyal Davis, when Nancy was around ten years old. Yet he did not adopt her until she was in her late teens, on the peculiar grounds that he wanted her to "earn" the right to his last name. She was educated at the Girls' Latin School in Chicago and Smith College. While a student at Smith, she fell in love with a Princeton student. The couple was considering marriage, when he died tragically in a train accident. She tried her hand at theater and then went to Hollywood in the 1940s, where she became a modestly successful actress. Yet her "greatest ambition," she confessed at the time, was to "have a happy marriage."

Nancy Davis found Ronald Reagan to be the decent and dependable man she was looking for. She was not fooled by his cheerful facade; behind it, she saw a furnace of ambition. She was quite willing to live with Reagan's detachment that Jane Wyman found so unbearable. He seems to have seen that in her he would find a fierce loyalist and a determined protector, who would promote his career as if it were her own. They were married in 1952, with William Holden serving as best man. From the outset, they seem to have found that they complemented each other perfectly.

They could have moved in glamorous Hollywood circles but chose not to do so. Other stars lived in a complicated and fast-paced social world, but not Reagan. "When the day's shooting was over," Nancy Reagan wrote in her autobiography, "he never stayed behind to have a drink with the fellows in the dressing room. He preferred to come home."[34] Nancy Reagan made one movie with her husband, *Hellcats of the Navy*. Then she quit her acting career, a decision feminists later deplored but one she says she never regretted, and she devoted herself to advancing Reagan's career, and to family life. Their marriage produced two children, Patti and Ron.

When Reagan met Nancy, his career was not going very well, and he was starting to lose interest in the parts he was getting. His lowest point came when he was forced to take an assignment as master of ceremonies for a Las Vegas floor show. He resolved to try something different. Through his union activities, he had developed a broader interest in politics, to which he now turned. His new wife encouraged him to pursue new opportunities. But as the late Jimmy Stewart, who knew how ambitious Nancy was for her husband, once put it, "If Nancy Reagan instead of Jane Wyman had been Ronald Reagan's first wife, he never would have gone into politics. Instead, she would have seen to it that he got all the best parts, he would have won three or four Oscars, and been a real star."[35]

As long as Reagan was an actor, he was a popular national figure who enjoyed the accolades of a celebrity. But as soon as he entered politics, he found himself the object of unrelenting opposition and derision, and much of that focused on his previous screen roles. In subsequent years Reagan noted the irony, telling aides: "Now that I am something else besides an actor, everybody is saying that I'm an actor. I'll probably be the only fellow who will get an Oscar posthumously."

The reaction to Reagan's political foray went beyond the normal surprise that can be expected to greet a movie star who seeks the highest office in the state. "All wrong," Reagan's old boss Jack Warner is said to have quipped when he heard about Reagan's gubernatorial bid. "Jimmy Stewart for governor, Reagan for best friend." Reagan loved this line and quoted it for two decades; he welcomed good-natured ribbing. Yet the pundits and intellectuals were not good sports about Reagan's political debut: they called him a dummy, a faker, a kook, and dangerous to boot.

This reception at the hands of the political and social elites cannot be entirely explained by the fact that Reagan came from Hollywood, land of make-believe. Nor, when Reagan ran for president, can it be attributed to the fact that he was from California, land of the screwballs. Reagan was not the first actor to seek political office. Indeed when he ran for governor of California in 1966, one of the U.S. senators from that state was a former actor, George Murphy. Moreover, other political candidates for national office like Richard Nixon had a California background, yet they didn't get the same treatment as Reagan. Many in the media detested Nixon, but at the same time they respected him as a formidable figure. So the incredulous reaction to Reagan was not primarily due to his origins. Indeed, that wasn't even the main factor. The main factor was his ideas.

Where did Reagan get his ideas that were the source of such consternation, and what gave him the confidence to persist in espousing those beliefs under circumstances that would make most men modify them to suit the prevailing mood? Reagan's real political education began in 1954, when he gratefully accepted an offer by the General Electric Company to host the show *General Electric Theater* and to travel around the country as a motivational speaker and corporate ambassador on behalf of the company. Reagan had one hesitation about taking the job: he didn't like to fly. But he accepted the $125,000 a year assignment on the condition that he would commute by land and rail.

Reagan worked for General Electric for eight years, from 1954 to 1962. Nancy Reagan estimates that he spent two of those eight years on the road, and through his extensive travels, former GE executive Edward Langley says, Reagan discovered "the native conservatism of working America."[36] Month after month Reagan would address workers on the factory floor, or stop in the cafeteria to chat with secretaries, or be forklifted into the air to converse with welders. By his own account, he sometimes gave as many as fourteen talks a day, visiting every GE plant and meeting all of the company's 250,000 workers.

His original speech to them focused on the virtues of the free market system and the benefits of GE's products. He attempted to establish a connection with people by telling them Hollywood stories. He was particularly eager to defend Hollywood against the charge of making debauchery seem glamorous. But he soon discovered that he was not addressing people's real concerns.

It was not what he said to them but what they said to him that was important. They were the kind of people with whom he grew up, and he saw them as hard-working, decent Americans for whom life had not been easy. He became a convert to their way of thinking and, in time, a champion for their interests. Indeed, what Reagan heard in the course of countless conversations formed the basis of a philosophy that was in touch with the sentiments of mainstream America—and utterly opposed to the conventional wisdom of elites at the time.

At first, this philosophy was an inchoate assortment of horror stories and personal incidents that Reagan picked up in his travels. People regularly told him about how their attempts to improve their lives were frustrated by high taxation and arbitrary and burdensome regulations. Reagan believed these stories because he heard them again and again, and he saw that they were not the product of theorizing but were based on experience. Recognizing their narrative power, he began to integrate them into his own presentations, often buttressed by news items and quips that illustrated his themes.

Sometimes stories got better in the telling, and the facts were stretched to make a point. If not as a radio announcer, Reagan acquired his irresponsible habit of padding his anecdotes at GE. This habit would stay with him for the rest of his life. Even the careful scrutiny of his White House aides could not prevent him from reciting an incident that he had read about somewhere but didn't verify, or the news item that he remembered with one or two embellishments. Yet Reagan was unapologetic, because to him the stories were "morality tales," and the particular incident at hand was only an illustration of a broader theme. As he saw it, just because this or that particular detail might be erroneous did not mean that the moral of the story was invalid.

Reagan's general theme was the intrusiveness and incompetence of government and its comical inability to solve human problems. He elaborated this message over the years with infinite variations, examples, and jokes. To Reagan, the government's approach to the economy could be summed up in the following way: "If it moves, tax it. If it keeps moving, regulate it. And if it stops moving, subsidize it." Reagan saw the wisdom of the bureaucrats in Washington, D.C., expressed by a sign that used to hang on the gigantic Hoover Dam: "Government Property. Do Not Remove." The federal government, Reagan noted, was spending millions "inventing miracle cures for which there are no known diseases." In his view, the most dangerous words in the English language were: "Hi, I'm from the government and I'm here to help."[37]

Reagan regaled his audiences with countless stories over the years. In one of his favorites, he dramatized what he saw as the bizarre and counterproductive effects of government benefits for the poor and underprivileged through the example of a man who discovers that "you can get subsidized housing, health and dental care, university scholarships and other welfare benefits, provided you're poor enough." So the man approaches his boss and asks for a pay cut. "If I make less," he explains, "we'd be eligible for an apartment in the city's new development, the one downtown with a pool, sauna and tennis court. Besides, my son would qualify for a government scholarship and we could get his teeth fixed at government expense." His boss says fine, but on one condition: "If your work slips, you'll get a raise!" The man is grateful, but on his way out the boss asks to be invited over for tennis and a swim some night when his employee gets into his new place. "Certainly sir," the man says. "I believe the poor should share with the less fortunate!"[38]

These quips and anecdotes could be meaningful and amusing, or offensive and irrelevant, depending on the context. Reagan tried them out in various situations, both formal and informal, keenly gauging how they were received and constantly honing his delivery. It was during his GE trips, not in Hollywood, that Reagan learned the skills that would earn him the title of Great Communicator. He developed his own system of shorthand in which he could record a forty-five-minute address on a series of four-by-six note cards. He was a perfectionist who constantly reworked his material and rehearsed his speeches until his delivery and timing were perfect. He learned how to read his audience, a talent he retained in the White House. Michael Deaver once tried to convince President Reagan that he didn't have to sit through every dinner but could arrive just in time to give his talk. "No," Reagan replied. "You'd be surprised how much I learn about my audience watching them during the meal and the early part of the program."[39]

Through years of practice on the road for GE, Reagan developed what came to be known as The Speech, a comprehensive statement of his outlook that had been test-marketed to middle America itself. In places, the speech was colloquial and implausible, but the whole was greater than its parts. This rough-hewn document contained within it a viewpoint that struck a responsive chord among many Americans, a social and political philosophy for a new era.

Reagan's standard speech soon became so popular that he was invited to address trade organizations and civic groups as well. He also began to speak on behalf of regional political candidates, so it was not entirely surprising when, in 1964, the Republican presidential nominee,

Barry Goldwater, agreed to have Reagan's speech aired on national television to raise funds and generate support for the Goldwater candidacy. For Reagan, it was a momentous opportunity, and he seized it. It was the speech that would change his life and put him on a course that would transform the Republican party and American history.

Chapter 3

Mr. Reagan Goes to Washington

FROM THE TIME THAT HE delivered his national television address for Barry Goldwater in 1964 until he won the presidency in 1980, Reagan faced a serious problem. How does a man who believes in principles that are out of touch with the prevailing public ethos get elected? The ordinary politician has an easy solution: modify principles to suit the regnant mood. The leader, however, is not interested in just getting elected. He seeks public office in order to vindicate his principles and realize his policy objectives. Thus the option of accommodation to the fashions of the moment is not open to him.

Fortunately, there is a second option. The leader can remain true to his principles, refusing to yield even when the elites and the people are against him. This does not mean he is condemned to virtuous defeat. It does mean he must be wily and opportunistic in finding issues that allow him to neutralize his strongest opposition and enable him to find the greatest common ground with his popular constituency. He must be patient when circumstances are difficult, self-disciplined in staying focused on his goals, and creative in his selection and presentation of issues, until the moment of opportunity presents itself. Reagan's political career from 1964 to 1980 illustrates this higher path.

The main reason Reagan faced so many obstacles and generated so much controversy in his pursuit of public office was this: he was running against the twentieth century. This is the real source of all the incredulity and scorn he provoked and the true message of the speech that he delivered on Goldwater's behalf. The political history of the twentieth century can be summed up by the growth of the power of central government. Communism and fascism were its two extreme versions, but throughout the industrialized world, the century has seen the growth and expansion of welfare states, reflecting the assumption that an engaged and powerful government is essential to promoting freedom, justice, and the general welfare.

Reagan disagreed with that assumption. His view was that a large, central government is an obstacle to freedom, a poor instrument to secure justice, and harmful to the common good. For him, the lesson of the modern era is the danger of placing too much power in the hands of a coercive state. Reagan's political life was defined by opposition to collectivism. Thus, for all the diverse issues on which he took positions over the years, there was a fundamental unity to his thought. He opposed the concentration of power in Washington, D.C., as counterproductive and inimical to freedom. He believed that the more the government does for us, the less we are able to do for ourselves. He opposed communism because he saw it as the logical conclusion of centralized state control, to the point where economic, religious, and civil liberties are completely extinguished.

"You can't control the economy without controlling people," Reagan said in his Goldwater address. "So we have to come to a time for choosing. . . . I suggest to you that there is no left or right, only an up or down: Up to the maximum of individual freedom consistent with law and order, or down to the ant heap of totalitarianism, and regardless of their humanitarian purpose, those who would sacrifice freedom for security have, whether they know it or not, chosen this downward path."[1]

Not only did Reagan frontally attack the notion that the federal government is the solution to the nation's problems; he went further, saying explicitly that the federal government itself was the source of the problem, because its expansion was endangering the control of free citizens over their own lives. This sentiment was iconoclastic in 1964, the year that swept Lyndon Johnson into office and inaugurated the Great Society, and it would remain so through the 1970s. All the Republican presidents of the postwar era—Eisenhower, Nixon, and Ford—criticized the excesses of the federal government and spoke of making it more efficient, but they did not question in principle the ability of the government to remedy the ills of society. In this sense Reagan's views were completely outside the mainstream of conventional thinking about the role of the state in the modern era.

The intellectuals were the ones who developed the idea that government should be the shaping influence of modern life. Many of them argued that society was simply too large and intricate to regulate itself. The old laissez-faire approach no longer worked; as they put it, "There are no easy answers to complex questions." They saw the free market as too unruly and inequitable for the nation to trust its invisible hand. Their point of view was vindicated by the Great Depression, which seemed to illustrate the complete failure of free market capitalism. And ever since Franklin Roosevelt established his brain trust, the wise men had come to take for granted their role as social planners and problem solvers, seeking to remedy perceived social ills as diverse as poverty, earnings inequality, financial insecurity in old age, and racism.

Suddenly, in the mid-1960s, just when they were implementing comprehensive new programs designed to go beyond the modest New Deal and establish a Great Society, here was this former movie star who questioned the very idea of government as a catalyst of social good. "There are no *easy* answers," he said, "but there are *simple* answers. Either we accept the responsibility for our own destiny, or we abandon the American revolution and confess that an intellectual elite in a far-distant capital can plan our lives for us better than we can plan them ourselves."[2] From the point of view of the intelligentsia, these views were more than impudent; they were outrageous.

It might seem a long way for Reagan, who began life as a Roosevelt Democrat, to end up as a Goldwater Republican railing about the evils of big government. And why would a hopeful leader leave the party that had dominated American politics since his youth for what seemed to be the losing side? From Reagan's point of view, he did not undergo any radical transformation; his basic values remained the same. "I am what I've always been," he said on the eve of the 1980 election, "and I intend to remain that way."[3] He didn't leave the Democratic party, Reagan liked to say; it was the Democratic party that left him. He saw in the Republican party a more likely conduit for his ideas and a better opportunity to lead the country. Let us examine why he made these assessments.

In his early years, Reagan writes in his autobiography, he was "an enthusiastic New Deal Democrat." His father was unemployed when Franklin Roosevelt ran against President Herbert Hoover in 1932. After Roosevelt was elected, Jack Reagan soon found a job as a local official in the Works Progress Administration. Reagan was twenty-two years old at the time. He never forgot what the New Deal did for his family; even more, he never forgot the visionary optimism of Roosevelt's first inaugural, including its famous affirmation that "the only thing we have to fear is fear itself." This was a philosophy that matched Reagan's own inclinations, and it was vindicated by events. During his twenties and thirties, Reagan saw the country pull itself through the depression and World War II. It strengthened his faith in America and in Roosevelt's leadership.

As a broadcaster and actor, Reagan remained, in his own words, a "near hopeless hemophilic liberal."[4] He identified liberalism with idealism and internationalism, with doing good for other people and improving the world. He joined organizations like Americans for Democratic Action, which he assumed were promoting those objectives. Yet when Reagan traveled the country for General Electric, he began to see instead a degree of government intrusion in people's lives that threatened their basic liberties. Nancy Reagan recalls that he came home one day from a speaking trip and told her that the Democrats he had campaigned for in election years were responsible for the very problems against which he was speaking out between elections.[5]

Slowly Reagan began to withdraw his allegiance from the Democratic party. He never lost his affection for Roosevelt, and even as president Reagan would evoke Roosevelt's memory, quoting his line that

America has a "rendezvous with destiny." When asked about his high regard for the founder of the welfare state, Reagan would point out that Roosevelt had attacked the dole as a "narcotic" and a "subtle destroyer of the human spirit." Roosevelt promised throughout the 1930s that the government "must and shall quit this business of relief."[6]

Yet there was another side to Roosevelt, which emerged in his 1944 State of the Union address. There, FDR outlined a vision of democratic citizenship quite different from what the American founders envisioned. For the founders, the primary function of government was to secure basic rights, such as the right to speak one's mind, the right to practice one's religion, and the right to keep one's property. The Constitution establishes a framework for the pursuit of happiness but does not guarantee the resources or the means to achieve it. Free citizens are expected to acquire these by themselves.

Roosevelt argued, by contrast, that an American who doesn't have a decent house or a good education or adequate medical care is not truly free. In 1944 he proposed a "second Bill of Rights," which would include a right to a "useful and remunerative" job, "adequate" clothing and recreation, and freedom from "unfair competition" and "the economic fears of old age, sickness, accident and unemployment." Roosevelt saw it as the government's duty to ensure that citizens were able to exercise these rights.

Roosevelt's critics pointed out that his argument confused wants—the product of our passions—with rights—the product of our nature. In any event, FDR's expansive concept of rights was an invitation to extensive government involvement in people's lives. It had to provide for those who lacked and had to confiscate the goods of other citizens to pay for this. In Roosevelt's own lifetime, government intervention in the economy remained quite limited, yet FDR's broader vision of an activist government outlived him and established the foundation for the Great Society.

"The press is trying to paint me as trying to undo the New Deal," Reagan wrote in his diary on January 28, 1982. "I'm trying to undo the Great Society."[7] Reagan viewed the New Deal as a response to an economic crisis: the Great Depression. Something had to be done, and FDR recognized that. The New Deal established a modest safety net to protect working people who lost their jobs, the elderly who could not work anymore, and widows and orphans who could not provide for themselves. Reagan was never a libertarian who opposed all government efforts to help the disadvantaged.

The Great Society was promoted as a continuation and fulfillment of the promises of the New Deal, but the circumstances that gave rise to it were quite different. In the 1960s, there was no economic crisis; on the contrary, it was an era of steady growth. Thus the Great Society was conceived out of affluence. It vastly expanded the reach of the central government with a battery of new programs and entitlements. Suddenly the federal government was building mass transit systems, funding college loan programs, subsidizing the arts, and getting involved in all kinds of activities that were previously reserved for the states and the private sphere. Reagan did not contest the entire Great Society agenda, but he opposed the hubristic notion that intellectuals should use the coercive power of government to organize society rather than allowing free citizens to do it on their own.

Even in the early 1950s, well before the Great Society, Reagan began to have doubts about remaining a Democrat. He campaigned for Harry Truman in 1948 and in 1950 supported the Democratic candidate for Senate in California, Helen Gahagan Douglas, against her Republican opponent, Richard Nixon. Yet in 1952 Reagan was a Democrat for Eisenhower. By 1960 he seemed willing to join the Republican party and promote the presidential candidacy of Richard Nixon, but Nixon's team, in characteristic Machiavellian fashion, told him he would be more effective if he campaigned for their man as a Democrat. Two years later, however, Reagan felt it was time to reveal his true colors; he changed his registration and joined the Republican party.

Reagan's 1964 speech for Goldwater was an inspirational *cri de coeur* and a fund-raising bonanza, bringing in unprecedented contributions to the Republican party, but nothing could have saved the Goldwater campaign. Fortunately for Reagan, his address attracted the attention of a group of self-made California businessmen. They saw that Goldwater was a loser, but they believed that Reagan could be a winner. They were right.

Reagan took his first step toward the presidency by deciding to run for governor of California in 1966. He was approached by a group of successful entrepreneurs, Holmes Tuttle, A. C. Rubel, and Henry Salvatori, who were greatly impressed by his uncompromising defense of freedom at home and abroad. A couple of years before his death in 1997, Salvatori told me that, after meeting Reagan, "We knew right away that he was our man." The group assured Reagan that if he was willing to work to implement the principles of his speech in California, they would raise the necessary money for his gubernatorial candidacy. Reagan procrastinated on the grounds that he liked campaigning for other people but hadn't considered public office for himself. But finally he relented, and political consultant Stuart Spencer knew Reagan was serious when he agreed to make airplane stops across the state despite his long-standing aversion to flying.

His opponent was the popular incumbent governor, Pat Brown, whose record seemed impressive. Brown was a big-government activist who claimed credit for completing construction of California's vast network of freeways and building the state's university system into one of the best in the country. He was considered politically formidable, having defeated Richard Nixon, the 1960 GOP presidential nominee, in the 1962 California governor's race.

By his own admission, Brown saw Reagan as "easy to beat."[8] The opponent who alarmed him more was San Francisco mayor George Christopher, a political moderate, so Brown campaign officials decided to help Reagan beat Christopher in the Republican primary by leaking to the press damaging information about Christopher's role in a regulatory price-fixing scandal. The ensuing controversy helped Reagan prevail by an overwhelming margin over Christopher. Then Brown set about what he considered to be a simple task: portraying Reagan as an inexperienced former movie actor who was also a dangerous reactionary.

Brown accused Reagan of being a supporter of extremist groups like the John Birch Society. He tagged Reagan with the epithet "crown prince of the far right." He said Reagan's transition from movie actor to "citizen politician" reminded him of an airline passenger: "You're sitting in a big jet. You're ready to taxi out and a nice-looking middle-aged man in a uniform comes up the aisle heading for the controls. You stop him and say you're a little nervous because it's your first flight. 'Mine too,' he says. 'I'm a citizen pilot. But don't worry. I've always had an active interest in aviation.'"[9]

Reagan's team was nervous about these accusations, especially when the John Birch Society endorsed his candidacy, but the candidate himself was unruffled. He laughed off suggestions that he was an extremist, noting that if the John Birch Society endorsed him, "they are accepting my philosophy, I'm not accepting theirs." He dismissed the pilot analogy because he rejected the notion that public office could only be discharged by trained professionals. Refusing to apologize for his lack of experience, Reagan insisted that it was his strength. "I don't know of anybody who was born holding public office," he said. "The man who currently has the job has more political experience than anybody. That's why I'm running."[10]

Instead of seeking to minimize his Hollywood background, Reagan flaunted it. He knew that people liked to go to the movies and suspected that most ordinary Americans regard actors and celebrities with affection and admiration. He solicited and won the endorsement of movie and entertainment figures, including Pat Boone, Frank Sinatra, Dean Martin, Bob Hope, and John Wayne. They traveled with him on the campaign trail and made television commercials on his behalf.

Reagan focused his attacks on high taxes, incompetent bureaucracy, welfare cheats, and judges who "coddled criminals." At a time when many in the elite sympathized with the burgeoning counterculture of the 1960s, which was just getting under way at Berkeley and other campuses, Reagan supported an antipornography initiative and said the radicals were lawless misfits who "engaged in sexual orgies so vile I cannot describe them to you." Some of Reagan's rhetoric was overblown, coming from a political neophyte, yet his general views in favor of smaller government and traditional cultural values resonated broadly with the voters.

National media coverage of the election portrayed a progressive governor being annoyingly menaced by a nostalgic throwback to an earlier era. "Reagan is anti-labor, anti-Negro, anti-intellectual, anti–twentieth century," the *New Republic* said. "We really can't believe the old bogey of federal government still scares Californians."[11] All the fashionable people had this smug feeling about Reagan in the fall of 1966, but the wise men weren't grinning when the election results came in. Reagan won by over a million votes, carrying middle-class voters in suburban and rural areas that were heavily Democratic in registration. Pat Brown will be remembered as the first of Reagan's many opponents who underestimated him and then vanished off the stage of history.

If Reagan's supporters expected him to arrive in the state capital of Sacramento and sweep out the bureaucracy, they were mistaken. His inaugural speech contained a broad-based critique of government: "If no one among us is capable of governing himself, then who among us has the capacity to govern someone else?" Reagan promised to put welfare recipients to work "to give the individual the self-respect that goes with performing a useful service."[12] Yet when he was asked about his first priority as governor, he replied, "I don't know, I've never played a governor." Reagan was being humorous, of course, but he was also being truthful. Those who enter politics from the outside are often initially mesmerized by the challenge of functioning in an utterly different world.

Reagan introduced to Sacramento an undemanding schedule and relaxed approach to state politics. He arrived at the office at 9 A.M. and left at 5 P.M. His aides told me that frequently, on his way out, he would stick his head into the conference room and call to his staff, "Hey, guys, get out. Go home to your wives." When aides asked him who would get all the work done Reagan often replied, "It's not that important. Go home." Richard Nixon once called to ask Reagan, who was California state chairman of Nixon's presidential effort, how he could have picked a particular individual to head the campaign in San Bernardino. "He's a jerk," Nixon snapped. Reagan put his hand over the receiver and said to his aide Michael Deaver, "Who is this guy he's talking about?" Nixon was sufficiently detail-oriented to be obsessed about who would manage his campaign in a mid-sized California county; Reagan, who had appointed the man, didn't even know his name.[13]

Reagan also confounded the political establishment with his abbreviated style of making decisions. Issues may be complex, Reagan believed, but none is so difficult that it cannot be summarized in a one-page memorandum. His cabinet secretary William Clark required that all policy issues be reduced to a single cover sheet with four paragraphs: one stating the problem, another detailing the facts, a third listing items for discussion, and a fourth recommending a course of action. Further documentation could be attached, but there was no guarantee that the governor would read it. Reporters ridiculed what they saw as a simple-minded approach to governance, yet Reagan insisted that the one-page memos gave him a bird's-eye view of the problem, and his aides said that his photographic memory enabled him to absorb and retain information on a wide range of issues.

All the same, Reagan got off to a poor start. Indeed in terms of substantive policy, his first term must be regarded as a failure. One of his early discoveries was that the Brown administration had left the state with a deficit of almost $200 million, which had been concealed during the campaign. Reagan told the citizens of California that he was forced to violate one of his campaign promises and raise corporate taxes, sales taxes, and income taxes. Reluctantly or not, he ended up signing the largest tax increase in California history.

Nor was Reagan able to reduce profligate state spending. In his inaugural address, he promised that "we are going to squeeze and cut and trim until we reduce the cost of government." Yet during his tenure, the annual state budget more than doubled, from around $4.6 billion to over $10 billion. In his defense Reagan maintained that he was limited by the power of a Democratic legislature and that the rate of growth of state government was slower than that of his predecessor, and of other states in the country.

Reagan also ended up signing the most liberal abortion law in the country. In 1968, five years before the Supreme Court's *Roe v. Wade* decision, the California legislature passed a bill permitting abortion in cases where the life or health of the mother was jeopardized. Abortion opponents, including the Catholic cardinal of Los Angeles, warned that the health exception applied to both physical and mental health and was drawn so broadly that it virtually permitted doctors to provide abortion on demand. Reagan, who emphasized his moral qualms about abortion, nevertheless signed the bill into law, and the worst predictions of the law's critics soon became a reality. The number of legal abortions in California skyrocketed from 518 in 1967 to an average of 100,000 in the years between 1968 and 1974.[14]

Although Reagan was undoubtedly not a strict pro-life governor, his subsequent private correspondence shows he was genuinely shocked by the magnitude of abortions under the new law. His subsequent correspondence suggests that he was intensely grieved by this outcome. Edwin Meese, a senior aide, told me that Reagan's regrets over his role in promoting abortion on demand in California may have intensified his pro-life convictions and led him, as a presidential candidate, to support measures like the human life amendment, which would establish a blanket prohibition on abortion.

Despite his undistinguished record, Reagan was reelected in 1970, an achievement in a state where Democrats outnumbered Republicans by three to two. Many California voters seem to have credited him with good intentions, despite his inability to enact most of his goals into policy. And Reagan proved that he could learn from his mistakes. When he was informed that a growing economy was bringing in surplus revenues for the government, his immediate reaction was: "Give it back to the taxpayers." His finance director, Caspar Weinberger, who recalled the incident for me, said that he reacted with surprise. "Give it back?" he told Reagan. "That's never been done before." Weinberger wasn't opposed to a tax refund; he simply doubted its practicality. He was right to worry: Reagan's proposal was not well received by the Democratic legislature. One state senator indignantly said, "I consider this an unnecessary expenditure of public funds."[15]

Reagan's experience in the statehouse taught him an important lesson about taxes and government spending. Over the years, he stated this lesson in the form of various jokes and quips. He once likened the government to a baby: "It is an alimentary canal with an appetite at one end and no sense of responsibility at the other." A government bureau, he liked to say, "is the nearest thing to eternal life we'll ever see on this earth." Reagan's serious point was that once new government programs are established, they are extremely difficult to eliminate, so the best way to prevent new programs is to keep the money out of the hands of the bureaucrats. During Reagan's tenure, he was unable to pass income tax reductions but did convince the legislature to refund several billion dollars to the taxpayers in the form of tax credits and rebates.

Reagan also achieved his most important legislative victory during his second term. This was the Welfare Reform Act of 1971, which passed with bipartisan support. By this time, Reagan had learned far better how to get results with Democratic lawmakers. When liberal Democrats in Sacramento turned down his appeal to address a joint session of the legislature, Reagan took his case directly to the citizens. "That speech they wouldn't let me give was like a book banned in Boston," he recalled many years later. "Everyone wanted to know what was in it." He barnstormed the state and made television appeals. Eventually the speaker of the assembly, Robert Moretti, was so inundated with letters that he begged Reagan to stop the juggernaut. The two of them sat down and worked out a compromise. The ensuing legislation tightened eligibility requirements and established job training requirements, but at the same time it paid higher benefits to those who were deemed truly needy. In the next two years, the state's welfare rolls were reduced by around 300,000 people, a 15 percent decline.[16] These results could not be entirely attributed to the legislation—a robust economy helped former welfare recipients find jobs—yet Reagan was justified in considering his welfare reform a success.

Equally important, Reagan had introduced the topic into the national debate and offered a new criterion for evaluating government programs. Until then, many public officials and policy experts considered a government program a good one if it covered a lot of people. The more people who received benefits, the more successful the pundits and bureaucrats regarded the program. This was the logic of the Great Society. Reagan, by contrast, said that the Great Society approach was a failure. "We declared war on poverty," he famously quipped, "and poverty won." Reagan did not dispute that government has a responsibility to help the poor, but he argued that you cannot free people by making them dependent on the state. "The best social program," Reagan liked to say, "is a job." He insisted that welfare programs be measured by the degree to which they encouraged self-reliance. The purpose of welfare, he said, "should be to eliminate . . . the need for its own existence."[17]

Throughout his career, Reagan's advocacy of reducing dependency on government would provoke accusations of insensitivity to the poor and disadvantaged. Sometimes Reagan would become defensive under fire, yet he never wavered in his conviction that his was the right approach. Occasionally he would use humor to deflect criticism. When a California state senator who supported prescribing birth control devices for teenage girls without parental consent charged that "illegitimate births to teenage mothers have increased alarmingly while Reagan has been in office," Reagan wrote back, "Thanks very much. . . . I have never felt so young and virile."[18]

Reagan's usual approach, however, was to seize the moral high ground. Responding to a letter from one of his constituents charging him with a lack of compassion, Reagan replied, "I'm sure everyone feels sorry for the individual who has fallen by the wayside or who can't keep up in our competitive society, but my own compassion goes beyond that to those millions of unsung men and women who get up every morning, send the kids to school, go to work, try to keep up the payments on their house, pay exorbitant taxes to make possible compassion for the less fortunate, and as a result have to sacrifice many of their own desires and dreams and hopes. Government owes them something better than always finding a new way to make them share the fruit of their toils with others."[19]

Around the country, Reagan was best known not for his gubernatorial record but for being one of the few governors in the nation to stand resolutely against the counterculture of the 1960s. In doing so, he earned the lasting enmity of the activists who defined their identity in that era; many of them became his lifelong critics. Reagan's reaction to the protest movements of the 1960s was a vital stage in his political development. He discovered the importance of the social issues that would help to broaden the Republican coalition beyond its familiar economic base to include many blue-collar Democrats who didn't like what the radicals of the 1960s were saying about them or their country.

The counterculture was officially launched by the "free speech" movement at Berkeley in 1964. Soon activism spread to other campuses and acquired its breadth and intensity because of opposition to the Vietnam War. The radicals saw themselves as apostles of civil rights, feminism, and the sexual revolution as well. They defined their cause in opposition to bourgeois American conformity. "Hell no, we won't go," they shouted. "We won't die for Texaco." Many, like Bill Clinton, found ways to avoid the military draft. Some fled to Canada.

The radical students and professors presented their cause as a moral crusade and portrayed their opponents as bigots and warmongers. Many of the antiwar protesters were genuinely opposed to what they considered an unjust and pointless war, but Reagan saw them as ingrates who wanted to enjoy their country's benefits but would not put themselves at risk to defend its ideals. Their moralism, in his view, masked a crass opportunism. He detected in the radicals' hostility to "bourgeois materialism" a naked contempt for the working and middle classes. They didn't just despise the average American; they despised American ideals.

Reagan opposed the way the war was being fought, which made achieving victory impossible, but he considered the objective of over-throwing communism a "noble cause." He sided with those he called "the unpampered boys of the working class" who responded when their country called and yet encountered hostility and neglect when they came home. As governor, Reagan held several receptions for American prisoners of war returning to California, and when they thanked him for his hospitality, he would reply, "No, we're here to thank *you* for all you've done for us."[20]

Many teachers and administrators felt that the antiwar radicals who sought to shut down the universities were inspiring moral leaders who only needed encouragement and, at times, a little forbearance. Some of them proclaimed themselves to be disciples of the students. A few extolled the North Vietnamese communist Ho Chi Minh, burned the American flag, and called for revolutionary socialism in the United States. From these examples of excess, Reagan saw that the new class of intellectuals seemed to have a much greater disposition for depraved lunacy than ordinary people did. They were the people of whom George Orwell said, "One has to belong to the intelligentsia to believe things like that; no ordinary man could be such a fool." Reagan was also struck by the pusillanimity of the intellectuals; he encountered many deans and professors who told him that they disapproved of the campus disruptions yet were immobilized by indecision when it came to doing anything about it.

Reagan started by confronting not the radicals but the administrators who let them run amok. The president of the University of California system, Clark Kerr, symbolized the problem. By refusing to discipline student activists who were taking over buildings and obstructing classes, Kerr, in Reagan's view, had only encouraged further disruptions. The regents of the university system were displeased with Kerr, but he was lionized by the media, and they were afraid to take him on. As governor, Reagan was an ex officio member of the board of regents and at his first meeting on January 20, 1967, told them that if they wanted to fire Kerr, they had his full support; he would handle the political fallout. Kerr was ejected, to his own evident disbelief.

Then Reagan turned to the activists. Initially he tried to engage them in dialogue, but he soon found that they only wanted to trade barbs and insults. Reagan's quick-wittedness is apparent from records of some of those exchanges. At one campus meeting, a student told Reagan that it was impossible for people of Reagan's generation to understand young people. "You grew up in a different world," he said. "Today we have television, jet planes, space travel, nuclear energy, computers." Without missing a beat Reagan replied, "You're right. It's true that we didn't have those things when we were young. We *invented* them."[21]

As the war expanded and the antiwar movement gained momentum, the radicals became more impatient and aggressive, and Reagan became one of their main targets. Burning the governor in effigy became something of a campus ritual. Reagan's aides told him to stay away from the universities and tried to arrange for rear-door exits so that the governor could leave his public engagements without encountering the protesters. "We tried to keep him away from the troublemakers," Ed Meese told me, "but he wouldn't listen." Reagan frequently faced his radical accusers. He saw that their threats were mostly bluster and wanted to show them he was not intimidated. He also guessed that many voters would not approve of unkempt activists' shouting obscene names at the governor. He understood the political value of making the right enemies.

The activists greeted him with banners that said "Impeach Bonzo and His Co-Star" and "Jane Wyman Was Right," so he decided to return their fire in his inimitable style. "Their signs say make love, not war," Reagan said. "But they don't look like they could do much of either." Of one particularly egregious demonstrator, Reagan observed that he "had a haircut like Tarzan, walked like Jane, and smelled like Cheetah." When the militants promised Reagan a "bloodbath," he told them that they should start by taking a bath. Reagan once witnessed a sidewalk lined with students staring him down and giving him the silent treatment. Reagan began to tiptoe, put his finger to his lips, and said, "Shhhhh." A few students broke out laughing, and Reagan ducked into his car with a smile. On another occasion when students chanted outside the governor's limousine and one held up a sign saying, "We are the future," Reagan scribbled on a piece of paper and held up his reply to the car window: "I'll sell my bonds."

Although he treated them as spoiled children, Reagan understood the real threat the activists posed to the normal functioning of the California university system. He said he would not permit protesters to stop students who wanted to learn from getting to class. For him, campus disruption, not free speech, was the main issue. He proved his seriousness at Berkeley in the late 1960s when a group of protesters occupied university facilities and hurled rocks and tear-gas canisters at local police, who tried to eject them. Reagan declared martial law and called in 2,500 members of the National Guard; order was promptly restored.

In May 1967, Senator Robert Kennedy, a Democratic presidential hopeful, debated the issue of the Vietnam War with Reagan in a town meeting format that was aired on national television. A number of student radicals were in the audience, and they denounced the United States and praised the North Vietnamese. Kennedy tried to placate and find common cause with the students, while Reagan opposed them in a tone alternately firm and bemused. RFK was later swamped with angry mail, while Reagan received congratulations for standing up for America. The pundits who expected the suave Kennedy to dispose easily of the shallow Reagan had to concede, based on the popular reaction, that Reagan had prevailed in the debate. Senator Edward Kennedy subsequently quoted his brother as saying that Reagan was the toughest debate opponent he ever had.[22]

RFK's ambivalent performance can be taken as one of the last stands of resistance to the counterculture within the Democratic party. Soon there would be the riots of 1968 at the Democratic convention, and by 1972, with the candidacy of George McGovern, the party would be largely taken over by the radicals. It would cease to be firmly anticommunist and become the party of disarmament and arms control. Its domestic policy became focused not on economic growth but on redistribution. Moreover, the cultural values of the Democratic party, far from reflecting those of the middle class, now came to be defined in opposition to the patriotism and moral traditionalism of millions of Americans.

The radicals, many of whom entered the academy and the media, never forgave Reagan for his conduct during the 1960s; indeed, over the years they continued to see him as the embodiment of everything they opposed. Indeed, the hostility of the contemporary revisionist view of Reagan owes much to the long-standing prejudices of this group. If Reagan proved to be right in what he believed, it would mean they were wrong in what they believed. But Reagan had no interest in what the radicals thought of him. He saw an opportunity to attract to the Republican side millions of Democrats whom their party had abandoned in its surrender to the counterculture.

Reagan's successful bid for the presidency in 1980 cannot be understood without seeing how he redefined the message of the Republican party to make it appealing to a majority of middle- and working-class Americans. Many conservative pundits do not understand this. Their view is that Goldwater pioneered the conservative takeover of the GOP, and they see Reagan as another Goldwater who happened to run at a more propitious time.[23] Shortly after Reagan was elected president, I attended an anniversary dinner for *National Review* at which George Will said in his keynote address, "It took approximately sixteen years to count the vote in the 1964 election, and Goldwater won."

Goldwater was a pioneering figure because he attracted a new generation of conservative activists to the Republican party. In 1964 they wrested the nomination from the moderate wing for the first time, and their grassroots organizing and political institution building grew in magnitude and sophistication over the next decade and a half. Reagan benefited from the fertile harvest of ground that had been first ploughed by Goldwater's recruits.

There were important differences between Goldwater and Reagan, however, which help to explain why the former failed and the latter succeeded. Goldwater was basically an Old Testament figure. He was anchored in the time-tested values of the past and seemed to regard the future as anathema. He was a reactionary who threatened to repeal much of the New Deal. He also had a hard, combative edge, evident in his boast that the United States could "lob one into the men's room of the Kremlin." He famously said that "extremism in defense of liberty is no vice." Goldwater could be charming on occasion, but as a political candidate he frightened people.

Reagan, by contrast, was a New Testament figure. Like Goldwater, he was capable of outrageous remarks. As president, he once said over the radio that he had signed legislation "which outlaws Russia forever. The bombing begins in five minutes." But he didn't know that his microphone was turned on; Americans understood that he was joking. Moreover, when Reagan said that "sometimes moderation should be taken in moderation," there was a twinkle in his eye. Reagan projected a warmer public persona than Goldwater; he was philosophically conservative but temperamentally genial.

The two men differed not just in style but also in substance. Reagan spoke as a former New Dealer—he was the original "Reagan Democrat"—and this gave his criticisms of government an authenticity and credibility they otherwise would have lacked. Moreover, the principles that Reagan upheld—anticommunism, economic growth, and traditional values—were once promoted by the mainstream of the Democratic party. Like Goldwater, Reagan looked to the past, but only to discover the foundation on which to build the future. He was forward-looking and optimistic and liked to quote the Revolutionary War pamphleteer Tom Paine, "We have it in our power to begin the world over again." Unlike Goldwater, Reagan was a populist whose conservatism was based on widely shared American values and was not afraid to place its trust in the good sense of the American people.

Yet Reagan was not ready to run for the presidency when he completed his second term in California in 1974. He may have had the general outlook and temperament, but he lacked national issues that would define his candidacy, distinguish him from others in the field, and win the assent of the voters. Nor, in truth, was the country ready for him. The Watergate crisis had destroyed the credibility of the Republican party. A new generation of left-leaning Democrats was elected to Congress, shifting the political center. In the mid-1970s, Reagan was seen as a far-right figure who appealed to a small constituency of reactionaries but had no future in national politics.

The six years from 1974 to 1980 were Reagan's wilderness years. He was a well-known figure but didn't really have a job. He founded a political action committee called Citizens for the Republic, wrote a syndicated newspaper column, recorded a daily radio commentary, and gave speeches for a living. He read widely, looking not for a new philosophy but for ammunition for his views. Reagan regularly excavated material from conservative publications like *National Review* and *Human Events.* He also began to peruse *World Marxist Review* to find out, as he put it, "what the other side is up to."

He read more seminal works, which he encountered through citations in conservative publications: Friedrich Hayek and Frederic Bastiat on economic liberty, and Whittaker Chambers and Aleksandr Solzhenitsyn on communism. He was especially interested in books about the American founding. One of Reagan's early biographers, Lee Edwards, told me he once spent a few hours perusing the books in Reagan's study and was surprised to discover that Reagan had gone through most of them, underlining passages of significance and making notes in the margin. Although Reagan read broadly and regularly, he was attracted not so much by the systematic analysis of works as by their trenchant observations, memorable turns of phrase, and revealing examples that he could use. Several aides told me that, as president, Reagan occasionally surprised them by citing the Roman emperor Diocletian's policy of wage and price controls or by invoking the medieval Islamic historian Ibn Khaldun's opinions on taxation and government revenues.

Reagan's understanding of communism, initially derived from his Hollywood experience, was undoubtedly deepened by the writings of Whittaker Chambers and Aleksandr Solzhenitsyn. He liked to cite a point that both Chambers and Solzhenitsyn made in different ways: communism is a false religion that seeks to destroy the family, private property, and genuine religious faith in order to achieve a kind of earthly paradise. Reagan was deeply moved by Chambers's autobiography and could recite from memory the lines in *Witness* wherein Chambers explains why he decided, for the sake of his children, to jeopardize his career and possibly his life in testifying about his past life in the Communist party. In that book, Chambers describes communism as "the focus of concentrated evil of our time."[24] Reagan, who had a vivid memory, did not forget this description.

Yet Reagan knew that ideas by themselves are not enough; they must be converted into the currency of politics. During his travels, he scavenged for issues that reflected his core beliefs and at the same time resonated with average Americans. He was like a political venture capitalist who was receptive to new ideas and willing to invest in them; he was not afraid to take big risks that offered the prospect of big gains. His market research was his radio show and his lectures, to which he carefully monitored the public reaction.

I reviewed some of the proposals Reagan advocated in those years. He recommended that the United States abandon détente and figure out a way to "roll back" the Soviet empire to its pre–World War II boundaries. He discussed the viability of distributing literature, including Bibles, to the citizens of the captive nations in Eastern Europe. He suggested that America return to the Monroe Doctrine and entertained schemes for getting rid of Castro. He speculated about eliminating the U.S. system of progressive taxation and returning to proportional taxation—what we now call the flat tax. He mused about the possibility of making social security voluntary. Some of these ideas he later jettisoned; others he kept; all of them he tested on the American people, trusting their judgment about whether a particular proposal made sense. He was searching for the common ground between conservatism and populism.

A researcher at the Hoover Institution has traced virtually all Reagan's presidential initiatives to ideas he propagated in the 1970s. In 1978, for example, Reagan said on his radio show, "Calling a Communist a liar is pretty frustrating. How do you insult a pig by calling it a pig? Communists are not bound by our morality. They say that any crime, including lying, is moral if it advances the cause of socialism."[25] Shortly after becoming president, Reagan would generate controversy by saying pretty much the same thing. Equally significant, in retrospect, is a visit that Reagan made to the Berlin Wall in 1978. Peter Hannaford, an aide who accompanied him, told me he remembers Reagan's "cold fury" as he gazed at the symbol of the divide between freedom and totalitarianism. Reagan's reaction was brief and to the point: "This wall has got to come down."

Reagan matured as a national politician during those years and yet understandably was restless about being out of the fray. In 1976 he decided to challenge Gerald Ford for the Republican presidential nomination. He had already made an earlier bid. Galvanized by ambition, he had allowed himself to be talked into submitting his name to the Republican convention as early as 1968, when he had not yet served two years of his first gubernatorial term. It was a rash and premature gesture, doomed from the start, because it soon became evident that Nixon was the clear front-runner who would have no trouble winning on the first ballot. "I'm not disappointed that I didn't get the nomination," Reagan told his political adviser Lyn Nofziger. "I wasn't ready for it."[26]

In 1976 Reagan was confident he could do better. His candidacy was a daring move, because Ford was the incumbent president and the Republicans tend to be loyalists who do not reward insurgencies. But this time he had his two-term gubernatorial record to establish his credentials for national office. He also had a major issue: foreign policy. The political climate had changed a great deal since the early 1960s, when both parties stood resolutely against Soviet expansionism, ready, as John F. Kennedy put it, to "pay any price" and "bear any burden" on behalf of liberty and democracy. But the Vietnam War changed all that. By the mid-1970s the Democrats had become the party of disarmament, seeking to protect American security through arms agreements aimed at limiting the growth of nuclear arsenals. The Republican party went along with the process of détente, merely adding the caveat that agreements should be verifiable. Nixon and Ford were both champions of détente, whose crowning achievement was the Strategic Arms Limitation Treaty (SALT).

Reagan attacked détente as a futile and dangerous attempt to accommodate an adversary bent on achieving military superiority and world domination. He noted that while the United States was busy negotiating "fatally flawed" treaties, the Soviet Union was building its nuclear stockpile, which had become at least as formidable in the mid-1970s as that of the United States. This new preeminence, Reagan argued, was beginning to translate into Soviet military and diplomatic victories in Africa, Asia, and South America. "The overriding reality of our time," Reagan said, "is the expansion of Soviet power in the world." He scorned the diplomatic initiatives of Henry Kissinger, the architect of foreign policy in the Nixon and Ford administrations, whose Machiavellian strategies were, in Reagan's view, diminishing American influence across the globe.[27]

Reagan introduced another issue into the campaign against Ford that was previously on no one's agenda. This was the Panama Canal treaty, negotiated during the 1960s and early 1970s, which transferred authority over the canal from the United States to Panama. Republicans and Democrats had both reconciled themselves to the treaty. Many people Reagan knew and respected, including William F. Buckley and John Wayne, supported it. But Reagan discovered during his travels that the Panama Canal "giveaway" struck a chord with many people, because they saw it as a matter of national honor. Of the canal Reagan said, "We bought it, we paid for it, it's ours and we're going to keep it," and the people applauded and cheered. When the professionals at the State Department objected to what they termed Reagan's irresponsible statements, Reagan said that he would consider giving up the canal after all "if we could throw in the State Department."[28]

Reagan was expected to win the first primary in the conservative state of New Hampshire, but Ford beat him narrowly and went on to win in Massachusetts, Florida, Illinois, and Vermont. The consensus within the GOP was that after five losses in a row, Reagan was finished. One after another, Republican governors, senators, and mayors urged Reagan to withdraw. Even Barry Goldwater endorsed Ford and called on Reagan to get out. Nancy Reagan pleaded with her husband to spare himself further embarrassment. Reagan's campaign manager, John Sears, on his own initiative set up a meeting with the Ford campaign to negotiate his candidate's withdrawal. Yet, sitting in his hotel room, with his campaign deeply in debt, Reagan refused to give up. Domestic policy aide Martin Anderson recreated the scene for me. "I'm taking this all the way to the convention," Reagan said, "even if I lose every damn primary between now and then." Anderson says he was struck by Reagan's immense courage to persist against unanimous advice and in the face of apparently hopeless odds.

With borrowed money, the Reagan campaign purchased TV time on local stations to air segments of his speeches. It worked: Reagan confounded the political establishment by winning the North Carolina primary. He then trounced Ford in several southern and western states, where his criticisms of détente and the Panama Canal treaty resonated with Republican voters. Using all the powers of incumbency, Ford fought back and eventually won the nomination, but his victory was extremely narrow: 1,187 delegates to Reagan's 1,070. Reagan gave a gallant speech at the convention, in which he declared that the Republican party would never be the same because it now had "a platform that is a banner of bold unmistakable colors with no pale pastel shades." The tumultuous reaction revealed that although many of the delegates were unwilling to dethrone a sitting president, their hearts were with the challenger. In a speech to his supporters the next day, Reagan paraphrased an English ballad: "Though I am wounded, I am not slain, I shall rise and fight again."

Privately Reagan confessed his frustration, knowing he had come so close. His son Michael presumed that Reagan was upset because so many of his allies, including Goldwater, had endorsed Ford. Yet Reagan said nothing about that; he seemed to understand the ephemeral allegiances of politics. He told Michael that his biggest regret about not getting the nomination and going on to win the presidency was that he was looking forward to sitting across the table from the Soviet general secretary and, after listening to his arms control proposals, walking over and whispering a single word, "Nyet," into his ear. Reagan said he was "really going to miss" not getting the chance to do that.[29]

Reagan resolved to try again in 1980. This time his opponent was Jimmy Carter, the peanut farmer from Georgia who had beaten Ford in 1976. Carter was vulnerable because his record on both domestic and foreign policy was one of the worst among modern presidents. The American people seemed willing to contemplate a fundamentally different approach and to consider a new type of leader to implement it. This time Reagan found an issue that proved critical for his success.

The issue was across-the-board tax cuts, and its chief political advocate was Congressman Jack Kemp of New York. Kemp himself was a convert to the new way of thinking, which he had picked up from a small group of economists and journalists. These men were mavericks outside the parameters of mainstream Keynesian economics. They had their meetings not in conference rooms but in New York bars and restaurants. They were "true believers" who saw themselves as the pioneers of a Copernican revolution in political economy. One of the supply siders, Jude Wanniski, was the author of a book modestly titled *The Way the World Works.*[30]

Reagan was attracted by these intellectual entrepreneurs, even though he knew some of them were cranks. Aide Martin Anderson told me that "Reagan understood that revolutionary ideas are often generated in unfashionable precincts." Not that he followed their abstruse theorizing. Reagan was never strictly a supply sider. He once joked that he didn't even know what the term meant. But he was outraged that high rates of inflation were pushing Americans into higher tax brackets—"taxation without legislation"—and he felt that working people were morally entitled to a tax cut that would allow them to keep more of their earnings.

He also appreciated the economic logic of the theory: if you tax people less, they have an incentive to produce more. He saw this in Hollywood, where marginal tax rates of 90 percent discouraged film stars from making more than one or two movies a year. In 1978 Congress reduced the capital gains tax, which immediately resulted in an increase in the venture capital available to new and expanding companies. That same year Reagan witnessed the breadth of public support for tax cuts in his home state, where voters by a two-to-one margin approved Proposition 13, which enacted deep cuts in property taxes. As a presidential candidate, Reagan instinctively understood the political potency of the issue: if you promise to tax people less, they are more inclined to vote for you.

One might expect that the Republican party would have figured this out long ago. But not for nothing have the Republicans been called the "stupid party." Prior to Reagan, the GOP was the party of balanced budgets and fiscal austerity. Its main political focus was to cut government spending or, failing that, to balance the federal budget by raising taxes. Goldwater himself had opposed John F. Kennedy's plan to cut income tax rates on the grounds that it was fiscally irresponsible and would exacerbate the deficit. When traditional Republicans did support tax reductions, they tended to favor tax cuts for corporations rather than for working families. No wonder the sadomasochists in the GOP had been losing elections since the 1930s. For decades, the Democrats were seen as the good guys. They had what Jack Kemp called a "Santa Claus strategy," promising the American people generous spending programs. The Republicans were seen as the bad guys. They had, in Kemp's phrase, a "Scrooge strategy." They tried to take away people's benefits some of the time, and the rest of the time they raised taxes to pay for Democratic programs. Unwilling to have his party continue its losing role as tax collector for the welfare state, Reagan hit upon a new strategy: let the Democrats pay for their own programs. The Republicans would concentrate on giving people back their hard-earned money. Breaking with Goldwater, Reagan embraced Kennedy's concept of sharp reductions in income tax rates.

Reagan integrated the concept of lower taxes into his broader campaign theme, which he defined for a Republican audience in the following way. The Democrats, he said, are the party of group interests. The Republicans will be the party of shared values, which he specified as family, work, neighborhood, peace, and freedom. Traditionally, Reagan said, we think about which side to take in the division between industry and labor, rich and poor, city dweller and suburbanite. Yet there is a "community of values" that cuts across these conventional barriers. The suburbanite who owns a small business, no less than the union member who lives in the city, both want tax relief, a dollar that holds its value, safe neighborhoods, and greater control over their own lives. These people, Reagan said, are angry because "they are victims of an undeclared war against the things they hold most sacred. And we are their allies in that war."[31]

Reagan pledged to restore people's confidence in a country where their security is protected and where they are permitted the freedom to fashion a decent life for themselves and their families. His campaign was based on three pillars. First, he promised large increases in defense spending in order to deter Soviet aggression and achieve "peace through strength." Second, he pledged to give Americans an across-the-board 30 percent income tax cut in the belief that this would help the economy to grow faster. Finally he resolved to have government policies that affirm traditional, commonsense values. Here, finally, was a conservatism at home with the shared beliefs and aspirations of the American people. It blamed any "malaise" in the country not on the inadequacy of the citizens but on a failure of presidential leadership.

President Carter and the Democratic leadership were not impressed by any of this. From the outset they made a familiar mistake: they regarded Reagan as the weakest of the Republican candidates.[32] Thus they were elated when he won the nomination. Carter and his advisers knew that they had a difficult record to defend, but they did not believe they needed a defense. They reasoned that if the best and the brightest could not solve the problems of stagflation and the energy crisis, they must be insoluble. Instead they decided to make Reagan himself the issue. They were confident that Americans would never elect a man they regarded as a washed-up actor whose political views were clearly outside the political mainstream.

Media coverage focused on Reagan's campaign "gaffes," such as his reference to a Chicago "welfare queen" whom he described as having eighty names, thirty addresses, and twelve social security cards and a tax-free income of $150,000 a year. The press tracked down the woman in question; it turns out that she had four aliases and was charged with a fraudulent collection of $8,000.[33] The gaffe didn't hurt Reagan politically, because voters accepted his general point that there was plenty of waste and fraud in government, and they were not reassured to discover that the Chicago woman was bilking taxpayers of "only" $8,000 a year.

Reagan was also ridiculed by his opponent and the media for stating that the U.S. economy was in a depression. "That shows how little he knows," Carter said, pointing out that Reagan failed to appreciate the difference between a recession and a depression. Reagan proceeded to give Carter a lesson in political terminology. "A recession," he said, "is when your neighbor loses his job. A depression is when you lose yours. And recovery is when Jimmy Carter loses his." This became one of his best-received lines on the campaign trail.

It soon became apparent that public disgust with Carter was thrusting many working- and middle-class Democrats into the Reagan camp. Polls had Reagan running strong even in Carter's home base, the South. Carter recognized that he had only one strategy that might defeat Reagan and he put it into effect: a sophisticated version of the so-called daisy strategy that Lyndon Johnson used against Barry Goldwater. In an infamous campaign commercial that showed a child being incinerated in a nuclear explosion, the Johnson team implied that if Goldwater was elected president, he would blow up the world in an atomic holocaust. The TV ad generated enormous controversy, but Johnson was elected in a landslide. Following in Johnson's path, Carter alleged that Reagan was a dangerous extremist who would bring the country closer to atomic war, destroy the social fabric, and set North against South, white against black, and Christian against Jew.[34]

This mode of rhetoric was generally beneath Carter, but with the presidency at stake, he was willing to use it. Carter's accusations were supported and echoed by the pundits and the intelligentsia. The strategy backfired, however, because Reagan wasn't Goldwater. During his public appearances and on television the American people for the first time encountered Reagan the man. Landon Parvin, a Reagan speechwriter, explains that "when he was governor of California, the rest of the country thought he was a hard-edged kind of guy. But once the nation got to know him, they realized that it was not the case at all. They'd been *reading* the lines; they hadn't been *listening* to them."[35] Reagan's famous riposte to Carter in the Cleveland debate, "There you go again," epitomized for many the incumbent's rhetorical excess and Reagan's reassuring self-confidence. Public opinion, uncertain to the last, finally turned decisively in Reagan's favor.

Reagan became, at sixty-nine, the oldest man to be elected president of the United States. Finally he had what biographer Lou Cannon termed his "role of a lifetime": he got to be John Wayne. Most Americans recognized that he brought to the job varied experience as sportscaster, actor, labor leader, motivational speaker, and public official. He was a friendly man whom people could identify with, and he had some new ideas—this too the people saw. What was not so apparent, and was indeed disguised by his simplicity and geniality, was that Reagan was a revolutionary who intended to change the existing order; a self-confident leader who trusted his beliefs and instincts and could not be seduced by the temptations of power or prestige; a lone warrior who was willing to withstand the disapproval of the intellectuals, the media, and even his own aides; and a shrewd gambler who was ready to take risks to achieve his objectives. These were the qualities that enabled him to win the presidency, and he took them with him to the White House.

Chapter 4

A Walk on the Supply Side

PRESIDENT REAGAN CAME TO Washington with the most ambitious program for America since the New Deal. In his inaugural address, Reagan called for deep, across-the-board tax cuts and limits on domestic spending. He predicted that if his program was implemented, the economic woes of the Carter era would end and the United States would enjoy lasting economic growth and prosperity. During his administration, his conservative allies supported his tax reductions but criticized his failure to reduce government spending substantially. His liberal critics opposed the tax cuts and faulted him for increasing spending on defense while slowing the growth of domestic programs. Both groups subsequently blamed him, at least in part, for the huge deficits that attended his tenure. Nearly a decade has passed since Reagan left office, and we are now in a good position to evaluate whether he made the best decisions under the circumstances and whether his economic policies succeeded.

In a sense, Reagan's agenda was more radical than that of Franklin Roosevelt. When FDR was first elected in 1932, he had only a vague idea of how to counter the depression; his policies were ad hoc responses to specific changes in economic and political conditions. Reagan, by contrast, had a comprehensive and explicitly outlined program for bringing down double-digit inflation and reviving economic growth after nearly a decade of stagnation and decline. He was determined to see it tried.

Moreover, FDR was moving with the flow of events in the industrialized nations. Welfare states had already been established in Europe, and Roosevelt was steering the United States down that familiar path. FDR also had the support of the American intelligentsia, in part because he entrusted the project of developing new programs to a brain trust drawn from the ranks of the wise men of his day. Reagan, by contrast, was swimming against the current. He sought to limit a government that had been growing for more than half a century. He provoked the opposition of political and intellectual elites because he sought to curb rather than expand their power.

Reagan believed intellectuals have no right to attempt to plan or manage the economy. He didn't think intellectuals knew how, and he didn't think the American people intended them to do it. Reagan held the view that individuals are the creative force in a society and should be given a greater control over their own destiny. Reagan believed that society was best served not by bureaucrats but by entrepreneurs, putting their own resources at risk in the hope of creating something new. The main objective of Reagan's economic policies was to create an environment in which the innovative energy of entrepreneurs could be unleashed.

For Reagan this meant steep, across-the-board tax cuts that would allow citizens to keep more of their money. It meant limiting the growth of government so that it consumed a smaller share of the nation's resources. It required reducing the magnitude of burdensome federal regulation to enable small business to prosper. It implied privatizing certain government services, so that they could be more efficiently performed by the private sector. Finally, it meant restoring power from the federal bureaucracy to the states, so that problems could be solved at the local level.

Yet, for someone with such a bold and far-reaching agenda, Reagan began his presidency with what seemed to many observers like extraordinary casualness. On the morning of inauguration day, Reagan's aide Michael Deaver arrived at Blair House shortly before 9 A.M. to help the Reagans prepare for the ceremonies.

"Where's the governor?" Deaver asked, and Nancy replied, "I guess he's still in bed." Astonished, Deaver walked into the bedroom, where the lights were out and the curtains were drawn. "Governor?"

"Yeah?"

"It's nine o'clock."

"Yeah?"

"You're going to be inaugurated in two hours."

"Does that mean I have to get up?"[1]

Even in the White House, Reagan persisted with his unhurried style. When he was informed that his first meetings were scheduled for 7:30 A.M., his response was that they would have to start without him, because he would be showing up at 9:00 A.M. The meetings were rescheduled for 9.30 A.M. Asked about his reluctance to do overtime at the White House, Reagan said, "I know that hard work never killed anyone, but I figure, why take a chance?"

Reagan's more relaxed approach to his work schedule was symbolized by his decision to remove Harry Truman's portrait from the cabinet room and replace it with one of Calvin Coolidge. Coolidge is regarded by historians as a do-nothing president because of his philosophy that a free society basically runs itself and politicians would do well not to interfere. Coolidge was also famous for taking a mid-afternoon nap and would actually change into his pajamas. When he opened his eyes, he would sometimes grin at his aides and say, "Is the country still here?" Despite this lethargic approach—or perhaps because of it—Coolidge presided over an era of unparalleled prosperity in the 1920s, and won reelection in a landslide. He was one of Reagan's favorite presidents.

Reagan also took an easygoing approach to his senior appointments, which distressed both liberals and conservatives. The right was alarmed to see men like James Baker and Michael Deaver as Reagan's close advisers. They were regarded as "pragmatists" or "business-as-usual" Republicans who were not fully committed to the Reagan agenda. Many liberals were disturbed at Reagan's indifference to the ethic of the idealistic public servant. Reagan said he had no intention of hiring people who *wanted* a job in government; he wanted people of accomplishment from private enterprise who had to be *persuaded* to join the public sector. Aides told me that when Reagan was presented with a list of economists to serve as his Council of Economic Advisers, his reaction was, "I've got several millionaires in my cabinet who have made their own money. Why do I need a bunch of economists?"

Sometimes Reagan made appointments based on instinct, with only cursory information about people. For example, he was considering Malcolm Baldrige for commerce secretary, but Baldrige had been a Bush supporter in the Republican primaries, and Reagan wasn't sure he wanted him for the job. Reagan asked to speak to Baldrige over the phone, but was told that he couldn't be reached, because he was somewhere out West riding in a rodeo. Reagan asked, "Is he actually riding?" He was told yes. "Don't bother to reach him," Reagan said with a smile. "Let's go ahead with the nomination. He'll be fine."

When the pundits and Washington insiders saw these signs, they exchanged meaningful looks. They were confident that Reagan would prove to be a weak and ineffective leader. He didn't have a mandate, they said; the American people hadn't voted for him; they had voted against Jimmy Carter. Besides, they said, Reagan is not even as intelligent as Carter, not to mention that Carter had a Democratic Congress. Under Reagan the Republicans had a slight majority in the Senate, but the Democrats controlled the House. Many political observers, including some seasoned Republicans, said publicly that Reagan could be expected to abandon his campaign dogma as soon as he encountered the realities of governing.

Reagan got the same condescending treatment when he stopped in to see Tip O'Neill, the powerful Democratic Speaker of the House. Reagan told O'Neill that he expected a good working relationship because he had gotten along well with the Democratic-run California legislature. O'Neill replied, "That was the minor leagues. You're in the big leagues now." It was an insulting remark to make to the new president on meeting him for the first time, but Reagan didn't seem offended, only a bit surprised.

It was only a matter of weeks, however, before the political establishment realized that Reagan was moving purposefully to get his campaign promises enacted into law. A headline in the *Washington Post* proclaimed, "Epic Political Struggle Looms: Official Washington Realizing Reform Crusade Is Not Business-As-Usual."[2] "We made quite a stir," Reagan later remarked to his aides. "Everybody found out that we were going to do just what we said we were going to do."

Immediately after delivering his inaugural address, Reagan performed his first official act as president: he signed an executive order eliminating the price controls on oil and gasoline that had been in place for a decade. The next day, Reagan abolished the Council on Wage and Price Stability. Although the price controls were promoted as a response to the energy crisis, they had in fact exacerbated it by distorting the market forces of supply and demand. Critics of Reagan's action, like Senator Howard Metzenbaum, warned that gas prices would rise to two dollars a gallon. Reagan predicted that oil and gas prices would fall dramatically, and he proved to be right. Not many people knew it at the time, but with two strokes of his pen, Reagan had ended the energy crisis.

Six months later, Reagan proved he was serious about dramatically changing the priorities of the federal government. Congress approved, and Reagan signed into law the central plank of Reagan's campaign platform: the largest tax cut in American history. The vote was relatively close in the House of Representatives, 238 to 195, yet several moderate Democrats—the so-called "boll weevils"—had defected from their party to vote with the president. The Reagan plan won decisively in the Senate, 89 to 11. Alternative proposals supported by the Democratic leadership were defeated in both houses. Noting that previous presidents seemed unable to manage the complexity of government, David Broder of the *Washington Post* called Reagan's tax victory "one of the most remarkable demonstrations of presidential leadership in modern history."[3] Even Reagan's critics were impressed. Author Ronnie Dugger conceded that "no ordinary person could have achieved what Reagan has."[4] The professional politicians were aghast that they were outmaneuvered by a man they had considered a hopeless amateur. In a sense Reagan had proved Tip O'Neill right: he wasn't in Tip's league, he was playing a different game.

So how did Reagan do it? The most pressing problem of the late 1970s was stagflation—stagnant growth and inflation occurring simultaneously. This posed a serious problem for the mainstream school of Keynesian economics, because these two evils were not supposed to go together. The Keynesian approach was premised on the notion that experts can control the ups and downs of the economy by manipulating government spending and the money supply.

A central principle of modern Keynesian thought is the Phillips curve, which specifies an inverse relation between unemployment and inflation. In practice, this means that policymakers can reduce unemployment or inflation but not both. If you bring one down, the other will go up. Economic policy is a matter of figuring out where you want to be on the trade-off between the two.

It all makes sense in theory, at least if you accept Keynesian assumptions, yet during the 1970s, the United States and other Western countries encountered high rates of inflation and high unemployment. Both variables were going up in tandem. Not only were Keynesian policies proving ineffective, but the Keynesian model itself was in crisis because it no longer described economic reality. Baffled, some Keynesians announced that the industrialized world had reached a point where it could not expand any more and began talking about our need to adjust to what a best-selling study of the period termed the "limits to growth."[5]

There were two conservative schools of thought that proposed an alternative approach: a mainstream view called monetarism, identified with the Nobel laureate Milton Friedman, and a maverick view called supply-side economics, identified with economists Robert Mundell and Arthur Laffer. The monetarists argued that price levels were rising because there was too much money in circulation; thus the best way to bring down inflation was to control the supply of money in the economy. The supply siders argued that the best way to promote economic growth was to cut marginal tax rates so that entrepreneurs would have a greater incentive to produce, thus invigorating the economy from the production or "supply" side.

Supply-side thinking first came to national attention in the late 1970s in the pages of the *Wall Street Journal*. Its main propagandist was Jude Wanniski, an editorial writer for that newspaper. Wanniski had converted Robert Bartley, editor of the *Journal,* and he was determined to proselytize the rest of the world. Yet Wanniski was only the evangelist. The man whose ideas he was propagating was a boyish-looking economist named Arthur Laffer, who lent his name to the famous Laffer curve. The Laffer curve, which Laffer is said to have first drawn on a cocktail napkin to explain the concept to a staffer in the Ford administration, posits that there are two levels of taxation that produce an identical level of government revenue.

Imagine two scenarios: a tax rate of zero percent and a tax rate of 100 percent. In both cases, the amount of revenue the government can expect in tax receipts is zero. In the first case the answer is obvious: the government doesn't tax people, and so it doesn't take in any money. But Laffer's point is that a 100 percent tax rate produces the same result; if the state takes away everything the citizens produce, then they have no incentive to work and so will produce nothing.

Once this principle is grasped, the Laffer curve becomes virtually self-evident. Laffer's broader argument was that once the marginal tax rate—the tax on an additional dollar of income—reaches a certain point, it has such a deleterious effect on incentives that entrepreneurs either stop producing more or move their money into tax shelters. Thus the government's objective in raising taxes, which is to secure more revenue, is thwarted. The supply siders argued that marginal tax rates in the United States, which had reached as high as 70 percent, had crossed the Laffer limit and were both stifling the economy and reducing tax receipts.

Reagan's approach was to combine the monetarist and the supply-side solutions. This was an unconventional strategy; only a few reputable economists, among them Milton Friedman and Robert Mundell, thought it could work. Moreover, Reagan's economic strategy brought political problems, because from the outset of his administration, the monetarists and the supply siders began to fight over whose philosophy should be emphasized. It was a veritable slugfest, with lots of well-known economists taking part—Alan Greenspan, Arthur Burns, Martin Anderson, and Paul Craig Roberts—and the ever-voluble Jack Kemp weighing in from the outside.

By and large the two groups rejected Friedman and Mundell's compatibility theory. Each group sought to place its advocates in high-level appointments at the Treasury, in the White House, and on the cabinet councils. Both groups warned the president that if the solutions of the other camp were accepted, disaster would follow. Some supply siders wanted Reagan to pressure the Federal Reserve Board to abandon its policy of restricting the money supply on the grounds that tight money would choke off the economic recovery. Some monetarists worried that Reagan's tax cuts would exacerbate the problems of inflation and the budget deficit.

As for the Keynesian experts who were advising the Democrats, their own inability to solve the problem of stagflation did not restrain them from vehemently denouncing the Reagan program as incoherent and destructive. Robert Reich, who would become President Clinton's labor secretary, found it "hopelessly contradictory: a tight monetary policy yoked to a profligate fiscal policy."[6] Reich argued that the tax cuts would release money into the economy, and restrictive monetary policy would have the opposite effect. From a Keynesian point of view, this was like putting one foot on the brake and the other on the gas pedal.

Reagan paid little attention to the outside criticism, and even less to the convulsions within his own administration. He listened to briefings from the rival conservative groups and always nodded in agreement, yet his real attention lay elsewhere, on the question of how to get the biggest and broadest tax reduction possible out of Congress. Here his main obstacle was Tip O'Neill; the man whom one Republican congressman had likened to the government itself: "big, fat and out of control." Reagan liked O'Neill; the two of them enjoyed swapping Irish stories and got along well together. On one occasion, after a glass of champagne in the Oval Office, Reagan said, "Tip, if I had a ticket to heaven and you didn't have one too, I would give mine away and go to hell with you."[7] But Reagan also knew that O'Neill was a truculent political linebacker who would do everything he could to block the new agenda. Once he called O'Neill to protest the vicious remarks O'Neill made about him to the press. "Ol' buddy, that's politics," O'Neill said. "After six o'clock we can be friends, but before six, it's politics."[8] Such is the modus vivendi of the Washington establishment.

The pundits continued to debate whether Reagan had a mandate, but he acted as if he did. He informed the Congress that there was no alternative to his tax cuts and they would have to be approved in their entirety or the nation's economic woes would continue indefinitely. When the Democrats protested, Reagan deployed the acumen and experience of his aides, especially chief of staff James Baker, a savvy political wheeler-dealer, to win the support of moderate Republicans in the Senate and conservative Democrats in the House. Without both these groups, Reagan could not possibly win a majority.

Then Reagan scheduled a national television address. One of his aides asked him what a TV presentation had to do with negotiating with Congress, and he replied, "When you can't make them see the light, make them feel the heat." In a prime-time appeal, Reagan asked the American people to call and send telegrams to their representatives demanding immediate support for his tax plan. The response was overwhelming.

Reagan didn't get everything he wanted, but he got almost everything, because he was able to use the negotiating skills he learned from his days at the Screen Actors Guild. As White House aide David Gergen recounted the process to me, at each stage, the Democratic leadership would make compromises and expect him to sign, but he wouldn't. So they would give a little more, and he still wouldn't sign. No, he would say; I cannot bring myself to do this. Again the Democrats would relent, and just when their patience was exhausted and they had given about everything they could, Reagan would prevail on them to concede a bit more, and then suddenly he would sign. Tip O'Neill protested that Reagan's style of bargaining was extremely unfair, verging on blackmail. Reagan responded with an injured expression.

According to the historic 1981 tax legislation, taxes would be reduced by 25 percent across the board, with a 5 percent reduction the first year and 10 percent for each of the two subsequent years. The top marginal rate would fall from 70 to 50 percent. This was the first tax cut. Then starting in 1985, taxes would be indexed to inflation, ending the phenomenon of bracket creep. The tax tables would be adjusted each year taking inflation into account, so it would no longer push people into higher tax brackets and force them to pay higher rates without a corresponding increase in their purchasing power. There were also reductions in estate and business taxes, while individual retirement accounts were expanded, allowing more people to make tax-deductible contributions toward retirement.

Against the odds, Reagan had achieved one of his major objectives: lightening the tax burden on the American people. Asked by an aide whether he liked being president better than being a movie actor, he replied, "Yes, because here I get to write the script too."

Yet problems remained on the spending side; if you cut taxes and don't reduce government spending, you encounter the green monster called the deficit. The deficit has been the primary political issue of recent years, so it is not surprising that many people remember the Reagan era as the unfortunate period in which the national debt began to spiral out of control. By this measure, the wise men's concerns about the economic legacy of the 1980s seem entirely justified. The deficit was around $50 billion when Reagan became president. Deficits during the Reagan years surged above $200 billion during the mid-1980s. The United States was $1.5 trillion deeper in debt when Reagan left office than when he arrived. That works out to one-fourth of our gross national product, or $15,000 for each American family.[9]

Many intellectuals and media pundits contend that the prosperity of the Reagan years was largely illusory because it was borrowed against the earnings of our children and grandchildren. As *Business Week* summed it up in 1990, "Charge it! That simple slogan was almost a battle cry for a generation that spent its way through most of the 1980s."[10] Reagan is faulted for abetting an intergenerational crime: during his administration, the federal government robbed future Americans to enrich those who merely happened to be around at the time. Thus economist Benjamin Friedman charges Reagan with intellectual incompetence "of the first magnitude" as well as "moral irresponsibility on a truly astonishing scale."[11]

The wise men also fault the way in which money was distributed and spent during the 1980s, a decade represented by many historians and political scientists as an era of greed and selfishness. It was "a golden age for financial wheeling and dealing," economist Paul Krugman writes.[12] "Not in decades, perhaps not in the century," journalist Haynes Johnson informs us, have "acquisition and flaunting of wealth been celebrated so publicly by so many."[13] Yet very little of this largesse is believed to have reached the middle class or the poor. The 1980s were, as President Clinton put it, "the trickle-down Reaganomics years." Michael Schaller speaks for many scholars when he sums up the era as one in which "the rich got richer and everyone else treaded water."[14]

Conservative politicians and scholars generally disagree with the characterization of the 1980s as a wanton and profligate era, but they are no less critical of Reagan for the deficit, which they too see as a sign of fiscal irresponsibility. Senator William Armstrong asked, "What's the sense of having a Republican administration . . . if the best we can do is a $200 billion deficit?"[15] The main source of the deficit, conservatives allege, is Reagan's failure to limit the growth of domestic spending. Pointing out that, under Reagan, federal spending as a percentage of the gross domestic product remained roughly the same as during the Carter administration, William Niskanen, a member of Reagan's Council of Economic Advisers and now head of the Cato Institute, contends that the president's economic policy fell short of its own stated purpose in the most important respect.[16] Worse, conservatives say, Reagan didn't even make a serious effort. Free market activist Fred Smith insists that "the Reagan revolution hasn't failed—it really hasn't been tried."[17]

Reagan, we are told, was too detached to figure out what was going on and make the tough choices. "His presidency would have been a lot more successful," columnist Fred Barnes concludes, "had Reagan not been so lazy."[18] Instead of exercising leadership and convincing the American people to endure some restraint on their entitlements, Reagan is said to have contented himself with a superficial feel-good politics. And so, writes author David Frum in *Dead Right,* the Reagan era is over, the federal government is larger than ever, and we are saddled with those deficits that must at some point be paid off.[19]

To evaluate these criticisms, we must recover the context of the issues facing Reagan when he arrived in Washington. The question is not, Are we living with challenges inherited from the Reagan era? People in every period of history must contend with the legacy of those who came before them. Yet, before we condemn our forebears for leaving us with problems, we must assess how responsibly they dealt with the ones they confronted. It makes no sense to denounce Lincoln for saddling the country with Civil War debt without asking whether the war was worth fighting in the first place. Nor are leaders, always constrained by external forces, able to achieve everything they want. The challenge of leadership is to establish priorities and make difficult choices. So the real question is, Given the situation facing Reagan in the 1980s, how well did he exercise his leadership, and how sound were his economic decisions?

Reagan's choice to head the Office Management and Budget (OMB) was David Stockman, a former congressman from Michigan and a recent convert to supply-side economics, who was charged with finding a way for government receipts to match government expenses. Stockman's solution was to reduce federal spending drastically in order to bring it down to the level of tax revenues. Yet it took Stockman only a few months to conclude that Reagan was a dim-witted sentimentalist who lacked the understanding and the nerve to follow through on this grand project.

Stockman's bespectacled elegance concealed the temperament of a social revolutionary. He went from being an antiwar activist with Students for a Democratic Society in the 1960s to being a true believer resolved in Reagan's first year to launch a "frontal assault on the American welfare state." Stockman recognized the costs of such a crusade, namely, that "forty years . . . of promises, entitlements and safety nets issued by the federal government to every component and stratum of American society would have to be scrapped or drastically modified." Stockman gave it his best effort, he says, yet laments that his crusade was rebuffed, and eventually the whole enterprise went up in flames. The man who was most to blame for this, Stockman alleges, was Reagan. Reagan was a nice man, Stockman writes, but not a true revolutionary. He was a simple fellow who did not comprehend the magnitude of budget cuts that must be obtained, and he was too good-natured for the scorched-earth policy that the times demanded. The president, Stockman bitterly charges, allowed Caspar Weinberger and the Defense Department to take over the budget process and obtain just about everything they wanted. In what he considers a failure of leadership, Stockman faults Reagan with refusing to be an "iron chancellor" who would refuse to permit the big spenders in the Defense Department and in Congress to get away with it.[20]

As a consequence, Stockman abandoned his supply-side convictions and went from being a true believer in tax cuts to being a true believer in tax increases. He conspired with Republicans and Democrats on the Hill to secure tax hikes that would undo the effects of the Reagan tax cuts and, he hoped, moderate the forthcoming deficits. He also went public with his disaffection, telling journalist William Greider that he had rigged his original economic projections to make the tax cuts look viable and that the supply-side rhetoric was a "Trojan horse" that concealed a trickle-down program of rate reductions for the wealthy.[21]

It is odd for a chief executive to open the morning paper and see his budget director calling his policies unworkable and even malevolent. Moreover, Stockman's critique was enthusiastically embraced by the liberal pundits, who had no sympathy for Stockman's budget-cutting zeal but who were eager to see Reagan undermined from within his administration. After Stockman's embarrassing disclosures, Reagan should undoubtedly have fired him for brazen disloyalty. "If it were up to me," Nancy Reagan wrote in her autobiography, "Stockman would have been out on the street that afternoon."[22]

Yet, despite his wife's urgings, Reagan didn't fire Stockman, which revealed a serious vulnerability in his management style. He simply hated to fire people, even those who had done him grave and unnecessary injury. This weakness saved Stockman's position, or what was left of it. Even though his influence was greatly diminished, Stockman remained in the administration until 1986, a strange and forlorn figure, until he finally left to take a job on Wall Street.

The larger question remains: Was Stockman's severe depiction of Reagan accurate, and was his disenchantment over Reagan's failure to reduce the size of government basically justified? While running for president, Reagan frequently denounced what he termed "waste, fraud, and abuse" in government. He said he would restrain the growth of old programs and avoid new ones but did not propose to eliminate programs, let alone the entire range of entitlements. In emphasizing this point during the 1980s, columnist George Will offered a toaster to anyone who could specify a single program that Reagan pledged to abolish during the campaign. No one has come forward, and Will still has his toaster.

It is possible that Reagan was understating his objectives during the campaign for the purpose of getting elected. So consider his 1981 inaugural address, which set forth his governing philosophy. "It is my intention to curb the size and influence of the federal establishment," he said. "It is not my intention to do away with government. It is rather to make it work—work with us, not over us; to stand by our side, not ride on our back. Government can and must provide opportunity, not smother it; foster productivity, not stifle it."[23] These remarks suggest that Reagan sought to slow the growth of government and make it a catalyst, not an obstacle, for individual self-reliance. Reagan's statements can hardly be interpreted as a call to arms for Stockman's frontal assault on the welfare state.

On the other hand, Reagan's campaign speeches as well as his inaugural address clearly specified his top priorities: tax cuts and the defense buildup. Defense Secretary Caspar Weinberger told me that Reagan knew America's defense spending had dropped from 50 percent of the budget in 1960 to around 25 percent in the 1970s.[24] Reagan directed Weinberger to develop a program for the restoration of the military. Weinberger told him what it would cost, and Reagan approved his general estimates. Stockman challenged these numbers: he saw Weinberger as a hawk who had no sense of budgetary reality. Weinberger took an equally dim view of Stockman, whom he saw as a peevish schoolboy with a calculator. Aides who were present at their meetings confirmed to me that conversations between the two became acerbic at times.

Yet there was never any doubt from the outset whose side Reagan was on. He agreed completely with Weinberger that defense needs should be dictated by the national security and could not be determined simply by looking at how much money the domestic budget had to spare. Reagan paid little attention to Stockman's budget-cutting arguments because he had no intention of economizing in this area. Stockman seems so infuriated with Reagan for deciding against him on this vital point that he concludes that Reagan must not have understood the facts or that

Weinberger had somehow conned him. Yet both men's account of these disputes make it clear that Reagan was in charge; he made the decision.

Stockman was right that the defense buildup would prove to be extremely expensive. Measured in 1987 dollars, the military budget soared from $187 billion in 1980 to $286 billion in 1989, an increase of more than 50 percent.[25] If Reagan had not spent roughly $2 trillion on defense during his tenure, no doubt the deficit would have been a lot smaller. Yet Reagan justified the military buildup on the grounds that the United States was fighting a cold war. Economist Lawrence Lindsey points out that it is not uncommon for nations to borrow money in such situations. Moreover, America won the cold war. Lindsey calculates that the country's defense savings since the collapse of the Soviet empire have more than compensated for the investment that Reagan made in the 1980s.[26] In purely economic terms, Lindsey told me, the cost of the Reagan military buildup was "a fantastic payoff—the best money we ever spent."

This is not to say that Reagan initially disapproved of Stockman's attempt to reduce domestic spending. On the contrary, Reagan encouraged him and gave him unprecedented powers to cut spending enjoyed by no previous budget director. Essentially Stockman could dictate terms to other cabinet secretaries, to the point that virtually the entire cabinet was terrified of his budget axe. Stockman kept finding new programs to eliminate and eventually produced a blueprint for cuts of a staggering $100 billion a year. Yet Reagan was undeterred. During a budget meeting, he was asked if he could take the political heat, and he replied, "I come from a warm climate. I can take the heat." At one point Reagan said to Stockman, "We won't leave you out there alone, Dave. We'll all come to the hanging." This was both a message of support and a gentle hint of the impracticality of Stockman's fevered enterprise.

Stockman soon realized that there was little support for his crusade to reduce entitlement spending in Congress. He expected opposition from the Democrats, whom he regarded as ravenous "hogs." Stockman confessed, however, that the Republicans on Capitol Hill really surprised him. Stockman observed that Congressman Richard Cheney, who later served as defense secretary in the Bush administration, was one of the few who didn't demand spending favors for his district in return for his vote to cut federal programs. "I was shocked to find that the Democrats were getting so much Republican help in their efforts to keep the pork barrel flowing and the welfare state intact."

Stockman discovered what Reagan already knew: that legislators of both parties place a high priority on getting reelected, and they are strong backers of spending programs in their home states that will help them in this effort. In the end it was Stockman, the economic genius, who turned out to be a political dunce. His ignorance and miscalculation rendered him ineffective, so he ended his memoirs on a note of despair. The American people, he wrote, basically support big government. They say that the state has become too large and inefficient, yet by and large they approve of entitlement programs that they benefit from directly. They are against Leviathan in theory but not in practice. Stockman concluded that his own efforts were a failure and that the Reagan revolution was a disaster waiting to happen because it was inconsistent with the wishes of the people.[27]

In a democratic society, what the citizens want, they usually get. As a believer in popular government, Reagan had no intention of thwarting the shared preferences of the people. Yet were these preferences really shared? Sure, we are all eager to play the role of the selfish looter; we all like to get money for nothing. Thus we are always tempted to support government measures that impoverish other citizens to enrich ourselves. The principle was stated by that Fabian socialist George Bernard Shaw: "A government which robs Peter to pay Paul can always depend on Paul's support."[28]

For a politician like Reagan who wants to reduce the size of government, this is a problem but not an insurmountable one, because the shrewd politician can appeal to the same selfishness in citizens that sustains programs for themselves to deny benefits to others. Even as we nobly insist that the national interest is vitally served when government programs benefit us, we are quite willing to support measures to deny others—those indolent freeloaders—their checks. In other words, there is a Madisonian solution to the problem of the selfish looter, outlined in the *Federalist* Number Ten. Factions are inevitable in a free society, Madison argued. They cannot be outlawed without destroying freedom. So let us design a system in which interests can be set against each other, a framework of competing interests, so that only interests broad enough to serve the common good can prevail.

Yet there is a practical problem with the Madisonian solution, which economists call the "public choice" dilemma. Imagine a government program that takes one dollar in taxes from each of 1 million citizens and then turns over the money to a beneficiary group, say, the National Endowment for Pornography. (This is just a hypothetical example.) The NEP soon proceeds to waste the money on exhibits that initially shock and eventually bore viewers. Yet, when politicians of the Reagan stripe attempt to get rid of the program, they discover that it is virtually impossible to do it because the NEP now has a constituency of bureaucrats and grant recipients who will fight desperately to retain their subsidies. Now the politician turns to the people who are paying for the program and tries to rouse them in unified opposition to the NEP. Yet they cannot be stirred, for the simple reason that they have each invested only a dollar. In other words, although the beneficiaries of the program are fewer in number, they compensate for that weakness by the intensity of their determination, and their interests prevail. Multiply this example a thousand times, and you will understand what Reagan first saw when he was governor of California: once established, government programs usually last forever.

As president, Reagan knew how hard it would be to cut government spending, partly because programs are popular with beneficiaries and partly because of the "public choice" dynamic. Throughout his presidency Reagan never changed his outlook toward the legislature, which feeds the process. That he knew exactly what to expect from Congress can be illustrated by what he said to the former Senate majority leader, Howard Baker. Baker, whose responsibilities included being the president's liaison with Capitol Hill during the second term, recalls Reagan's call to offer him the job of chief of staff. Baker had taken his five-year-old grandson to the zoo, so his wife, Joy, answered the phone and Reagan said, "Joy, where is Howard?" She replied, "Mr. President, Howard is at the zoo." Reagan chuckled and said, "Wait until he sees the zoo I have in mind for him!"[29]

The problem for Reagan was that he knew he would have to do business inside this menagerie. Most important, he had to convince

PUYALLUP PUBLIC LIBRARY

Congress to approve the massive increases in defense spending he considered absolutely necessary. The Democratic leadership in the House was strongly opposed to the magnitude of the proposed buildup. Tip O'Neill and others made it absolutely clear that there was no way they were going to approve huge defense increases while at the same time voting for huge domestic spending cuts. On this point, White House domestic adviser Martin Anderson told me, no amount of presidential persuasion would change their minds. Reagan finally accepted the political reality that if he wanted a big increase in the defense budget, he would have to leave domestic spending roughly at existing levels. In a sense, Reagan reconciled himself to presiding over a large federal government as the price worth paying for his defense policy.

In 1981, the Reagan administration was able to get $35 billion in domestic spending reductions by tying them to the package of across-the-board tax cuts. Congress reluctantly agreed to cutbacks in food stamps, Medicaid, public service jobs, housing subsidies, unemployment compensation, urban mass transit, student loans, and welfare. One boondoggle make-work program from the 1970s, the Comprehensive Employment and Training Act (CETA), was eliminated. These were relatively modest savings, yet the reaction from Reagan's critics was tumultuous. Reagan was "soaking the poor to subsidize the rich," Tip O'Neill protested, dubbing the president "Herbert Hoover with a smile."[30] Senator Daniel Patrick Moynihan accused Reagan of "slashing government" with "devastating cuts" that would produce "radical disruptions of social programs."[31] Noting that government cutbacks disproportionately harmed blacks and other minorities, columnist Carl Rowan charged that the Reagan administration "encourages, subsidizes and defends racism."[32] Economist Robert Reich foresaw "the return of social Darwinism."[33] These were by and large the same critics who would subsequently blame Reagan for large budget deficits.

Anticipating a rising deficit, Reagan tried again in 1982 to obtain cutbacks in domestic spending. The seriousness of his concern about the deficit can be gauged from the fact that he even agreed to a tax increase as a bargaining chip to obtain spending reductions. Ed Meese told Reagan that the White House had a verbal assurance from the Democratic leadership on the Hill that for every dollar Reagan would approve in tax increases, Congress would approve three dollars in spending cuts. Reagan was instinctively averse to a tax hike, but he relented on the condition that only business and excise taxes be increased and the individual income tax cuts approved the previous year be preserved unchanged. Yet, as Meese describes it, this bargain turned out to be a ruse. Congress approved the tax increase, and Reagan signed it. "The country is still waiting for the spending reductions," Ed Meese told me. The lesson Reagan learned in California—if you raise taxes, government will immediately find a way to spend the money—was painfully reaffirmed. As president, he vowed never to repeat what he considered the biggest political blunder of his first term.

Instead he decided to try a different route. In 1982 Reagan asked businessman J. Peter Grace to establish a commission to investigate waste and fraud in government and to propose ways to reduce inefficiency. The Grace Commission uncovered many egregious examples of government practices that offended common sense and made over two thousand recommendations that covered everything from privatizing many government functions to eliminating processing and paperwork costs. The administration was able to implement a number of these recommendations, yet a substantial proportion proved politically untenable, because they required congressional approval, and politicians knew that there were constituencies that benefited from these spending measures. According to the motto on the Hill, one man's waste is another man's subsidy. The Grace Commission saved the government some money, but it was modest in relation to the overall budget.

Eventually Reagan abandoned any serious effort to reduce domestic spending substantially. Sometimes his frustration would give way to grim jokes. At a cabinet meeting he was informed that as part of congressional subsidies to the dairy industry, the federal government was stabilizing market prices by buying butter from producers, with the result that government warehouses currently had 478 million pounds of surplus butter. "Four hundred and seventy eight million pounds of butter!" Reagan gasped. "Does anyone know where we can find four hundred and seventy eight million pounds of popcorn?"[34]

There arose a deficit standoff between the Reagan administration and its Democratic critics. The Democrats warned of escalating deficits and demanded that President Reagan agree to tax increases and reductions in military spending. Reagan wouldn't agree to any further tax increases, which he believed would stifle the incentives of entrepreneurs and inhibit economic growth. He insisted that the defense buildup, costly though it might be, was vital to reverse the tide of Soviet expansionism and to affirm American principles of freedom and democracy around the world. From the very beginning, Reagan was clear about his priorities. He said in 1981, "I did not come here to balance the budget—not at the expense of my tax cutting program and my defense program."[35]

The deficits of the 1980s arose out of the imbalance produced by sharply reducing taxes on the one hand and lavishly increasing domestic and military spending on the other. Reagan accepted this situation not because it was ideal, but because it was the best he believed he could get under the circumstances. Yet he could take some solace in the fact that his two major priorities, tax cuts and the defense buildup, had been achieved. Although the size of the federal budget remained the same, its shape was quite different. No president since Franklin Roosevelt, *Time* rightly pointed out, had "done so much ... so quickly to change the economic direction of the nation."[36]

Reagan's failure to reduce domestic spending and control the deficit was a reversal for his principles and provoked sharp criticism from conservative intellectuals and activists. Yet there was no such reaction from the American people, because to them the deficit was an abstraction. Once accustomed to hearing about billions and trillions, they began to regard these figures as meaningless—just a matter of adding zeroes. Far more serious, as a political matter, was the fact that the U.S. economy had plunged into a deep recession in 1982. Only a year into his first term, Reagan found himself facing the most serious domestic challenge of his administration. All those who remember Reagan as the purveyor of feel-good sentiments—"the economics of joy," as Herbert Stein put it[37]—should carefully observe his leadership during what turned out to be the worst economic slowdown since the Great Depression.

The recession was not the consequence of tax cuts; indeed, the first 5 percent tax cut had barely gone into effect. Rather, it was produced by the restrictive monetary policies of the Federal Reserve, under the leadership of Paul Volcker. Volcker was a Carter appointee and no favorite of supply siders like Treasury Secretary Donald Regan or Congressman Jack Kemp, who warned that his tight money approach was dragging down the U.S. economy. Nevertheless Reagan supported Volcker's policies as a difficult but necessary solution to runaway inflation. Interest rates were already high, but Volcker raised them still further. Soon this harsh medicine worked; inflation came down and stayed down. This was the good news.

Yet, as inflation plummeted, unemployment skyrocketed. The Phillips curve seemed to be back with a vengeance. The unemployment rate rose from 7 to nearly 11 percent, which meant that more than 10 million Americans were out of work. Businesses began to close their doors. Farmers suffered foreclosures. The poverty rate rose from 12 to 15 percent. Homeless men and women, many of them alcoholics and drug addicts unable to take care of themselves, began appearing on the streets of major cities, their plight a reminder of the depths of the nation's economic problems.

Reagan's critics had predicted that his policies would prove inflationary, yet they immediately blamed him for the recession and dubbed his economic program "Reaganomics." Technically, those who attributed the recession to Reaganomics were being unjust, since even they recognized that Volcker was the prime mover and that his agency is independent of executive control. Yet, in a broader sense, they were right to hold Reagan accountable. He was the one who had been elected, after all. Moreover, Reagan reaffirmed his support for Volcker in 1983 when, against the recommendation of Donald Regan and others in his administration, he reappointed Volcker to a second term.

In the depths of the recession, CBS television aired a documentary, *People Like Us,* narrated by Bill Moyers. The show presented an emotional account of how Reagan's policies were making ordinary Americans suffer unbearable hardship. An Ohio man with cerebral palsy had been dropped from the welfare rolls. A Wisconsin mother who cared for her comatose daughter at home was forced by new Medicaid regulations to move her to an institution. A Hispanic woman whose welfare and health benefits were cut off could not afford cancer treatment for her teenage son. The Reagan administration protested the premise of the program, but to no avail.[38] Other media reports were equally unfavorable, profiling the anguish of the unemployed on a daily basis.

The pundits were also on hand to inform Reagan smugly they told him so. "It didn't take a genius to predict on Inauguration Day that Reaganism would unravel," wrote political consultant Kevin Phillips. It was foolish, Phillips suggested, to think that Reagan could solve the nation's serious problems with policies based on "maxims out of *McGuffey's Reader* and Calvin Coolidge."[39] The *New York Times* was equally triumphal: "The stench of failure hangs over Ronald Reagan's White House."[40] Keynesian economists seized the opportunity to demand that Reagan adopt their counsel and change direction. To avert economic disaster, economist Lester Thurow warned, "A new, completely different strategy is needed."[41] The intelligentsia and the Democrats proposed massive public works projects to put Americans back to work.

Reagan said no. Aides confirmed to me that he was under enormous pressure, not just from the Democrats on the Hill but also from Republican senators and congressmen, to acquiesce to further spending increases. Even Nancy Reagan, who was perturbed to see her husband portrayed as an unfeeling monster in the press, thought he should "do something." Annoyed by what he saw as a one-sided portrayal of his policies, Reagan said, "Is it news that some fellow out in South Succotash someplace has just been laid off?"[42]

This insensitive remark shows that the pressure was getting to Reagan, but he resisted all attempts to change direction. "He saw his role as one of maintaining steadiness of purpose," White House communications director David Gergen told me. More than anything else, Reagan believed, it is the responsibility of a leader under trying circumstances to avoid succumbing to quick fixes that would prove harmful over the long run.

So Reagan counseled patience. He told the American people that the economic crisis he had inherited took a long time to create, and it wasn't going to be solved in a year. He met criticism with his usual savoir faire. "Mr. President," reporter Sam Donaldson yelled at him after a press conference, "In talking about the continuing recession tonight, you have blamed the mistakes of the past and you've blamed the Congress. Does any of the blame belong to you?" Without missing a beat, Reagan replied, "Yes. Because for many years I was a Democrat."[43]

"Stay the course" was the theme he adopted in the 1982 midterm congressional election. Unlike Bush in 1992, Reagan did not attempt to deny that there was a recession and that people were suffering. Rather, he did what leaders must do in such circumstances: he appealed to a higher cause. "Stay the course" was an attempt to confer dignity to struggle. It was a message of hope because it reaffirmed to the people that there *was* a course. It was also a message of resolution because it suggested that Reagan was a president of firm beliefs who would not be easily swayed. And it asked of the American people endurance, in the expectation that the situation was going to improve.

Did the people respond with "three cheers for the Gipper"? They did not. According to the Gallup Poll, Reagan's popularity rating fell to 35 percent, the lowest for a president in the postwar era. The Teflon president suddenly seemed vulnerable. The 1982 election proved to be painful for Republicans, who lost twenty-six seats in the House. Yet since there were twice as many Democratic as Republican seats at stake in the Senate, the GOP managed to retain its majority of fifty-four to forty-six. The Democrats also did well in state and local races, winning seven additional governorships. The American people had rebuked but not routed the Republicans. Public patience with Reagan's policies was strained but not quite exhausted. At best, one could say, there was one cheer for the Gipper.

Even if Reagan had shown the resolve that we expect in a leader, his prospects looked bleak in January 1983. His attempt to reduce federal spending had produced few results. Indeed even his modest reductions looked insensitive, given the magnitude of poverty and unemployment. His effort to privatize government assets and restore government functions to the states and localities had gone nowhere. His tax cuts appeared a risky and needless gesture, as deficits soared. The country seemed in worse shape than it was under Carter. Just two years after he assumed office, Reagan was beginning to look like another failed one-term president.

Chapter 5

They Don't Call It Reaganomics Anymore

IDEAS HAVE CONSEQUENCES, conservatives like to say, and consequences matter. We can admire Reagan for being a politician of conviction who did not waver when the going was rough. Yet it remains to be seen if Reagan's convictions were the right ones. What is the point of staying the course through a recession if it turns out to have been the wrong course? Leaders are judged not just by a functional standard that measures how successfully they got their programs enacted into law; they are also liable for the results of those policies. Accordingly, we must consider whether Reagan was correct to subordinate the problem of the deficit to his other priorities—in this case, tax cuts.

In 1983, the final year that the Reagan tax cuts went into effect, the U.S. economy commenced a seven-year period of uninterrupted growth. These were "the seven fat years," as *Wall Street Journal* editor Robert Bartley calls them—the biggest peacetime economic boom in U.S. history. At a growth rate of 3.5 percent, well above the nation's historic average, the gross domestic product expanded by nearly a third in real terms.[1] Measured in 1990 dollars, median family income, which had declined during the 1970s, climbed from $33,409 in 1980 to $38,493 in 1989, a 15 percent increase.[2] While

European countries were facing chronically high unemployment rates, in America 5 million new businesses and 20 million new jobs were created, largely solving the nation's unemployment problem. Interest rates fell from 21 percent in 1980 to less than 10 percent. Despite sporadic ups and downs, including the steep fall of Black Monday in October 1987, the stock market more than doubled in value. Most spectacular, these results were achieved with low inflation. The double-digit price increases of the Carter years simply vanished; inflation became an insignificant problem in the Reagan era.[3]

The recovery took Reagan's critics in the press and among the intelligentsia by complete surprise. Their first impulse was to deny that the economy was improving. When it became obvious that the recovery was here to stay, they said that it "had little to do with Reaganomics," as historian Robert Dallek put it.[4] Rather, they insisted that it was a Keynesian recovery, produced by the conventional Keynesian remedy of a "tax cut stimulus." Yet if this was the obvious cause of the recovery, why had not one of the nation's Keynesian economists predicted it? Most of them had warned instead that Reagan's policies would lead to higher rates of inflation.[5] Not only did this prove to be false, but the very economic facts of the recovery had once again falsified the Phillips curve. Throughout the 1980s, we had low inflation and low unemployment. The two did not move in opposite directions, as the Phillips curve would lead us to expect.

The American people, however, didn't care whether it was a Keynesian recovery, or a monetarist recovery, or a supply-side recovery. People were back to work, gas prices were down, mortgages were affordable again, and with the government taking less in taxes, there was even money left over, in many cases, for a new car or that long-overdue vacation. As far as most people were concerned, if it made sense to speak of the "Reagan recession" of 1982, it made sense to call this a "Reagan recovery." No one could be surprised that Reagan easily won reelection in 1984. The world seemed to be working not as the liberal Democrats said it would but just as Reagan predicted.

Consider the promises that Reagan made when he campaigned for office. He promised to reduce the inflation rate, and it came down. He promised to cut taxes, and he did. He said that tax cuts would lead to an economic recovery, and they did. He said he would reduce unemployment, and it happened. He said he would lower interest rates, and they declined. What other president in the modern era can boast of a better record of keeping his promises?

Reagan permitted himself a little humor at the expense of his critics. He told reporters at the White House Correspondents' Association dinner, "It's my job to solve the country's problems, and it's your job to make sure no one finds out about it." He defined a Keynesian economist as "someone who sees something happen in practice and wonders if it would work in theory." He told the story of a friend of his who was asked to a costume ball: "He slapped some egg on his face and went as a liberal economist." Reagan quipped that "the best sign that our economic program is working is that they don't call it Reaganomics anymore."

Unable to disconnect the recovery from Reagan's economic policies, his critics advanced a more plausible criticism. America is doing well, they said, but not all Americans are doing equally well. In particular, they alleged that the 1980s were an epoch of greed, a "second Gilded Age," characterized by a "new plutocracy" indulging itself in "too many stretch limousines . . . too much high fashion . . . an ostentatious celebration of wealth," in the words of author Kevin Phillips.[6] This cultural critique was reinforced by Oliver Stone's film *Wall Street* in which the unscrupulous tycoon Gordon Gekko proclaims that "greed is good." Reagan's critics warned that while the modern-day robber barons were making their millions, the poor were getting poorer and the country was losing its bulwark, the great middle class.[7] The *Atlantic Monthly* featured a cover article on "The Declining Middle" and the *New York Times Magazine* followed suit with "The Disappearance of the Middle Class."

Even if all these facts were true, it is not obvious that they proved much. "The first object of government," Madison wrote in *The Federalist,* is "the protection of different and unequal faculties of acquiring property." Madison's point is not that inequality is the regrettable but necessary outcome of economic growth. He contended that it is a central purpose of the newly established Constitution to enable people to attain different levels of income and wealth. Reagan himself agreed with this view. The American dream, he frequently said, is that each individual has the right to fly as high as his abilities permitted. Consequently Reagan never seriously attempted to rebut criticisms based on the "fairness issue." During the 1984 campaign, presidential candidate Walter Mondale made income disparities one of his main themes. As Reagan was leaving the Rose Garden on one occasion, Andrea Mitchell of NBC News yelled out to him, "What about Mondale's charges?" Reagan replied, "He ought to pay them."[8] Yet this is perhaps too flippant an approach to the liberal concern with social justice, so we should investigate these criticisms, beginning with the poor.

When Reagan took office, the poverty rate had been rising, from 11.4 percent in 1978 to 14 percent in 1981. After climbing to a high of 15.2 percent during the recession of 1982, the poverty rate fell to 12.8 percent in 1989.[9] There were proportionately fewer poor people during Reagan's administration, and the poor as a group made modest financial gains in this period. The average real income of the poorest fifth of the population, as measured in 1989 dollars, increased from $6,494 in 1980 to $6,994 in 1989.[10]

Why such a small increase? The reason is that the majority of poor people do not work—they are not, strictly speaking, part of the economy—and therefore when the economy grows, they do not benefit from that growth. "A rising tide lifts all boats," John F. Kennedy famously said, but for this to happen, the boats have to be in the water.

To understand this better, consider the composition of the group that makes up the broad category of the poor in America.[11] A good number are single people who are just starting out on an upward earning curve but who are counted as poor because their current income is low. Another substantial group is the elderly, whose monthly income may be small but who are not in fact "poor" because their assets such as homes, cars, and savings typically give them a standard of living well above what we think of as poverty. The largest group of poor people consists of single-parent households, disproportionately black. Many of these are teenage unwed mothers. Their educational levels tend to be very low, and many have little, if any, work experience. This group does not benefit directly from tax cuts because it does not pay taxes. Poor people who do not own their own homes do not benefit from low mortgage rates. Even high-paying job openings are of little value to those who have neither the skills nor the work habits necessary to become members of the workforce.

As for the middle class, Reagan's critics are quite right that this group became measurably smaller during the 1980s. Measured in 1993 dollars, the percentage of families earning between $15,000 and $50,000 fell by nearly 5 points during the decade from 53.9 percent to 49.2 percent. These were the members of the "disappearing middle class." Yet their plight is an occasion for celebration, not alarm. The reason is that during the Reagan era, a substantial number of middle-class Americans became rich. They moved up rather than down. The percentage of families earning more than $50,000 in 1990 dollars rose by 5 points from 30.9 percent to nearly 35.9 percent. During the 1980s, millions of middle-class Americans disappeared into the ranks of the affluent.[12]

If the numbers of affluent Americans increased, did the rich also get richer during the 1980s? Indeed they did. Measured in constant dollars, the average income of the top 20 percent of the population increased from $70,056 in 1980 to $85,529 in 1989.[13] There was a veritable explosion of wealth at the very top end of the spectrum. In 1980 there were too few billionaires to count; by 1989, there were over fifty. When Reagan came to office, fewer than 5,000 people listed their annual income as $1 million or above; when he left, more than 35,000 people did. During Reagan's tenure, the number of Americans who had more than $1 million in assets increased from half a million to almost three times as many. Kevin Phillips sniffs that during the Reagan era so many Americans made so much money "that the term *millionaire* became meaningless."[14]

As Phillips's example suggests, the prosperity of the 1980s has provoked a good deal of antagonism. This reaction is natural. After all, when we do well, we call it success. When someone else does well, we call it greed. And there is a word for that: envy. Yet, in calmer moments, we would do well to ask: Was the burgeoning wealth of the Reagan era really a bad thing? What the Reagan policies seem to have fostered is an economic environment in which affluence, once the ancestral prerogative of the few, suddenly became accessible to a large and growing number of Americans. For the first time in history, a nation could honestly boast of mass affluence. It is easy to see why this change might upset members of the old order, whose millionaires' club started to get fairly crowded in the 1980s. But there is no rational reason for the rest of us to rue the phenomenon of a plethora of rich people. May the club expand so that there will be room for all!

Did the 1980s produce what author Haynes Johnson terms a Reagan-inspired "national climate of selfishness"? Well, there were those corporate raiders on Wall Street—Michael Milken, Carl Icahn, Saul Steinberg, and the rest—but then greed has never been in short supply on Wall Street. There was Leona Helmsley, but Leona Helmsley would be Leona Helmsley in any era. Certainly Ronald Reagan cannot be held responsible for the Reverend Jim Bakker's air-conditioned doghouse.

Yet what these examples suggest is that an era of prosperity like the 1980s is likely to produce its share of wheeling and dealing, as well as a good deal of conspicuous consumption. When people have a chance to attain affluence for the first time, we have the familiar phenomenon of the nouveaux riches, whose avarice is rivaled by their atrocious taste. Greed was clearly on display during the Reagan era; to see it, one had only to visit one of America's major cities and search out that distinctive product of the 1980s, the yuppie.

These were the characters of novels like Jay McInerny's *Bright Lights, Big City* and Tom Wolfe's *Bonfire of the Vanities*. The posh neighborhoods of Boston, New York, Chicago, and Los Angeles were teeming with them, young couples earning six figures whose lifestyles were defined by their Porsches and BMWs, fully equipped with compact disc player and telephone; their designer clothes, including special gear for jogging and tennis; their exercise machines, sometimes attended by a personal trainer; their electronic equipment, such as built-in recorders and video screens; and their gourmet food and coffee beans purchased at specialty stores.

The yuppies were Reaganites in the sense that most of them wanted to be bankers, not social workers. Their motto was not "Bread for the World" but "Poverty Sucks." Yet, while the young urban professionals were economically conservative, they were also socially liberal. They were pro-choice on abortion. They were avid consumers of recreational drugs. These yuppies undoubtedly were self-centered and narcissistic, but there have been greater villains in Western history, and it remains questionable whether this group was any more selfish than all those young men who didn't want the Vietnam War to interrupt their life-styles of sex, drugs, and rock and roll and so they ducked the draft or ran away to Canada. In some cases, these two groups were made up of the same people.

Moreover, most Americans who were successful during the 1980s did not satisfy the stereotype of the profligate yuppie. During the 1984 campaign, Mondale routinely denounced the extravagance of rich people and proposed that their taxes be increased. By "rich" Mondale meant any family making more than $60,000, which inspired one Los Angeles executive, John Adams, to observe in the "My Turn" column in *Newsweek:* "Me rich? Good lord, I live in a three-bedroom house in a nice but hardly chic neighborhood. Our family car is a '79 Mercury sta-tion wagon. The children attend private schools, but to offset part of that cost my wife keeps a sharp eye out for sales and shuts off the air-conditioner on all but the worst summer days to save on energy expenses. I inherited nothing from my parents when they died, did not attend a money-college with an old boy network, and have basically worked like a Trojan to get where I am and own what I do."[15]

Reagan would have smiled had he read this article. He understood people like John Adams very well. To him, they were the real Americans, nice guys who paid their dues and had every right to seek a better life. Yet, we may ask, was Reagan right to take such a benign view of the upwardly mobile citizens who made it in the 1980s? This question can be answered by examining the effect of the prosperity generated by Rea-ganomics on how much well-to-do Americans paid in taxes and how much they gave away in charity. The facts confound the stereotype of the 1980s as an era of greed and selfishness.

Contrary to the expectations of all the pundits, even after their tax cuts the affluent paid a *greater* amount of federal taxes than before. Rich people who used to pay a marginal tax rate of 70 percent and saw their tax rate decline dramatically still paid about 50 percent more in taxes to the government. Not only did the rich pay more in absolute terms, the proportion of federal taxes collected from those in the top 1 percent of income went from 18 percent of all revenues in 1981 to 28 percent in

1988. The top 5 percent of income earners, who paid 35 percent of the Treasury's tax revenue in 1981, bore 46 percent of the tax burden in 1988. Meanwhile, the tax share of middle- and lower-middle-income Americans declined.[16] The Reagan tax cuts, which were attacked as a bonanza for the rich, actually extracted a bigger share of tax revenue from upper-income taxpayers.

This remarkable result occurred for a simple reason: sharply lower marginal tax rates gave many Americans a greater incentive to move their money out of tax shelters and into the productive economy and also to work harder and produce more wealth. Thus their total income rose, and even though their marginal rates were lower, they ended up paying more to the IRS. Yet if this seems obvious today, it was considered a bizarre line of reasoning by Reagan's critics. Consequently these results were anticipated by only one group, the supply siders, who said, based on the Laffer curve, that a lower tax rate would, for those in the higher tax brackets, produce greater government tax revenues.

Critics of supply-side economics, including some conservative skeptics, have tried to discredit the doctrine by attributing to supply siders in the Reagan administration the view that a reduction in tax rates would produce an overall increase in government revenues, so the tax cut would "pay for itself."[17] This obviously didn't happen, but no prominent supply sider said it would, and neither did the Reagan administration, whose budget projections, available for inspection in public documents, all show an expected loss in revenue due to the tax cuts.[18] Indeed, the expectation that tax cuts will increase total government revenues is based on an obvious misreading of the Laffer curve, which clearly specifies that beyond a certain point, marginal tax rates become prohibitive, and reductions for those taxpayers alone can be expected to increase the share of government revenues collected from that group. Tax data from the Reagan years have thoroughly vindicated the Laffer curve.

Not only did the rich and the middle class pay more in taxes, but they also gave more in charity. Indeed, the 1980s saw the greatest outpouring of private generosity in history. Americans who contributed about $65 billion (as measured in 1990 dollars) in charity in 1980 gave more than $100 billion annually by the end of the decade, a real increase of 57 percent. The average American who gave $377 to charity in 1980 raised his or her contribution to $493 in 1990. The rate of increase in charitable contributions, economist Richard McKenzie calculates, was greater than at any other time in the postwar era. Moreover, he observes, it was greater than the growth of expenditures on personal extravagances like jewelry purchases, eating out, and health club memberships. Nor did Americans merely contribute their money: more people volunteered their time for churches and civic groups than ever before.[19]

No one has challenged the accuracy of these figures. Yet, oddly enough, the articles in *Time* and *Newsweek* that summed up the 1980s as a decade of selfishness conveniently omitted any discussion of the entirely relevant issue of private charity. Perhaps this can be attributed to carelessness and ignorance of the facts that were available at the time. Yet, unless one's definition of charity is limited to involuntary giving—government programs funded by compulsory taxation—the evidence now compels us to revise the facile characterization of the 1980s.

Reagan showed little interest in these empirical data, but undoubtedly the results would have pleased him. Reagan's philosophy was never "rugged individualism" pure and simple. He did not believe in solitary Americans going it alone. He did accept that competition is essential to the production of knowledge and wealth. "Without a race," he would say, "there can be no champion, no records broken, no excellence."[20] If the competitive drive was motivated by self-interest, so be it. But what is so selfish, Reagan sometimes asked, about people working hard to get a better job or save money to buy a bigger house or make a weekend getaway or pay for the college education of their children? American self-interest, in Reagan's view, was broad enough to encompass the betterment of one's family and community. He saw it work in his home town of Dixon, as well as in his own life. In his high school and college years, being a lifeguard was the job that Reagan liked best. He did not take the up-by-their-bootstraps view often attributed to him in media caricature: "Why don't those drowning kids get their own life rafts?"

Reagan's America was a vision of voluntary communities in which people work together to help each other and improve their lives. In his inaugural address in 1981, he praised "individuals and families whose voluntary gifts support church, charity, culture, art and education." He added, "How can we love our country and not love our countrymen, and loving them, reach out a hand when they fall, heal them when they are sick, and provide opportunities to make them self-sufficient?"[21] An excessively paternalistic government, Reagan believed, got in the way of that. Reagan believed that as citizens of a free society we should demand less of the state and more of ourselves.

Yet even amid the prosperity of the Reagan years, there was a serious problem: millions of Americans found themselves laid off their jobs and facing long-term unemployment. This problem had nothing to do with Reagan's meager budget cuts, which took a small number of people, many of them bureaucrats, off the federal payroll. Rather, as even some of the president's critics conceded, it was a trend connected to profound changes in the U.S. economy.[22] Advances in automation ensured that machines could more efficiently perform tasks once reserved for manual labor. Moreover, America was becoming integrated into a global market. Foreign countries, which pay their workers less, were able to sell many products more cheaply than their U.S. counterparts. This meant that many American industries became uncompetitive in world markets, and they began to lose money and lay off workers.

The problem affected major sectors of the economy. Layoffs reached serious proportions in such industries as automobiles, steel, textiles, shoes, rubber, and machine tools. The decline of the steel industry is illustrative. In the World War II era, the United States produced two out of three tons of the world's steel. Steel built railroads, bridges, manufactured goods, and war equipment. Yet by the 1980s the United States was responsible for only about 15 percent of global steel production.[23] There was no mystery behind the reason: other countries were doing it more cheaply and better. All the same, the collapse of the industry in America created a rust belt, which hit hard all the local economies based on steel.

Layoffs were not limited to blue-collar workers or to industries on their way out. Major companies throughout the U.S. economy found themselves pressured by the demands of international competition. They had to downsize their workforces and become more competitive if they were going to stay profitable. This meant the end of a stable career for workers as well as managers, even at places like General Electric and IBM, which were seen at one time to offer lifetime employment, with prospects for continuing promotions and raises. For many Americans, that job security ended in the 1980s.

Nor were things going well down on the farm. It was worse than that: the small-size family farm was becoming obsolete. Many small farmers were not able to compete against the highly automated farming conglomerates. Exacerbating their problems was the fact that many small farmers had taken out large loans during the 1970s, in a period of high interest rates, and in the 1980s their profits were not sizable enough for them to make their payments. Consequently thousands of farmers found themselves compelled to turn over their land and equipment to the banks and mortgage companies.

In the era of the welfare state, all these problems become the government's problem, as even private hardships are converted to claims on the taxpayer's wallet. So, bewailing the end of a traditional institution, one that Thomas Jefferson had considered a repository of American virtue, the farmers came before Congress demanding a reprieve for their loans and increased federal payments for them not to grow and produce things. (As in the case of welfare, here was a case of the government's rewarding unproductive economic behavior.) The cause of the farmers was even taken up by three noted Hollywood actresses—Jessica Lange, Sissy Spacek, and Sally Field—who had developed a special interest in the subject after recently starring in farm movies.

The farm constituency was joined by representatives of the steel, shoe, and other industries that were losing market share and profits. Lobbyists for these industries located the source of the problem as one of cheap foreign products, allegedly produced by "slave labor." They proposed that the United States tax these goods heavily or prevent them from coming into the country, so that American industries would once again be competitive and workers would get their jobs back. In the view of most lobbyists, such measures were not merely the quickest path to shielding uncompetitive companies from ruin; they were required by the national interest itself.

Many intellectuals understood the misery of the farmers and steelworkers as part of a general problem with U.S. competitiveness.

America, they said, was "deindustrializing." Manufacturing jobs were all going abroad. Something must be done about this at the policy level. Yes, it was time for the intellectuals to take charge. The new theme was "industrial policy." The Japanese do it, the pundits said, at a time when such a phrase was often enough to settle an argument. Instead of leaving things to the free market, many intellectuals offered to produce extensive blueprints for planning the future of the American economy. They volunteered to invest taxpayer money in "sunrise" sectors they felt would be profitable in the future and protect jobs in "sunset" industries where U.S. workers were losing out to foreign competition.[24]

President Reagan contemplated these problems and demands, and then settled on a general course of action: he did nothing. This may seem to be both an easy and insensitive approach, but in fact it was extremely difficult, and it proved the most compassionate option under the circumstances. It was difficult because Reagan genuinely sympathized with the plight of hardworking farmers and steelworkers who found themselves in acute distress. Many of the blue-collar workers laid off in Pennsylvania, Illinois, Minnesota, and elsewhere were Reagan Democrats who had voted for him. Also, farm country was Reagan country. There was enormous political pressure on Reagan to consent to measures that would bail out such friendly constituencies.

Reagan wasn't going to do it. He acknowledged the problem, but his view was that industrial policy, and all the attendant rhetoric about government partnerships with the private sector, basically amounted to "government coercion, political favoritism, and old-fashioned boondoggles nicely wrapped up in a bright colored ribbon."[25]

Reagan did, however, seek to address the problems of people who were being hurt by changes in the U.S. and world economy. Farmers, he pointed out, were already receiving government subsidies. In principle these should be reduced, he admitted, because there is no good reason for taxpayers to pay farmers to keep their products off the market and to keep prices artificially high. Reagan did not propose the immediate elimination of these farm subsidies, but he was unwilling to undertake new bailouts either.

On trade Reagan adopted a similarly prudent stance. He recognized the unfairness that the Japanese were free to sell their cars in America while U.S. companies faced heavy restrictions and tariffs in selling their cars in Japan. Reagan would not agree to a quota bill restricting imported foreign cars, but in order to give the U.S. auto industry time to get its act in gear, he authorized his trade representatives to negotiate with Japanese car manufacturers to show voluntary restraint in their volume of exports to the United States. Seeing that far more stringent protectionist legislation was making its way through Congress, the Japanese trade ministry consented to the Reagan solution.

Yet Reagan's general position was that protectionism is bad for all parties, and just because one country engages in it does not mean that the United States should follow that foolish precedent. "If one partner shoots a hole in the bottom of the boat," Reagan said, "does it make sense for the other partner to shoot another hole in the boat?"[26] While many of his critics were demanding tariffs, Reagan began negotiations with Canada to establish a free trade zone completely devoid of tariffs between the two countries. It laid the groundwork for more extensive free-trade negotiations with Latin America and Asia during the Bush and Clinton administrations.

Sometimes Reagan had to be shrewdly diplomatic in the way that he handled protectionist demands. Senior aides told of an incident in which a group of northeastern shoe manufacturers came to see Reagan. These men, big Republican donors who had contributed to his campaign, wanted him to help block cheap foreign shoes from being sold in the United States. Their business was suffering, they said, and their employees were being laid off. Reagan could have disputed the claims of these lobbyists and argued that their companies were losing money because of their inability to compete, and that the American consumer benefited from free trade which enabled him to purchase more inexpensive shoes.

Reagan didn't say anything of the sort, however. Instead he launched into a lengthy reverie about how much he liked to wear cowboy boots on his ranch in Santa Barbara, finishing up with a lament about how difficult it was to find a good pair these days. The businessmen listened politely and then left, commenting among themselves that Reagan was an awfully nice man but had seemed not to follow their line of reasoning at all. As the press reported it, this was another one of those "anecdotal non-sequiturs," as Morton Kondracke put it in the *New Republic*.[27] Yet it turns out that Reagan knew exactly what he was up to.

Under the guise of being distracted, he was doing something that we all do when pressed to discuss something we don't want to talk about: he was changing the topic. When the shoe manufacturers left, Reagan commented to his aides, "No way was I going to give in to that crew."

Even amid the gut-wrenching problems facing many U.S. industries, Reagan took the tough line that American workers who were in the business of making things that no one wanted to buy at the prices they charged had only one sensible course open to them: get out of uncompetitive industries and find work in the productive sectors of the economy. Undoubtedly this would involve retraining and a painful period of transition, but Reagan did not believe that there was an alternative. "America's open market is its strength, not its weakness," Reagan said to audiences who were sometimes openly skeptical. At a time when many workers were discouraged about their future prospects, Reagan professed confidence in their ability to prepare themselves for the global economy of the future.

Early in his second term, Reagan decided that he would support measures to reform the tax code further. He had long believed it to be far too complex for the average citizen, with too many loopholes that could be exploited by those with access to lawyers and other experts. Reagan's determination to restructure the tax system fundamentally was strengthened after a conversation with his Treasury secretary, Donald Regan. Regan asked him what his old corporate sponsor, General Electric, had in common with Boeing, General Dynamics, and more than fifty other big companies. Reagan didn't know. Regan said that they paid no taxes at all. Reagan said he didn't believe it, but Regan confirmed that it was true. Both men agreed that it was wrong.[28] In his 1984 State of the Union address, Reagan announced his intention "to simplify the entire tax code so all taxpayers, big and small, are treated fairly."

The pundits said that popular though Reagan was with the voters, it was highly doubtful that a president could engineer a second dramatic overhaul of the tax system. Reagan was proposing to eliminate many of the deductions available to special interest groups such as the real estate and banking industries. A broad coalition of lobbying groups, representing oil drillers, insurance agents, drug companies, credit unions, and the manufacturers of luxury yachts, had vowed to use their political influence to kill tax reform. Moreover, Reagan's plan basically eliminated the complex and steeply graded curve of tax rates and reduced it to a simple three-bracket system in which the only tax rates were 15 percent, 25 percent, and 35 percent. The pundits were convinced that the liberal Democrats in Congress would never tolerate further cuts in marginal rates, especially the hefty reduction in the top rate.

Yet Reagan knew that two influential Democratic legislators, Senator Bill Bradley and Congressman Richard Gephardt, as well as Congressman Dan Rostenkowski, the powerful chairman of the Ways and Means Committee, favored tax reform as a way to close loopholes for the rich and simplify the tax code. The Reagan administration worked with these Democrats and negotiated a compromise. Reagan would agree to close existing loopholes if the Democrats would agree to Reagan's proposal for lower marginal rates for individuals and families. The two parties worked out a deal, and on October 22, 1986, Reagan confounded his critics once again by signing into law a comprehensive tax reform bill that gave the administration most of what it wanted.

Stunningly, the new law brought down the top marginal rate from 50 percent to 28 percent. When Reagan assumed office, it was 70 percent, so the cumulative effect of Reagan's two tax cuts was to more than halve the top rate. Multiple tax brackets were simplified to just three. The personal exemption and standard deduction were increased, removing millions of low-income taxpayers from the rolls. An alternative minimum tax was established to ensure that wealthy taxpayers could not escape paying tax altogether. Hundreds of special interest provisions, such as full deductibility of the three-martini business lunch, were curtailed or eliminated.

The consequences were far-reaching. Reagan had proved that the special interests were not invincible; despite their permanent presence and concentrated power in Washington, they could be outmaneuvered. He had produced a tax code whose structure was vastly simpler and fairer than the byzantine one it replaced. Most important, Reagan had essentially repealed the notion of steeply progressive taxation, so that it would be much more difficult in the future for the liberal Democrats to manipulate the tax code as an instrument of social policy.

Some conservative Republicans opposed tax reform on the grounds that it imposed too many burdens on business. The effect, they warned, would be to stifle the economic recovery. Yet tax reform seemed only to strengthen the Reagan boom. The widely anticipated recession of Reagan's second term never materialized. Instead the country found itself in the vanguard of what has been described as the Third Industrial Revolution.[29] The technology driving this revolution was that of the silicon chip, a universe of knowledge contained in what amounted to little more than a few grains of sand. "At the very time that the intellectuals were complaining about America's inability to compete," technology guru George Gilder told me, "the United States took global dominance."

It is easy to forget that when Reagan was first elected, very few Americans owned a computer. Videocassette recorders were a novelty. Hardly anyone had an answering machine. Only one in six American families possessed a microwave oven. All of this changed during the 1980s. Cellular phones were introduced only in 1983, yet by the end of Reagan's tenure, more than 20 million Americans owned one. By 1989, 50 million homes had microwave ovens, and more than half of American households owned a VCR.[30] The Sony Walkman became a symbol of the mobility and versatility of technology. Computers ceased to be used primarily by businesses and became a regular feature of the American home. So did the fax machine. These conveniences have become so widespread that we take them for granted; indeed it would be hard to imagine life without them.

Reagan didn't create this revolution. Its actual course had more to do with Bill Gates, the founder and chairman of Microsoft, and other ingenious entrepreneurs. But where did all the venture capital for the new industries of the 1980s come from? There was very little of it around in the 1970s. George Gilder points out that the number of major venture capital partnerships surged from 25 in the mid-1970s to more than 200 in the early 1980s. The total pool of venture capital nearly doubled, from $5.8 billion in 1981 to $11.5 billion in 1983.[31]

Why did this happen? I put this question to several Silicon Valley entrepreneurs at a recent conference sponsored by *Forbes* magazine. Many of them gave credit to two men: Michael Milken and Ronald Reagan. Whatever his flaws, they said, Milken more than anyone else found a way to use high-yield or "junk" bonds to make capital more widely available for mergers, acquisitions, and business expansion. The entrepreneurs also credited Reagan's policies of limited government, deregulation, and open markets with creating an atmosphere in which the revolution could flourish. Michael Dell, who founded Dell Computers in the mid-1980s, argues that Reagan did this in part by championing the entrepreneur as an American hero who defies limits to the imagination and creates new things. "Reagan was the inspirational leader of the technological revolution," remarks T. J. Rodgers, founder and chief executive of Cypress Semiconductors. Other entrepreneurs who got their start in the 1980s echo Rodgers's judgment that without Reagan the technological surge of the past two decades "would not have happened this way, and this fast."

So what about those deficits? A funny thing happened during the 1980s and 1990s: none of the dire warnings about the deficit came true. All the bad things that Reagan's critics insisted would transpire did not transpire. The American public's relatively cavalier view of the deficit as a jumble of big, meaningless numbers proved to be a fairly accurate appraisal of the significance of the issue. The intelligentsia were absolutely befuddled by the deficit's failure to wreak economic havoc and inflict political damage on Reagan.

So at the risk of once again embarrassing the pundits by citing them, let us revisit their warnings about the deficit, issued without respite throughout the 1980s. The deficits, *Time* predicted, would release huge amounts of money into the economy, and this would foster inflation. Yet inflation rates dropped sharply and remained low throughout the Reagan era. *Time* also warned that deficits would raise nominal interest rates, on the theory that when the government borrows money, it competes with and crowds out private borrowing, and this drives up the interest rate.[32] Yet when deficits were running at $50 billion in 1980, the prime rate of interest was over 20 percent, whereas during the Reagan era, deficits exceeded $200 billion for several years and the interest rate was around 8 percent. These are, of course, nominal interest rates. Even when inflation is taken into account, real interest rates during the Reagan era averaged 5 percent, lower than the 8 percent real rate that Reagan inherited in 1980. Finally, deficits were supposed to retard growth and choke off the economic recovery; this too did not happen in the 1980s, nor has it occurred in the 1990s.

None of this means, of course, that deficits are a good thing. They are a bad thing, and for a very simple reason: at some point, the money has to be paid back. If a nation keeps borrowing, interest payments add up to such an extent that they begin to put a serious strain on the federal budget. This is exactly what has happened to the U.S. government. Interest on the national debt rose to the point where, along with social security, Medicare, and defense, it became (and remains) one of the largest items in the budget.

Yet even this storm cloud contains a silver lining. It occurred to Congress during the mid- to late 1980s that if it kept up its pace of expenditures, interest payments would continue to rise each year to the point where there would be no discretionary funds left. In other words, the prospect of an end to future spending suddenly began to impose constraints on current spending. Of the big spenders in Congress, one may say that they began to run out of other people's money. Thus, by a strange turn of fate, the deficit accomplished for Reagan what he was unable to achieve directly: for the first time in this century, Congress began to impose limits on the growth of government. Of all the measures we know, economist Milton Friedman writes, "the deficit has been the only effective restraint on congressional spending."[33]

This notion of limiting their appetite for new programs was so novel to liberal Democrats like Senator Daniel Patrick Moynihan and Congressman Barney Frank that they were convinced that they had been victimized by an ingenious plot. Moynihan and Frank accused Reagan and his aides of planning and executing a conspiracy to manufacture gigantic deficits and thus starve the government of future revenue.[34] This claim is overstated, of course. There was no scheme to produce deficits. Reagan didn't pursue them as a positive good; he settled for them as a necessary evil under the circumstances. Indeed here was a rare case when Reagan was overestimated by his critics.

Yet if one is going to err about Reagan, it is always safe to err on the side of overestimation. Sure enough, there is some truth to Moynihan and Frank's allegations. From his days as governor, Reagan had developed what he called his "children's allowance" theory of government spending. His attitude was that the government is like an irresponsible adolescent: if you raise the kid's allowance, he'll promptly find a way to spend the money. The only way to produce restraint is to limit the amount of funds available. Reagan realized early in his first term that the deficits would produce a serious political dilemma for the liberal Democrats. They would be hard-pressed to generate new spending schemes, since they would have to specify how to pay for them, through either new taxes or additional deficit spending. Most of them would simply sulk; a few might even become born-again budget balancers.

This is exactly what happened. During Reagan's second term, the Congress passed with bipartisan support the Gramm-Rudman legislation, a "bad idea whose time has come," as Senator Warren Rudman put it. The law placed strict limits on deficit spending and sought to balance the budget by the end of the decade. Gramm-Rudman was flawed because it exempted too many entitlements, and some of its crucial provisions were held to be unconstitutional by the Supreme Court. Nevertheless, it helped to instill in lawmakers of both parties a newfound sensitivity to the issue of the deficit, and if they weren't willing to eliminate programs, they were willing to contemplate modest reductions in existing ones, and they were essentially rendered mute in proposing new spending schemes.

As a result of economic growth and spending restraint, the deficit in the late 1980s began to decline in both absolute terms and as a proportion of the economy. The deficit, which consumed 6.3 percent of the gross domestic product in 1983, shrank to around 3 percent during 1987–1989, which is just where it was when Reagan first took office.[35] During the 1990s, largely due to a continuation of the Reagan economic boom as well as huge defense savings resulting from the end of the cold war, the deficit has fallen so dramatically that some economists believe that the budget will soon balance itself. Thus, even on the objectives that proved most elusive throughout his administration—controlling the rate of growth of government and limiting the deficit—Reagan achieved, in the end, a measure of success.

Reagan came to office in 1981 when the American economy faced two seemingly insoluble problems: economic stagnation and runaway inflation. His domestic achievement was twofold: he supported monetary policies that practically eliminated the problem of inflation, and his tax cuts produced a juggernaut of economic growth and corporate restructuring that continued through the 1980s and whose effects persist in the 1990s. These were not victories obtained without pain: he had to steer the country through a serious recession and a gut-wrenching reorganization of major sectors of the economy. Yet his vision was such that he never allowed himself to lose sight of his major goals.

He vindicated capitalism and free markets at a time when many people wondered if industrialized economies could grow any more. Many other countries have absorbed the lessons of Reaganomics, reduced their marginal tax rates, and witnessed a rapid surge in economic growth. Yet America gained most of all: today the nation is an economic colossus, more competitive, more innovative, and more technologically advanced than Japan and Europe. Yet aides told me that whenever Reagan was asked whether he was responsible for this American resurgence, he would always reply, "Oh no, it wasn't me. The American people did it. They deserve the credit."

Chapter 6

*Confronting
the Evil Empire*

ON JUNE 4, 1990, MIKHAIL Gorbachev delivered a speech to the students and faculty at Stanford University. The audience listened with rapt attention as Gorbachev outlined how far his policies of *glasnost* and *perestroika* had advanced. When he proclaimed that the cold war was over, people clapped with evident relief. Then Gorbachev added, "And let us not wrangle over who won it." Now the crowd went into raptures, as thousands leaped to their feet and applauded thunderously.[1]

If you think about it, this was a very strange reaction on the part of the Stanford audience. The collapse of the Soviet empire, writes Sovietologist Martin Malia, was a "total implosion of a sort unheard of in history. . . . A great state abolished itself utterly."[2] Zbigniew Brzezinski, Jimmy Carter's national security adviser, terms the defeat of Soviet communism an outcome "no less decisive and no less one-sided" than the defeat of Napoleonic France in 1815 or of Nazi Germany and Imperial Japan in 1945.[3] With it, the most ambitious political and social experiment of the modern era ended in failure, and the supreme political drama of the century—the conflict between the free West and the totalitarian East—came to an end. What will probably prove to be the most important historical event of our lifetimes has already occurred. We are unlikely to live through anything else of comparable significance.

Given these remarkable developments, it is natural to wonder what caused the destruction, or self-destruction, of Soviet communism. Gorbachev's desire to avoid this topic was perfectly understandable. Losers typically don't want to talk about the game after it's over. It is in the interest of one who has suffered a resounding defeat to deny that a battle has even occurred. What was mysterious was the reaction of those in the audience. Why were the apparent winners of the cold war equally resolved not to celebrate their victory or analyze how it came about? Not only did the Stanford community that night display a striking lack of curiosity about a question of paramount importance; it revealed a passionate determination to change the subject, to put the cold war behind us. Inquiring minds didn't want to know.

The peculiar reaction of the Stanford community is not an aberration; it is typical of the American intelligentsia. Hawks and doves, liberals and conservatives all share a notable aversion to the subject of how the cold war really ended. In an era where a plane crash is extensively studied for the slightest evidence of what happened, the collapse of the Soviet Union has produced few postmortems to discover what they did wrong and few self-appraisals to find out what we did right. Unlike our reaction to the Holocaust and the defeat of the Nazis—"We must not forget"—our response to the gulag and the defeat of the communists seems to be, "We must not remember."

This self-imposed amnesia cannot be attributed to a reasonable desire on the part of Americans to "get on with our lives" and "face the future." We would be able to do those things better if we were equipped with a clear understanding of the events that brought us to our current pass. Nor can we justify our lack of enthusiasm for exploring the end of the cold war on the grounds that it was an anticlimactic collapse, a hollow victory, achieved with no outbreak of nuclear war. The absence of heavy casualties makes the disintegration of the Soviet empire more incredible and mysterious: how many other empires in history have dissolved themselves without resorting to force?

Perhaps the true reason that hardly anyone in the intellectual and political communities wants to talk about the end of the cold war is simply this: virtually everyone was wrong about the Soviet Union. The doves or appeasers were totally and ignominiously wrong on every point. They showed a very poor understanding of the nature of communism. They misunderstood Soviet objectives. Their strategy was not merely flawed; it was the precise opposite of what was required. If the doves' approach of conciliating Soviet demands had been followed, Soviet totalitarianism might well remain intact today. The hawks or anticommunists had a better understanding than the doves of totalitarianism and a superior strategy for meeting the Soviet threat, but they too were mistaken about what steps were needed in the final stage to bring about the dismantling of the Soviet empire. Why would the intellectuals want a postmortem when it would only call their expertise into question and expose their lack of foresight?

It is extremely difficult for intellectuals to admit that they were wrong and equally painful to concede that Reagan was right. Consequently the past few years have seen a determined attempt at revisionist history, mainly generated by doves like diplomat George Kennan, political scientist Raymond Garthoff, and journalist and Clinton administration official Strobe Talbott. There is no mystery about the end of the Soviet Union, the revisionists say. It suffered from chronic economic problems and collapsed of its own weight. "The Soviet system has gone into meltdown because of inadequacies and defects at its core," Strobe Talbott writes, "not because of anything the outside world has done or not done." George Kennan echoes Talbott in his insistence that "nobody won the Cold War." In this view, communism was not defeated; it committed suicide. To the extent that it was an assisted suicide, Raymond Garthoff contends, Mikhail Gorbachev was the Soviet Dr. Kevorkian.

In retrospect, we know that "the Soviet threat is not what it used to be," Strobe Talbott writes. "The real point, however, is that it never was. The doves in the great debate of the past 40 years were right all along." The revisionists charge the Reagan administration with greatly exaggerating the Soviet threat based on fears that turn out to have been misplaced. To be sure, the revisionists say, the United States was justified in standing up for U.S. interests during the 1980s, but this was nothing more than an extension of a bipartisan policy of containment initiated by the Truman administration. To the extent that Reagan went beyond containment and attempted to roll back the Soviet empire, the revisionists argue, this approach backfired. The "extreme militariza-tion" pursued by Reagan and the hard-liners in the Pentagon, George Kennan writes, "consistently strengthened comparable hard-liners in the Soviet Union." Far from accelerating the end of the cold war, it may have actually postponed it.[4]

This analysis is impressive if only for its audacity. The revisionists are certainly right that the Soviet Union during the 1980s suffered from debilitating economic problems on account of its inefficient socialist system. But why would this factor by itself bring about the end of the political regime? Historically, poor economic performance is common-place, but the peacetime implosion of a great political regime is rare. Never have food shortages or technological backwardness been suffi-cient causes for the destruction of a large empire. The Roman Empire survived internal corrosion for centuries before it was destroyed by the invasion of the barbarian hordes. Despite equally serious domestic strains the Ottoman Empire persisted as the "sick man of Europe" for generations and ended only with catastrophic defeat in World War I. The Soviet economy had been ailing for most of this century, at least since the bolsheviks came to power. Chronic shortages were routinely blamed on bad harvests. So the economic argument cannot explain why the empire collapsed at the particular time that it did, when the Soviet Union was previously able to sustain itself in the face of comparable— and in some cases worse—economic conditions. The revisionist claim seems based on the determinist view: it happened; therefore it was inevitable. Moreover, if Soviet collapse was so certain, why wasn't it foreseen by the revisionists who, we shall see, were embarrassingly wrong in their claims throughout the 1980s?

The revisionist argument that fears of Soviet power in the Reagan era were both exaggerated and misplaced is equally open to question. Consider the image of Napoleon on the island of Saint Helena in 1815. He was a forlorn figure who didn't pose much of a threat. But does that mean that he was never very dangerous and that Wellington was being paranoid to prepare for the Battle of Waterloo? One cannot infer from the fact that the Soviet empire proved to be fragile in the late 1980s and early 1990s that it was never politically potent or militarily threatening in the late 1970s and early 1980s. Moreover, if the policies the doves advocated were the best way to undermine an already brittle Soviet

Union, it remains a mystery why the communist empire did not collapse during the Carter era.

It is no less problematic to assert that Gorbachev was the designer and architect of the collapse of the Soviet Union. He was undoubtedly a reformer and a new kind of Soviet leader—quite different from the Brezhnev-Andropov-Chernenko type. But this itself poses an interesting dilemma: why did the Politburo in 1985 feel the need to turn over leadership to this kind of man? Certainly the communist bosses did not wish him to lead the party, and the regime, over the precipice. Nor did Gorbachev see this as his role. On the contrary, he insisted throughout the second half of the 1980s that he intended to strengthen the Soviet economy and military. As we shall see, Gorbachev understood himself as the preserver, not the destroyer, of socialism. He was appalled at the result. No one was more surprised than Gorbachev when he saw himself swept out of power. He is still bewildered that he gets less than 1 percent of the vote in Russian elections. The wise men of the West may regard Gorbachev as the savior of the Russian people, but clearly the Russian people do not agree with this assessment. Nor is Gorbachev a big hit in the former Eastern bloc. Indeed, if Mikhail Gorbachev had given his Stanford remarks at a shipyard in Gdansk, he would certainly have been booed and might have had rocks thrown at him.

The next few chapters are not about Gorbachev but about the man who was the true victor in the cold war: how he foresaw it, how he planned it, and how he brought it about. Yet, by all indications, this is not a postmortem that he would have sought. He encountered the revisionist view, of course, but he never worried about that kind of postgame analysis. How the wise men cover their tracks, what they say in their articles and textbooks about who won the cold war: these were secondary matters to him. He told them it was coming, and they laughed at him. He was crucial in bringing it about, while they jeered from the sidelines. He knew this in his heart; they knew it too but could not bring themselves to admit it. Yet his attitude was not to mind. It happened, and millions of people now have a chance to live in freedom.

This man who got things right from the start was, at first glance, an unlikely statesman. He became the leader of the noncommunist world with no experience in foreign policy. Some people thought he was a dangerous warmonger; others considered him a nice fellow but a bit of a bungler. Yet the man they called a lightweight turned out to have as deep an understanding of communism as Aleksandr Solzhenitsyn. He knew from the outset what its weakness was and that it could be defeated. This rank amateur developed a complex, often counterintuitive strategy for dealing with the Soviet Union that hardly anyone on his staff fully endorsed or even understood, and which he implemented over the objections of hawks as well as doves. During his first term, he was tough with Moscow, and he faced harsh criticism from the doves; during his second term, he was conciliatory with Gorbachev, and he endured strong opposition from the hawks. In both cases he proved to be right. Through a combination of vision, tenacity, patience, and improvisational skill, this implausible statesman produced what Henry Kissinger terms "the greatest diplomatic feat of the modern era."[5]

To see how Reagan's understanding of Soviet communism differed from all the mainstream approaches of his day, let us begin by considering his famous reference to the Soviet Union as an "evil empire." This was a phrase from a speech that Reagan delivered to the National Association of Evangelicals in 1983, although he had been saying essentially the same thing from the time he entered the White House.

At the president's first press conference in the Old Executive Office Building, barely ten days after he was inaugurated, the press demanded to know how serious Reagan was about arms control and when he would approach the Soviet leadership to propose a summit. Reagan responded that an arms control treaty at that point was not a priority with him. The reason, he said, was that signed agreements meant nothing to the Soviets. They had "openly and publicly declared that the only morality they recognize is what will further their cause, meaning they reserve unto themselves the right to commit any crime, to lie, to cheat."[6]

There was an audible gasp from the audience, as if to say, Did he really say that? Secretary of State Alexander Haig, standing in the corner of the room, conspicuously rolled his eyes. The next day the *Washington Post* would set the tone for editorial exasperation in the nation's newspapers by condemning Reagan's "good-versus-evil approach" on the grounds that it seemed to leave no room for "honorable accommodation" with the Soviets.[7] The pundits would later cite Reagan's remarks to suggest that he had once again proved himself a "simple-minded ideologue" and reinforced his image as a "reckless cowboy."[8]

At the time, Reagan seemed oblivious to the reaction he had caused. The only sign that he was conscious of having said anything unorthodox came after the press conference, as he walked back to the White House with national security adviser Richard Allen following behind him. Reagan beckoned to him, and Allen jogged to catch up with the president. "Yes sir?" As Allen recounted the story to me, Reagan asked him, "Isn't it true that communism gives the Soviets the right to lie?" Allen replied, "I believe it is." Reagan continued, "And don't we know for a fact that the Soviets steal and cheat?" Allen answered, "They do, sir." Reagan permitted himself a chuckle. "I thought so."

In his "evil empire" speech on March 8, 1983, Reagan described the cold war as a "struggle between right and wrong, good and evil." He repeated his charge that the only morality the Soviets recognized "is that which will further their cause, which is world revolution." Reagan asked the evangelicals in the audience to "pray for the salvation of all those who live in totalitarian darkness" so that "they will discover the joy of knowing God." But until then, Reagan said, the West should recognize that "they are the focus of evil in the modern world."[9]

This was the single most important speech of the Reagan presidency, a classic illustration of what Václav Havel terms "the power of words to change history."[10] When Reagan visited Poland and East Berlin after the collapse of the Soviet Union, he received a hero's welcome. Somewhat to his chagrin, he discovered that many people had a picture of him in their homes. Several former dissidents told Reagan that when they heard he had called the Soviets an "evil empire," it gave them hope, and they said to each other that America finally had a leader who clearly understood the nature of communism.

Drafted by speechwriter Anthony Dolan, Reagan's speech carried such power not because it conveyed Dolan's views, as recited by Reagan, but because it conveyed Reagan's ideas, forcefully expressed in prose by Dolan. Yet Dolan told me he had previously attempted to insert the "evil empire" phrase into speeches that Reagan was scheduled to deliver. Each time, the State Department insisted that the language be removed. Finally Reagan himself demanded that it stay in, and it did.

Reagan's central argument with communism occurs in many of his speeches but is nowhere better summarized than in his "evil empire" address. He defined the conflict between the West and the Soviet Union as fundamentally a moral conflict. Thus he regarded it as his first duty to state the obvious: despite its flaws, our system is basically good and their system is basically evil. Reagan saw himself as doing nothing more than clarifying what America stood for, and against. In doing this he became the first president in the post-Watergate era to speak in this way about communism. Indeed no other Western leader since Churchill had so unapologetically asserted the moral superiority of the West.

Reagan's view was that the buildup of nuclear weapons was not the cause but the result of this fundamental conflict between two inherently different systems. As he put it on numerous occasions, "Nations do not distrust each other because they are armed. They are armed because they distrust each other." To Reagan, the Soviet Union was like a gangster and the United States was like a policeman. Both were armed and willing to use force, but for different purposes. Reagan's objective from the outset was to frustrate the gangster's objectives and disarm him. His goal was to ensure the triumph of the good society over the evil empire.

Reagan was willing to be patient in the abatement of evil but was not willing to do business as usual with it. He recognized that he would have to deal with the adversary, and he was not opposed to discussions on how to reduce tensions. Cops sometimes have to negotiate with gangsters. But he was in no hurry to pursue arms agreements; indeed, he believed it was a mistake to negotiate with the Soviets too soon. First he wanted to assert American leadership of the Western alliance and build up the nation's defenses to the point where the West would not have to fear a Soviet attack or attempts at nuclear blackmail. These measures, he was certain, would convince the Soviet Union of the West's unity and collective will and bring Moscow to the bargaining table. The Soviet Union, Reagan argued, would give up at the conference table only that which it could not hope to win through force or threats of force. Reagan gave simple expression to this view with his slogan: "Peace through strength."

How these sentiments offended the conventional thinking of the doves can be gauged by a brief look at the tumultuous reaction to the "evil empire" speech. Typical was the indignant response of columnist

Anthony Lewis of the *New York Times,* who searched his repertoire for the appropriate adjective: "Simplistic." "Sectarian." "Terribly dangerous." "Outrageous." Finally Lewis settled on "primitive . . . the only word for it."[11] A year later, Lewis had still not recovered. Reagan, he charged, had a "confrontational style" based on the premise that "insult and intimidation were the keys to dealing successfully with the Soviet Union." Yet Lewis was convinced that "the notion that a diplomacy of abuse would make the Russians cry 'uncle' is fantasy." The Soviet Union, Lewis asserted, "is not going to disappear because we want it to." Therefore "in the real world . . . there is no escape from the hard work of relating to the Soviet Union."[12]

Lewis's views are important because they echo those of the doves in the foreign policy establishment. The doves' perspective was this: the United States and the Soviet Union are both superpowers. Their systems are different, but that does not mean one is inherently superior. Indeed they are basically the same: "two scorpions in a bottle." There is a moral equivalence between them: both are basically aggressive and expansionist. Their irredentism is mutually reinforcing.

Moreover, many doves held, the overriding concern is not to determine which society is better. That is irrelevant. The main concern is nuclear weapons. All rival principles pale in the face of the possibility of global annihilation. The Soviet Union has nuclear weapons, which are not going away, so America's relations with the Soviets must be based on "peace" and not "confrontation." The United States should abandon the foolish and dangerous notion of trying to "roll back" Soviet advances, which should be accepted as permanent. Since there is no way to change the Soviet system, the best we can do is to influence Soviet behavior.

Even more, the doves argued, the United States should avoid saying or doing anything that Moscow might view as "provocative" and "destabilizing." Rather, the United States should establish a working relationship with the Soviets and attempt to negotiate arms control agreements that will limit the growth of those dangerous arsenals. The West should also offer economic and political concessions that may help to moderate Soviet expansion abroad and internal repression at home. If we are nice to them, this view held, they'll be nice to us. Historian Barbara Tuchman urged that the United States ingratiate itself with the Soviets by exploring "the stuffed-goose option—that is, providing them with all the grain and consumer goods they need."[13] If Reagan had taken this advice when it was offered in 1982, the Soviet empire would probably be around today.

Hawks applauded Reagan's willingness to confront the Soviet Union rhetorically and initiate an ambitious military program to rebuild America's defenses in order to deter Soviet aggression. The right had been calling for such measures for years. Yet beneath this agreement about the fundamental nature of the Soviet Union and what needed to be done in the short term to meet the Soviet threat was a crucial disagreement between Reagan and the hawks about the durability of Soviet communism. This disagreement meant that, under certain conditions, the two might have entirely different strategies for dealing with Moscow. These conditions were realized during Reagan's second term. During that period many on the right were critical, and some even denounced Reagan as a "useful idiot," when he changed course in his dealings with the new Soviet leader, Mikhail Gorbachev.

Let me clarify in what respect Reagan's view of the Soviets differed from that of the hawks. The hawks were in agreement with the doves about the permanence and immutability of Soviet communism. For hawks, the evil of communism was no bar to its success. Rather, communist victories were attributed to its virtually unlimited capacity for deceit. Hawks regarded the communist ideology as inspiring in its followers a fanatical determination and a willingness to win by any means necessary. They saw Communist states as implacably unified behind a goal of global domination. It was for this reason Whittaker Chambers told the House Un-American Activities Committee in 1948 that he knew that in abandoning communism, he was "leaving the winning side for the losing side."[14] In his novel *Nineteen Eighty-Four,* George Orwell offered the unforgettable description of a totalitarian future as "a boot stamping on a human face—forever."

Not everyone on the right shared this degree of Spenglerian gloom, yet the hawks generally believed, as Jean-François Revel argued in his 1983 book, *How Democracies Perish,* that democratic countries are inherently vulnerable to the kind of ruthless challenge posed by totalitarian states. Revel complained that democratic societies tend to be fickle and easily paralyzed by division and self-doubt. We were Athens, and they were Sparta. In Revel's view, the West faced an eroding position against an adversary that was confident, efficient, and willing to endure enormous sacrifice to achieve its long-term purpose. Lest we have illusions, Revel assured us that "communist totalitarianism is both durable and immutable."[15] Short of destroying the Soviet Union in a nuclear war—a gruesome prospect—most of the hawks did not see how Soviet communism could possibly go away.

Even before he became president, Reagan had a much more skeptical view of the alleged omnipotence of Soviet communism. This position is most evident in his jokes, which contain a profound analysis of the working of socialism. Since his days at General Electric, Reagan had developed an extensive repertoire of humorous anecdotes that he attributed to the Soviet people themselves. One of Reagan's stories involved a man who goes up to a grocery store clerk in Moscow and asks for a kilogram of beef, half a kilogram of butter, and a quarter kilogram of coffee. "We're all out," the clerk says, and the man leaves. Another man observing this incident says to the clerk, "That old man must be crazy." The clerk replies, "Yeah, but what a *memory!*"

Another favorite anecdote concerned a man who goes to the Soviet bureau of transportation to order an automobile. He is informed that he will have to put down his money now, but there is a ten-year wait. Nevertheless, he fills out the various forms and has them processed through the various agencies, and he signs in countless places, and finally he gets to the last agency, where they put the stamp on his papers. He pays them his money, and they say, "Come back in ten years and get your car." He asks, "Morning or afternoon?" The man in the agency says, "We're talking about ten years from now. What difference does it make?" He replies, "The plumber is coming in the morning."

Reagan could go on in this vein for hours. What is striking, however, is that Reagan's jokes are not about the *evil* of communism so much as they are about its *incompetence*. Reagan agreed with the conservatives that the Soviet experiment that sought to transform nature and create a "new man" was immoral. At the same time, he saw that it was also basically stupid. It couldn't be done. Reagan did not need a Ph.D. in economics to recognize how laughable it was to espouse a philosophy that denied the obvious fact that people work in proportion to the reward that they receive. He drew the commonsense conclusion that any economy based on centralized planners' dictating how much factories should produce, how much people should consume, and how social rewards should be distributed was doomed to disastrous failure. Thus Reagan was confident, as he frequently stated in his speeches, that history was on the side of freedom. For Reagan the Soviet Union was a "sick bear," and the question was not whether it would perish but when.

Yet even if the Soviet Union had a faltering economy, Reagan also knew that it had a highly advanced military. No one doubted that Soviet missiles, if fired at American targets, would cause enormous destruction, so there was a contradiction between the regime's internal economic problems and its expansionist political and military ambitions. Reagan knew that this could be exploited. He believed from the estimates of the CIA and from Team B, a study group that examined the Soviet threat, that the evil empire was spending as much as 20 percent of its gross national product on defense. (The actual figure proved to be much higher.) Thus Reagan formulated the notion that the West could use the superior economic resources of a free society to outspend and outcompete Moscow in the arms race.[16] Sovietologist Richard Pipes, who briefed Reagan on the Team B project, told me that Reagan "understood the fundamental vulnerability of the system." Senior officials like George Shultz and Caspar Weinberger confirmed to me that Reagan had a conscious strategy to impose intolerable strains on the Soviet regime, perhaps bankrupting it altogether.

What these aides say is supported by the public record. Reagan outlined his "sick bear" theory as early as May 1982 in a commencement address at his alma mater, Eureka College: "The Soviet empire is faltering because rigid centralized control has destroyed incentives for innovation, efficiency and individual achievement. But in the midst of social and economic problems, the Soviet dictatorship has forged the largest armed force in the world. It has done so by preempting the human needs of its people and, in the end, this course will undermine the foundations of the Soviet system."[17]

It is hard to believe that when Reagan uttered these words, he did not have before him a script outlining how the rest of the plot would turn out. Reagan sounded an equally prescient note a month later, in his speech to the British Parliament: "The decay of the Soviet experiment should come as no surprise to us. . . . The constant shrinkage of economic growth combined with the growth of military production is putting a heavy strain on the Soviet people. What we see here is a political structure that no longer corresponds to its economic base."[18]

Yet sick bears can still be dangerous—even more dangerous than when they are well, because sick bears tend to lash out. What resources they cannot find at home, they seek through plunder. Imperialism becomes a life-support system for the dysfunctional society. Moreover, in this case we are not discussing animals but people, so there is also the question of pride. The leaders of an internally weak empire are not disposed to acquiesce in an erosion of their power. They typically turn to their primary source of strength: the military. Precisely because of domestic weakness, the empire is more likely to increase its adventurism abroad. The rulers can then invoke their foreign conquests as the measure of their greatness. These conquests also enable them to satisfy the people. If they don't have enough bread, at least give them circuses. Parade the heavy missiles on the street during national holidays, to the roaring applause of the multitude.

All of these things were going on in the late 1970s and early 1980s, and their meaning was evident to Reagan, if to no one else. As Reagan told the British Parliament in 1982: "it has happened in the past that a small ruling elite either mistakenly attempts to ease domestic unrest through greater repression and foreign adventure, or it chooses a wiser course."[19] Reagan was determined to adopt a tough stance, in both rhetoric and action, to convince the Soviet Union that it could gain nothing abroad, and therefore its wisest course would be domestic reform. Consequently Reagan believed it was imperative for the United States to be strong, not conciliatory, in dealing with the Soviet bear. Appeasement, he was convinced, would only increase the bear's appetite and invite further aggression.

Thus Reagan agreed with the anticommunist strategy for dealing firmly with the Soviets. But Reagan was more confident than most hawks that Americans were up to the challenge. "We must realize," he said in his first inaugural address, "that . . . no weapon in the arsenals of the world is so formidable as the will and moral courage of free men and women." What was most visionary about Reagan's view was that it rejected the assumption of Soviet immutability. The Soviet Union had advertised itself as surfing on the wave of history, and virtually everyone across the political spectrum in the West seemed to acquiesce in this boast. Reagan did not merely envision the rollback of the Soviet empire to its pre–World War II borders. At a time when no one else could, Reagan dared to imagine a world in which the communist regime in the Soviet Union did not exist.

It is one thing to envision this condition, and quite another to bring it about. The Soviet bear was in a blustery and ravenous mood when Reagan entered the White House. Between 1974 and 1980, the Soviet Union had, through outright invasion or the triumph of its surrogates, brought ten countries into the communist orbit: South Vietnam, Cambodia, Laos, South Yemen, Angola, Ethiopia, Mozambique, Grenada, Nicaragua, and Afghanistan. Moreover, the Soviet Union had built the most formidable nuclear arsenal in the world, with thousands of multiple-warhead missiles aimed at the United States. The Warsaw Pact also had overwhelming superiority over the North Atlantic Treaty Organization (NATO) in conventional forces poised for an invasion of Western Europe. Finally Moscow had recently deployed a new generation of intermediate-range missiles, the giant SS-20s, targeted on Western Europe with the capacity to destroy all its major cities.

Reagan's strategy at the outset could not help being reactive, because he could not let these developments go unanswered. Nevertheless Reagan was determined not merely to respond to Soviet initiatives; rather, he developed from the outset a broader counteroffensive strategy designed to frustrate Soviet objectives and promote Western interests and values around the world. There were many elements to this strategy: the military buildup, the deployment of Pershing and cruise missiles, the Strategic Defense Initiative, the Reagan doctrine of assistance to anticommunist guerrillas, the global crusade to promote democracy and capitalism. Eventually, as we shall see, Reagan took the battle into the Soviet empire itself. Let us examine the crucial elements of the Reagan strategy as they unfolded.

The military buildup was the largest in peacetime history, yet Reagan believed it was overdue in order to match the Soviet buildup of the previous decade. Weinberger asked his division heads to request full funding for their top priorities. When the money came rolling in, the army added new divisions, the air force had several thousand new combat aircraft, and the navy pursued (but never quite reached) its goal of 600 ships. The Defense Department also developed the B-1 bomber that President Carter had canceled, as well as the Stealth bomber and Trident submarines, furnished with D-5 missiles.

Some of the programs were of questionable value. Reagan inherited from the Carter administration a program to build MX missiles. The MX with its ten warheads is a lethal and accurate missile, but it is based on land, so the question was where the missiles should be located so that they would be invulnerable to destruction in a Soviet first strike. The Carter administration proposed a "racetrack" system, in which the missiles would be shuttled along highways and railroad tracks through Nevada, Utah, and other parts of the West. Not surprisingly, this was not appealing to the residents of those states. The Reagan administration proposed an alternative: placing the MX missiles in specially hardened silos. Yet since the location of these silos could be discovered, it remained an open question whether the missiles could survive a preemptive Soviet attack.

Even worthwhile programs suffered many instances of inefficiency and waste, as may be expected whenever the government undertakes any extensive venture. Media reports highlighted such extravagances as Air Force planes sporting $200 coffeepots and $800 toilet seats. "Our critics used those examples to bash the Defense Department," Weinberger told me. "They forgot that we were the ones who uncovered the problem, and set about correcting it." Most of the funds in the Reagan military budget, Weinberger points out, went toward pay raises, child care centers, spare parts, and modern communications centers, all of which had been neglected in previous years. In a short time, the United States had rebuilt its defenses; equally important, Reagan restored the morale of the armed forces by cultivating in Americans a sense of patriotism and pride in the military.

In its first two years in office, the Reagan administration faced its first serious test. The Western allies had agreed to station 108 Pershing II and 464 Tomahawk cruise missiles in Europe to counter the threat of the Soviet SS-20s. Reagan believed that the deployment of these intermediate-range missiles was essential to convince the Soviet Union that it would never achieve one of its major goals, which was Finlandization: to reduce Britain, France, and Germany to impotent countries, independent in name but always vulnerable to Soviet pressure and control. Equally important, Reagan was determined to demonstrate to Moscow that the United States had the capacity to lead the Western alliance and the will to follow through on its defense commitments.

Rather than permitting this effort to go unopposed, the Soviet Union struck back. Its goal from the outset was to break the will of the West, and its main ally in this effort was the "peace movement" in the United States and Europe. The Soviet Union invested heavily in the peace movement, mainly through its front organizations like the World Peace Council.[20] Some of the leaders of the peace movement reflexively adopted the Soviet line, rationalizing Moscow's nuclear buildup while excoriating the United States for escalating the arms race and bringing the world to the brink of nuclear holocaust.

Of course, the rank-and-file supporters of the peace movement were not Soviet apologists. They were ordinary people who were frightened by the prospect of being destroyed in a nuclear war. These fears were assiduously cultivated by books like Jonathan Schell's *The Fate of the Earth,* which describes in macabre detail what would happen to an American city in the event of an atomic explosion.[21] Scientists like the late Carl Sagan predicted that even a limited exchange of nuclear weapons between the superpowers would lead to nuclear winter, a life-extinguishing arctic night for the human species.[22] The message to the nation was clear: Be afraid. Be very afraid.

In June 1982 I visited Central Park in New York to witness what was billed as one of the largest protest rallies in recent history. More than half a million people assembled to demand an end to the arms race. The mood was reminiscent of the antiwar demonstrations of the Vietnam era. Speaker after speaker portrayed Reagan as a frightening figure; in one case, he was likened to the nuclear maniac in the 1964 film *Dr. Strangelove.* Clergy read passages from the Book of Revelation about the last days of the universe. I saw protesters carrying banners that said, "There Are No Winners In a Nuclear War" and "You Can't Hug Your Kids with Nuclear Arms."

These platitudes conveyed a certain naiveté, but no one could mistake the depth of popular concern. Helen Caldicott, the head of Physicians for Social Responsibility, told *Life* that disarmament was the human race's top priority. "No other issue really matters."[23]

The antinuclear movement's lurid images of apocalypse were aimed at applying pressure on the Reagan administration to make unilateral concessions in its dealings with the Soviet Union. Four prominent former diplomats—McGeorge Bundy, George Kennan, Robert McNamara, and Gerard Smith—demanded that the United States issue a declaration that under no circumstances would it ever be the first superpower to use nuclear weapons.[24] The Reagan administration refused to do this, because it would make Western Europe much more difficult to defend in the event that the Soviet Union invaded with its massively superior conventional forces. The administration contended that in order to discourage such an attack, nuclear weapons were an important deterrent.

The main concern of the antinuclear leadership, however, was with preventing the Pershing and cruise deployments and halting the Reagan administration's military buildup. Its strategy for achieving this goal was to demand that the Reagan administration consent to a "nuclear freeze" with the Soviet Union. The concept of the freeze, which would require both superpowers to maintain their nuclear arsenals at existing levels, was first raised by antinuclear activists in New England town meetings. It soon spread across the country. Many city councils and several state legislatures approved nuclear freeze proposals. The idea was taken up by Senators Edward Kennedy and Mark Hatfield, and the House of Representatives endorsed a freeze resolution in a close vote. In 1982, polls showed that more than 70 percent of Americans supported the concept of a nuclear freeze.[25]

The Reagan administration contended that a nuclear freeze at that point would simply codify the existing nuclear imbalance in favor of the

Soviet Union. Reagan offered a counterproposal, which had been devised the previous year by Assistant Secretary of Defense Richard Perle. This was the zero option. Perle told me that what appealed to him about the zero option was its simplicity. It said that if the Soviet Union would withdraw its intermediate-range missiles targeted on Europe and Asia, the United States would not deploy the Pershing and cruise missiles. As Reagan told the American people in a televised address, "We're willing to cancel our program if the Soviets will dismantle theirs."[26]

Reagan also developed a strategy of his own to guide negotiations on strategic missiles. As Reagan put it to his aides, why be content with a freeze? Why limit ourselves to the parameters of the Strategic Arms Limitation Treaty (SALT) when we can work to negotiate strategic arms reductions? Alexander Haig confirms in his memoirs that it was Reagan himself who came up with the new concept of Strategic Arms Reduction Talks (START).[27] Reagan proposed that the United States would cut the size of its strategic nuclear arsenal in half as long as the Soviet Union would agree to proportionately large reductions in its stockpile.

These might seem like measures that would make the freeze activists ecstatic, yet the leadership of the antinuclear movement, as well as the foreign policy establishment, scoffed at Reagan's zero option and arms reduction proposals. Typical was the reaction of Strobe Talbott, who branded the zero option "highly unrealistic," adding that it had undoubtedly been offered "more to score propaganda points . . . than to win concessions from the Soviets." Writing in *Time,* Talbott argued that "the Kremlin will hardly be in a negotiating mood if the U.S. sets as a precondition for agreement that the Soviets engage in what to them looks like unilateral disarmament." He urged the Reagan administration to keep its arms control proposals "within the realm of the possible."[28]

Officials in the Reagan administration publicly dismissed these concerns, but privately they were shared by some of Reagan's senior staff who were by no means doves. Alexander Haig worried that the zero option had been devised by hawks who had no intention of finding common ground with the Soviets but were engaged in a "frivolous propaganda exercise."[29] Paul Nitze, the top negotiator for the United States, once approached the president with the apparent difficulty of raising the zero option with the Soviet Union. Reagan said he didn't see the problem: if the West could live without the Pershing and cruise missiles, the Soviets should be able to live without the SS-20s. Nitze protested that Reagan was asking the Soviets to get rid of missiles already in the field, while the United States would merely agree not to proceed with planned deployments. If this point was raised by Soviet negotiators, Nitze asked, what should he say? Reagan replied, "Well, Paul, you just tell them that you're working for one tough son of a bitch."[30]

Reagan adopted a more benign rhetoric in dealing with the nuclear freeze activists. Noting that he hadn't seen "any anti-nuclear demonstrators in Red Square," he expressed his concern that the freeze movement would weaken the U.S. negotiating position without placing reciprocal pressure on the Soviet Union. Yet he never treated the activists as disloyal to their country or somehow in league with the enemy. They were, he said, "well intentioned but mistaken."[31] At his daughter Patti Davis's request, Reagan agreed to meet privately with Helen Caldicott, to engage in a candid discussion of nuclear weapons. Reagan specified one condition: the meeting should be off the record.

The discussion did not go well. Reagan was characteristically hospitable and courteous, but Caldicott was rude and condescending to the president. When Reagan expressed his concerns about the Soviet propaganda offensive to prevent the Pershing and cruise deployments, Caldicott interrupted, "Where did you get that? Did you get that from *Reader's Digest?*" After the meeting, Caldicott promptly called a press conference and proceeded to denounce Reagan as an ignoramus with psychological problems. "Almost everything he said to me was wrong. He doesn't understand much of this." Caldicott diagnosed Reagan as suffering from "missile envy." Reagan confined his reaction to a lament in his diary, "I'm afraid that our daughter has been taken over by that whole gang."[32]

As the date for the scheduled Pershing and cruise deployments neared, the political offensive against the missiles reached fever pitch in both Europe and the United States. In October 1983, more than 2 million people demonstrated in London, Rome, Stockholm, Vienna, Paris, and at various other European sites. In the United States, ABC television scheduled a film, "The Day After," to run in prime time nationwide three days before the first Pershing missiles were to be deployed. As the *New York Times* previewed it, the film featured "scenes of enormous destruction by firestorm, people being vaporized, mass graves, the irretrievable loss of food and water supplies, vandalism and murder, the breakdown of medical care and disfigurement and death from radiation sickness."[33]

The Soviet Union tried a final gambit: if the West deployed its intermediate-range missiles in Europe, Soviet general secretary Yuri Andropov threatened that the Soviet Union would withdraw from all arms control negotiations. The peace movement went berserk at this prospect, and some proclaimed that nuclear war was now imminent. Yet, several senior aides told me, Reagan directed U.S. negotiators in Geneva not to make any new concessions. If the Soviet team wanted to walk away, Reagan said, let them go; they will eventually be back.

Reagan's will, and that of the leaders of the Western alliance, did not break. In 1983, the missiles were finally deployed. The Soviet Union suspended arms control talks, giving new political impetus to the Western peace movement. But the Soviet propaganda offensive had failed to stop the missiles. Western leaders who had stood most strongly with Reagan, such as Helmut Kohl in West Germany and Margaret Thatcher in England, were reelected. The Western alliance under American leadership had withstood its toughest test of will in the postwar era.

Chapter 7

Making the World Safe for Democracy

IN ADDITION TO THE nuclear intimidation, a second challenge facing Reagan in his first term in office was the expansion of Soviet influence around the world. This trend began with the fall of South Vietnam and accelerated through the 1970s. Under the Nixon, Ford, and Carter administrations, the United States unsuccessfully attempted to pacify the Soviet Union through trade and arms control concessions. While the United States retreated in Asia, Africa, and Latin America, the Soviets escalated their involvement in conflicts around the world. So many countries fell into the clutches of the Soviet bear that I remember a grim joke that began to circulate in the early 1980s: "Lose a country, gain a restaurant." Sure enough, immigrants fleeing communist tyranny opened up Vietnamese, Cambodian, and Ethiopian restaurants in the Georgetown and Adams Morgan areas of the nation's capital and elsewhere. The Soviet invasion of Afghanistan with more than 100,000 troops in 1979 was the most spectacular demonstration of Moscow's confidence and power. In December 1981, the year Reagan took office, strikes broke out in Poland. The head of state, General Wojciech Jaruzelski, acting on instructions from Moscow, declared martial law and imposed a ruthless crackdown.

In the face of these developments, the United States needed a new strategy. Jimmy Carter took pride in the fact that his foreign policy was based on an affirmation of human rights. This was an excellent idea in principle, yet in practice, it began to downplay human rights violations in communist countries while applying diplomatic and trade sanctions to U.S. allies that restricted the freedom of their citizens. Carter gave in to the argument of the doves that in dealing with the Soviet Union, the paramount concern was preventing nuclear holocaust, so he subordinated his human rights agenda to what he perceived as the higher cause of arms control. Carter justified his emphasis on changing the behavior of U.S. allies by pointing out that, with countries as with people, it is easier to influence friends than enemies. Yet the unintended consequence of his strategy was to strengthen enemies and turn friends into foes.

This had happened in Iran, where the United States turned on its old friend the shah only to discover that his successor, the Ayatollah Khomeini, was a theocrat and an implacable foe of America. Similarly in Nicaragua, the Carter administration in the late 1970s helped to depose the reigning dictator, Anastasio Somoza, a pro–United States tyrant, only to find him replaced by the Sandinistas, who promptly suspended civil liberties and declared their allegiance to the Soviet Union. Not only were Khomeini and the Sandinistas violators of human rights, they did not even recognize human rights as the West understood them. Moreover, since the Soviet Union was the most systematic foe of political, economic, and civil liberties since the Nazis, the consequence of its growing hegemony in the Third World during the late 1970s meant that, contrary to Carter's objectives, human rights around the globe were in worse shape when he left office than when he arrived.

Reagan, determined to find an alternative to Carter's self-defeating human rights policy, discovered the intellectual framework for it in the writings of political scientist Jeane Kirkpatrick, whom he recruited as the U.S. ambassador to the United Nations. Kirkpatrick, who discussed her ideas with Reagan on several occasions, recently told me that "he was very well informed about foreign policy and could grasp the essence of an argument very quickly. Those who keep repeating that he never did his homework haven't done *their* homework."

Kirkpatrick argued in her writings that U.S. policy should distinguish between authoritarian and totalitarian regimes. An authoritarian regime is a tyranny of the traditional sort. A dictator runs a poor country, enriching himself at the expense of his people, and he outlaws political dissent and cracks down on anyone who is a threat to his power. These regimes can be more or less oppressive, depending on whether the dictator is merely a megalomaniac or also a sadist. Yet, Kirkpatrick pointed out, there is always hope for change. Dictators eventually die or are ousted, and because there are independent sources of power, such as the business sector and the clergy, "right-wing autocracies do sometimes evolve into democracies." For Kirkpatrick, Chile under Pinochet and the Philippines under Marcos typified the authoritarian regime.

Totalitarian regimes, by contrast, are based on ideology and characterized by systematic control of the basic lives of its citizens. Unlike traditional despots, who typically don't care where you live or what religion you practice or what you do for a living, totalitarian regimes in Kirkpatrick's view seek "jurisdiction over the whole life of the society." All aspects of social and even private life are subordinated to the state. The goal is to "revolutionize society, culture, and personality." This, Kirkpatrick argued, is historically unique. Only in a totalitarian regime does your neighbor or even child turn you in to the authorities if he sees you reading the Bible. In some cases, people are politically liable even for what they say in their sleep. Under such a system, Kirkpatrick argued, human rights violations are not an aberration; they are systemic imperatives. Indeed there cannot be any hope that things will get better, because the oppression is part of the structure of the regime. Totalitarianism is forever. The Soviet Union and its satellites were the model for the totalitarian regime.[1]

Reagan was far more convinced than Kirkpatrick of the vulnerability of Soviet communism, but he enthusiastically endorsed her main argument that it was entirely defensible for the United States to ally itself with authoritarian regimes, despite their imperfect human rights records, in order to check the advances of totalitarian regimes, whose human rights abuses were more systematic and which were also hostile to the United States. Critics charged Kirkpatrick and Reagan with espousing a double standard in which they condemned Soviet repression while overlooking the human rights violations of pro-American despots.[2] Yet at no time did either Kirkpatrick or Reagan condone the indefensible conduct of U.S. allies. Rather, theirs was a doctrine of the lesser evil. In the real world, one sometimes has to choose between the bad and the terrible. Just as it made sense for America to ally itself with Stalin in order to defeat Hitler, a greater immediate threat, so also the United States was justified in befriending authoritarian despots for the larger goal of stopping the spread of Soviet communism.

Reagan used the foundation of Kirkpatrick's ideas to construct a doctrine for responding to the Soviet Union that bore his distinctive stamp. This was the Reagan doctrine, so dubbed by columnist Charles Krauthammer, and it was a major departure in the annals of American postwar strategy. It involved U.S. military and material support for people who were struggling to overthrow the yoke of Soviet totalitarianism.

The Reagan doctrine can be clarified by contrasting it with other well-known doctrines that have come to define American and Soviet leaders. The Truman doctrine, for example, was based on the idea of containing Soviet influence and preventing it from spreading further. The Nixon doctrine of the 1970s involved U.S. support for friendly countries to prevent them from going communist. Yet both these doctrines were concerned with preserving freedom, not with extending it. The Reagan doctrine went beyond them in that it sought, for the first time, to reverse Soviet gains. Thus it was a direct challenge to the famous Brezhnev doctrine that once a country goes communist, it remains communist.

Reagan conceived of his doctrine primarily in moral terms. He told the Irish Parliament in Dublin in 1984, "All across the world today—in the shipyards of Gdansk, the hills of Nicaragua, the rice paddies of Kampuchea, the mountains of Afghanistan—the cry again is liberty."[3] In 1985 Reagan told the American people in his State of the Union address, "Freedom is . . . the universal right of all God's children. Our mission is to defend freedom and democracy. . . . We must not break faith with those who are risking their lives on every continent, from Afghanistan to Nicaragua, to defy Soviet-sponsored aggression and secure rights which have been ours from birth."[4]

While Reagan emphasized the universal right to freedom and self-government, his actions made it clear that the United States was unable to secure that right for all people living under communist tyranny. From the outset, George Shultz told me, Reagan's implementation of his doctrine was not indiscriminate but prudent. "The president was not willing to place the lives of large numbers of American soldiers at risk," Shultz explained. Rather, under the Reagan doctrine, the United States would provide military and material assistance to indigenous peoples who were fighting for their own freedom. Moreover, the nature and timing of U.S. support would vary according to the circumstances in each country.

In Poland, for example, Reagan signed a top-secret national security directive authorizing a series of diplomatic, economic, and covert measures to undermine the Soviet-backed regime of General Jaruzelski. The Reagan administration worked with the international division of the AFL-CIO to establish direct contacts with the trade union Solidarity and secretly provide assistance in the form of literature, electronic and communications equipment, and much-needed funds. Moreover Reagan established a close personal rapport with the Polish Pope John Paul II. In addition to their ideological anticommunism, the two men shared a close personal bond because they had both recently been victims of assassination attempts. Building on this relationship, the Reagan administration colluded with the Vatican to strengthen the Polish churches as a base of resistance to communist tyranny. From the American side, this campaign was directed by CIA director William Casey. Without these efforts, Lech Walesa and many others have conceded, Solidarity would have been destroyed by the Polish authorities.[5]

In Afghanistan, the Reagan administration won bipartisan support for the provision of small arms, artillery pieces, and grenades to the *mujahedin* tribesmen who had taken to the hills to launch a guerrilla war against Soviet occupation. Shultz emphasized that no one in the administration had any illusions that the Afghan rebels were democrats. Yet Reagan and many in Congress supported them because they were fierce patriots who wanted to free their country from Soviet hegemony.

I remember seeing a group of Afghan children who came to the White House to meet the President. At first I was struck by their innocent faces and exotic outfits; then I noticed that several were missing an arm or a leg, probably as a consequence of stepping on Soviet mines. Aides told me how moved Reagan was to see these children. Determined to resist Soviet barbarism, the Reagan administration convinced Pakistan to provide facilities which the CIA used as training camps to show the brave but sometimes inexperienced *mujahedin* how to blow up bridges, fuel depots, and ammunition dumps. Eventually the administration provided satellite intelligence for the *mujahedin* to target Soviet aircraft, and rocket launchers and Stinger surface-to-air missiles to shoot them down. The administration was determined to make Afghanistan the "Soviets' Vietnam."

In Angola, the Reagan administration sought support for the army of Jonas Savimbi, which was fighting to free the country from the Popular Movement for the Liberation of Angola (MPLA), the ruling communist government. The MPLA had imported Soviet advisers and more than 40,000 Cuban troops to consolidate its power. Savimbi's UNITA forces, with its headquarters in Jamba, controlled about a third of the country. I attended a lecture that Savimbi gave at the Heritage Foundation in the mid-1980s. His rhetoric was pro-Western, although few in the audience were convinced he was a democrat. Still, in the Reagan administration's view, Savimbi, like the *mujahedin,* was fighting for national self-determination and deserved support in his effort to expel the Soviets and Cubans from Angola. Yet Congress was initially reluctant to intervene in the Angolan civil war and did not approve support for Savimbi's forces until 1985.

In Cambodia, the United States had a problem. In 1978, Vietnam had invaded Cambodia with more than 150,000 troops and established a puppet government. The Reagan administration sought to punish this aggression by making Cambodia "Vietnam's Vietnam," but it was not going to be easy. The 50,000 Cambodian rebels struggling to expel the Vietnamese were made up of several groups: one was led by Prince Norodom Sihanouk, the former royal ruler of Cambodia; a second was headed by Son Sann, the former prime minister and a democrat; and a third, outnumbering the other two, was led by the Khmer Rouge army, which had, under the sanguinary Pol Pot, engaged in widespread torture and mass murder in the 1970s. Reagan showed no personal interest in Cambodia, but his State Department sought to strengthen the democratic forces within the resistance while keeping aid out of the hands of the Khmer Rouge. Congress was justifiably skeptical that the United States could manage such a feat, and aid to the Cambodian rebels remained modest through the Reagan years.

In Mozambique, the Frelimo ruling party of Samora Machel had established ties with the Soviet Union, but this socialist government was also eager to expand trade with the West. A guerrilla movement, Renamo, had arisen, with the support of the South African government, to overthrow Machel's Frelimo regime. Some conservatives within the Reagan administration advocated U.S. aid to Renamo, but Reagan, who knew and cared little about Mozambique, accepted George Shultz's view that Renamo's use of torture and other wartime atrocities had alienated its potential base of support among the people, and thus it was undeserving of U.S. support. Shultz argued, and Reagan agreed, that in this case, the United States was better off using its trade leverage with the ruling government to attempt to reduce its Soviet ties.

Ironically, Reagan's first opportunity to overthrow a communist regime came not in any of these places but in the island nation of Grenada. The Grenada operation is frequently described today as a vain and pointless display of American power. Haynes Johnson writes, "Real patriotism involves much more than jingoistically . . . invading small countries like Grenada with overwhelming power."[6] This criticism entirely misses the significance of the Grenada operation, which represented the first American effort to restore democracy to a communist country. Thus Grenada was an attempt to invalidate the premise of the Brezhnev doctrine: that communism was being carried by the inevitable current of history.

On October 23, 1983, Reagan received an urgent message from Eugenia Charles, prime minister of Dominica and chair of the Organization of Eastern Caribbean States. The situation in Grenada had become precarious, she said, and asked that the United States provide military assistance to protect the security of the small nations of the Caribbean. That evening, Reagan and his top advisers, including William Clark, Ed Meese, George Shultz, and Caspar Weinberger, gathered to discuss the request.

Since 1979 Grenada had been ruled by a Marxist dictator, Maurice Bishop, whose New Jewel movement came to power through a coup. Now Bishop himself had been murdered by a rival Marxist faction whose leaders considered him insufficiently committed to revolutionary principles. There were several thousand Cubans in Grenada at that time, who were working on constructing a 10,000-foot runway, possibly for the use of Soviet and Cuban military planes. The neighboring island nations felt deeply threatened by the Cuban presence, the continuing civil war, and the new regime's rule by violence. Reagan also had a special reason to be concerned about the presence on the island of some 1,000 U.S. citizens, most of whom were medical students at St. George's Medical College. Under Grenada's martial law, any of these students seen on the streets after hours could be shot on sight.

As Meese and Weinberger recounted the incident for me, Reagan's advisers conducted a vigorous debate among themselves on the question of whether the United States should intervene. The difficulty of military action was compounded by the fact that on that day, a suicide bomber had crashed his explosive-laden truck into the U.S. embassy in Beirut, killing 241 marines stationed there as a peacekeeping force. Reagan was informed in no uncertain terms that he could hardly afford another foreign policy debacle. Until this point in the discussion, Reagan had listened intently but said little. Finally he asked the Joint Chiefs of Staff whether they believed that a military operation was likely to succeed. They expressed reluctance to undertake it because of the expected political outcry over American casualties, but if they were asked to do it, they said they believed it could be done. "Very well," Reagan said, "in that case, let's go ahead." The day before the invasion, Reagan informed Tip O'Neill and a group of congressional leaders of the impending U.S. action. O'Neill expressed distress at being notified so late and warned the president that if the invasion went badly, Reagan could not count on his support.

On October 25, 1983, about 2,000 U.S. troops, along with units from six Caribbean states, stormed the island of Grenada. Fierce fighting broke out between the Americans and the soldiers of the Marxist regime. In the middle of the action, the Cuban "construction workers" showed up heavily armed and fired at the U.S. troops. The battle lasted three days. Given its overwhelming superiority in numbers and firepower, the United States prevailed, and the Marxist regime was ousted from power. Nineteen American soldiers were killed, and about a hundred were injured. In one mishap, U.S. troops had aimed a bomb at Marxist forces firing from the parapet wall of what turned out to be an asylum for the mentally ill. The bomb hit the main structure of the asylum, and several civilians were killed.

America had won. What would be the reaction? From the Democrats, it was one of outrage. They ridiculed the notion that Grenada was part of the Soviet bloc, dismissed the idea that the Cubans on the island were mercenaries, and were openly skeptical that any American lives were in danger. The thrust of the criticism was that the United States was simply throwing its weight around in the traditional manner of the neighborhood bully. Some said the United States even intended to occupy Grenada and establish a form of colonial rule. How did such aspirations and behavior, the Democrats asked, make America any different from the Soviet Union?

Walter Mondale warned that the Grenada intervention "undermines our ability to effectively criticize what the Soviets have done in their brutal intervention in Afghanistan, in Poland and elsewhere." Senators Chris Dodd and Daniel Patrick Moynihan expressed similar sentiments. Moral equivalence was also the theme at the *New York Times,* whose editors complained that the invasion was "a reverberating demonstration to the world that America has no more respect for laws and borders, for the codes of civilization, than the Soviet Union."[7] The press was especially bitter that media coverage of the invasion had been severely restricted.

There were calls for Reagan to resign, and a handful of congressmen, including Ted Weiss, John Conyers, Julian Dixon, Henry Gonzalez, and Parren Mitchell, submitted a resolution that called for the president to be impeached for violating international law. The reaction abroad was equally strident. The United Nations voted to condemn the U.S. action. Even Reagan's close ally, Margaret Thatcher, sternly protested that Grenada was a commonwealth country and the United States had no right to intervene.

Amid this firestorm of criticism, the American public also heard the case in favor of the invasion of Grenada made by Eugenia Charles, the prime minister of Dominica, who had implored the Reagan administration to take action in the first place. Contrary to those who said that the danger posed by Marxist revolutionaries was minimal, Charles called it very serious. Reagan himself challenged the notion that the Grenada expedition made the United States indistinguishable from the Soviet Union. "Let me just say," he said, "there's something seriously wrong with anyone who can't see the difference between 100,000 Soviets trying to force a dictatorship down the throats of the Afghan people, and America and eight Caribbean democracies joining to stop Cubans and local Communists from doing the same thing in Grenada."[8]

A few days after the military operation, the American students from Grenada returned to a U.S. Air Force base in Charleston, South Carolina. On the day of their arrival, Oliver North, who had helped plan the Grenada operation, came rushing into the president's office. He said that the students had not been briefed on the reasons for the invasion, and no one knew what they would tell the press. "Come with me," Reagan said. He led North into a room with a television monitor. There the two of them watched as the first young man got off the plane, walked over to the runway, dropped to his knees, and kissed the soil of the United States. "You see, Ollie," Reagan said, "you should have more faith in the American people."[9] Reagan knew that with the student's dramatic gesture, the national debate over the legitimacy of the Grenada invasion was effectively over.

Upon searching the island, U.S. troops uncovered large stockpiles of military equipment and thousands of pages of documents on the island that showed in detail the Marxist regime's secret arms pacts with other communist countries and its plans to make the island a military base for Soviet bloc activities. The Grenada papers also included a contingency plan for kidnapping the American medical students. The documents proved that the Cubans were military advisers who were identified in their duty rosters by their mortar companies and machine gun units.[10] U.S. troops also located on the island several Soviet, East German, Libyan, North Korean, and Bulgarian advisers, all of whom were sent back to their home countries.

Soon Grenada held free elections and joined the ranks of the democratic nations. To the surprise of those who predicted that the United States intended to occupy and colonize Grenada, American troops promptly left. On the first anniversary of the rescue, President Reagan landed in Grenada to a delirious welcome by more than half the citizens of the island. There were no signs that said, "Yankee Go Home." Instead there were several banners that said, "God Bless America."

As a military venture, Grenada was a small operation, yet the political risks were enormous. Reagan's leadership was exercised in the face of apprehension on the part of his staff and skepticism on the part of the congressional leadership. The real importance of the Grenada invasion was that, for the first time since the Vietnam War, the United States had committed ground troops abroad, sustained casualties, emerged victorious, and won the support of the American people.[11] The Grenada rescue helped to exorcise the ghost of Vietnam from the American psyche. Equally important, Grenada represented the first time in postwar history that a communist takeover of a nation had been reversed by overt military action. The Brezhnev doctrine was dead.

The Reagan doctrine faced its most serious challenge in Nicaragua. Nicaragua was viewed as important, by both Reagan and his critics, because it produced a clash of fundamental ideological worldviews. For the Reagan administration, Nicaragua was seen as another Cuba. For the Democratic leadership and many pundits, Nicaragua was seen as another Vietnam. Both sides were determined to prevent the other from achieving its policy goals in order to avoid dangers they saw as imminent. Both saw themselves acting in the vital interests of the United States. Only one could be right.

Like many other Latin American countries, Nicaragua met the Kirkpatrick definition of a traditional autocracy. The country had been ruled for most of the century by the Somoza dictatorship, and a handful of wealthy families controlled most of the land and wealth. The United States had pursued friendly relations with the Somozas; indeed Franklin Roosevelt once said of the dictator, "He's a son of a bitch, but he's *our* son of a bitch." By the late 1970s, however, the elder Somoza had been succeeded by his son, Anastasio Somoza Debayle, whose brutishness and vulgarity alienated just about everyone in the country; a broad coalition of political activists, businessmen, and clergy united to overthrow him. The Carter administration supported the revolution, at least in its last stages, and pledged financial assistance to the new government.

Yet, in precisely the pattern that Kirkpatrick described, the United States contributed to Somoza's downfall without paying much attention to his replacement. This turned out to be the Sandinistas, who seized the capital city of Managua and abandoned their promise to the Organization of American States (OAS) to hold free elections and pursue policies of political pluralism and nonalignment. Rather, the Sandinistas moved quickly to consolidate their power, destroy independent sources of dissent, and establish the framework for a totalitarian regime.

The Sandinistas proclaimed themselves socialists and established close relations with the Soviet Union. They confiscated land and other property, which they used for collectivized farming and the private gain of the Sandinista directorate. They took over control of radio and TV stations and imposed censorship on the country's largest newspaper, *La Prensa.* The activities of the Catholic church were curtailed. The Sandinistas seized the land of the Miskito Indians on the Caribbean coast and began to relocate them to other parts of the country. Neighborhood committees were established to report on persons disloyal to the tenets of socialism. The Sandinistas also built the largest military force in the region, seemingly with the intention of exporting their Marxist revolution to other Latin American countries.[12]

The Reagan administration was determined to prevent Nicaragua from making the transition to a communist dictatorship and a surrogate of the Soviet empire. Under the supervision of CIA director William Casey, the administration began to support the small band of guerrillas who had taken to the bush to fight the Sandinistas. This fledgling army of counterrevolutionaries, which came to be known as the contras, was initially only a few hundred strong. But with the assistance both of the United States and the Sandinistas, whose heavy-handedness proved to be a rapid recruitment mechanism, the ranks of the contras swelled to around 15,000 in the mid-1980s. At their peak they made up the largest peasant army in Latin America since the Mexican revolution.

Reagan supported what he saw as the contras' struggle for freedom. In March 1985, he called the contras "the moral equivalent of our founding fathers and the brave men and women of the French resistance." Speechwriter Peggy Noonan, who drafted Reagan's remarks, told me he specifically asked for those analogies to be used. The founding fathers analogy was ridiculed at the time—could these *campesinos* in the bush with names like José and Pablo be compared with George Washington and James Madison?—but Reagan's point was that freedom is not the prerogative of the English-speaking world. Rather, Reagan believed in the universality of American ideals. The Declaration of Independence and the Constitution of the United States, he once said, were "covenants we have made not only with ourselves, but with all mankind."[13] In this, Reagan was in the tradition of Lincoln, who in 1848 invoked the Declaration to proclaim: "Any people anywhere, being inclined and having the power, have the right to rise up and shake off the existing government and form a new one that suits them. This is a most valuable and sacred right, which we hope and believe is to liberate the world."[14]

The Reagan administration was aware that the contras, with their limited numbers, poor training, and inadequate weapons and equipment, had little chance of a clear military victory over the Sandinistas. But Reagan always maintained that if the contras were willing to put their lives on the line, they deserved American help. Officials in the State Department hoped that the contras would pressure the ruling government to open up the political process and perhaps even hold free elections. In his speeches to U.S. audiences, Reagan also stressed the American stakes involved: "If the Soviet Union can aid and abet subversion in our hemisphere, then the United States has a legal right and a moral duty to help resist it."[15]

From the outset, the battle over the contras occurred on two fronts: in the Nicaraguan bush and in the corridors of the U.S. Congress. Many liberal Democrats bitterly resisted the Reagan administration's requests for contra funding. Some openly worked with the Sandinistas, inviting them to their Capitol Hill offices and collaborating on strategies to undermine Reagan's policy.[16] These actions were hard to justify, but the conduct of the Democrats was driven by the intensity of their objection to the administration's course of action. Reagan, they said, was getting the nation into a war that would end up costing American lives. The contras, they alleged, were former Somocistas who routinely engaged in barbaric atrocities and sought to restore the ancien regime.

These were legitimate concerns. The Reagan administration insisted that contra aid was an alternative, not a prelude, to the commitment of U.S. forces, yet it was entirely possible that an escalation of the war might require a direct deployment of American troops. Most of the contras were too young to have been involved in the Somoza regime and were part of a genuinely indigenous uprising, but several senior officers, including Enrique Bermudez, the contra military commander, were former members of the National Guard. Moreover, despite the denials of the administration and many American conservatives, there were ample documented cases of contra atrocities; indeed, it is hard to imagine a guerrilla war without excesses on both sides. The Reagan administration established a human rights committee to monitor contra abuses; those found guilty of atrocities were forced to resign from the resistance.

Yet opposition to Reagan's Nicaragua policy went beyond these reasonable objections. For the American left, the Sandinistas were seen as peasant troubadors and authentic heroes who were implementing the mandate of a popular revolution. They were also the last hope for proletarian rule that would provide a real alternative to Western bourgeois capitalism. Disgusted by the political and economic system in their own countries, political and religious activists in the West had for much of the twentieth century projected their hopes for a better world onto socialist countries and movements abroad. In the 1930s, the designated worker's paradise was the Soviet Union. But Stalin's murder of millions made the illusion of a utopia difficult to sustain. It didn't perish, however, but simply moved elsewhere. In the 1950s, it settled on Mao's China where, once again, the brutality of the regime became so chilling and widespread as to dampen Western enthusiasm. The next stop, in the 1960s, was Castro's Cuba. Alas, here too evidence surfaced to discredit the leftist fantasy, which had to keep migrating in order to endure.[17]

In the 1980s, these hopes descended on Nicaragua, where William Sloane Coffin, Noam Chomsky, Ramsey Clark, and other Western leftists developed what can only be termed a romance with the Sandinistas. Officials at the U.S. Catholic Conference and the World Council of Churches were elated to see former clergymen like Ernesto Cardenal and Miguel d'Escoto serving in top positions in the Sandinista hierarchy, where they identified the promise of heaven with the cause of the revolution. As Cardenal expressed this tenet of so-called liberation theology: "There can be no effective eucharist except in a classless society."[18] In the literary societies of New York and London, there were raptures over the discovery that leading Sandinistas like Daniel Ortega and his brother Humberto Ortega were part-time poets. *Playboy* reprinted one of Daniel Ortega's poems:

> The shit and piss,
> Hot damn, so many people . . .
> Jail man!
> Don't let nobody talk with this man;
> Let 'im sleep on the floor,
> And if he makes a move, belt 'im one . . .
> The galleys, Auschwitz, Buchenwald
> Nicaragua.[19]

It isn't *Lycidas,* but at least give a politician credit for effort. And at the leftist Institute for Policy Studies, the research fellows shared the story of Nora Astorga, the Sandinista beauty who had lured one of Somoza's top generals into her bedroom, only to have him castrated and then murdered by guerrillas concealed behind the drapes. As the incident was recounted to me, the policy analysts present confessed that they had all studied the rhetoric of revolution, but confronted with the real thing, their only reaction was, "Wow."

Many of these Western leftists packed their bags and headed to Nicaragua. There these *internacionalistas* picked coffee, taught literacy, or simply sat in the cafés of Managua and sang the praises of the Sandinistas. Rock stars from the West performed in the streets; Woodstock had come to Managua. Tens of thousands of American visitors, many from churches led by a group called Witness for Peace, toured Nicaragua and returned home with wonderful tales of peasants dancing around trees and reciting proletarian verse.

Occasionally leading Sandinistas like the Ortega brothers reciprocated by visiting the West, where they went on lavish spending sprees on Rodeo Drive and the Champs Elysées. On a 1985 trip, Daniel Ortega and his wife stopped by Cohen's Fashion Optical on the Upper East Side of New York to purchase $3,500 worth of designer glasses.[20] During these junkets, the Sandinista officials also took time to regale gullible Western audiences with heroic accounts of their efforts to construct a brave new world, all in the face of senseless opposition from those spoilers in the Reagan administration.

In Washington, meanwhile, an acrimonious debate raged throughout the 1980s on whether Congress should fund the contras. What emerged was a schizophrenic approach to U.S. aid: now you see it—now you don't. Congress even placed sporadic and increasingly draconian restrictions on the Reagan administration's effort to assist the contras. Reagan became frustrated with the legislature's willingness to provide economic but no military aid. On February 18, 1986, he told reporters, "You can't fight attack helicopters piloted by Cubans with Band-Aids and mosquito nets."[21] Congress did not relent. Eventually, through a series of amendments—named after their sponsor, Democratic congressman Edward Boland—Congress prohibited cabinet and intelligence agencies in the executive branch from any involvement in the civil war in Nicaragua.

Despite congressional opposition, the Reagan administration was determined not to permit the contras, who had placed their trust in the United States, to be mercilessly shot down by the Soviet-made Hind helicopters consigned to the Sandinista armed forces. So CIA director William Casey, national security adviser John Poindexter, and his aide, Oliver North, pursued other sources of funding. They approached friendly allies like Brunei, Taiwan, and Saudi Arabia, as well as anticommunist donors in the United States. The funds thus obtained enabled the contras to purchase vitally needed ammunition and supplies. Finally, Poindexter and North went too far in seeking to fund the contras with profits from secret American arms sales to Iran. The Iran-contra scandal of the late 1980s—discussed later in more detail—paralyzed the Reagan administration's Central America policy and jeopardized the presidency itself.

Nevertheless, through its shenanigans, the administration had somehow managed to keep the contras alive through the decade. Finally, in 1990, a year after Reagan left office, President Bush and House Speaker Jim Wright prevailed on the Sandinistas to hold elections. Both diplomatic initiatives, as well as contra pressure, seem to have contributed to

Managua's decision. The Sandinistas seem to have gambled that if they could establish their legitimacy through elections, the United States would have no justification for continuing to support the guerrillas.

The opposition candidate was Violeta Chamorro, whose husband, Pedro, had founded the newspaper *La Prensa*. The Chamorros were opponents of Somoza, and Violeta had served in the coalition government that replaced him, but in 1980 she resigned to protest the increasingly repressive measures of the Sandinistas. After her husband's death, she became editor of *La Prensa,* where she waged a futile battle against the Sandinista censors. They accused her of being an "enemy of the people," and she finally had a chance to prove them wrong at the ballot box.

The elections were watched with great interest in the West. The press, which had been interviewing and polling Nicaraguans for months, predicted an easy victory for the ruling party. On ABC, Peter Jennings announced that the imminent Ortega triumph demonstrated "the failure of U.S. policy." Even American conservatives seemed prepared for the democratic opposition to lose and protested that the Sandinistas had used the state-run media and government resources to gain an unfair campaign advantage and steal the election.

When the results came in, however, the opposition candidate, Violeta Chamorro, and her UNO party won a stunning victory. The 55–40 percent outcome in UNO's favor was especially striking because Chamorro, who did not hide her American sympathies and was portrayed throughout the campaign as a Yankee dupe, did not seem hurt by her U.S. association. Even more significant, the demographic spread of the election results solved the puzzle of how thousands of contras managed to hide out for so many years without detection: they were supported and protected by peasants and natives, who saw them as fighting to recover the original promises of the revolution that overthrew Somoza. Reagan was no longer in the White House, but his administration's claims about the Sandinistas were vindicated by the election results, the best available test for determining the regime's level of popular support.

At Managua's International Hotel, Western journalists and *internacionalistas* wept bitter tears as the election results were tallied. In the view of many American and European leftists, the peasants had betrayed Daniel Ortega. A California doctor told American reporters that not she, but the Nicaraguan people, had made a terrible mistake. With scarcely concealed condescension, the Reverend William Sloane Coffin said the Nicaraguan people had "voted with their bellies, not their hearts." The head of Witness for Peace blamed U.S. imperialism for making Nicaragua ungovernable and contributing to the defeat of the Sandinistas.[22]

Yet all this crying after the fact could not alter the people's choice, and so the "political pilgrims," as Paul Hollander calls them, returned home. They were now missionaries without a mission. Their quest for a peasant utopia in Nicaragua turned out to be a deluded sham. Yet this time the wishful thinkers had run out of new places to go, new regimes to rhapsodize. The dove had no place to fly. With the rout of the Sandinistas, a century of illusion on the part of Western leftists finally came to an end.

If the Reagan administration was proving itself relentless in opposing Soviet totalitarianism and its surrogates, what of its conduct toward right-wing dictatorships that his critics worried would be given a free rein to oppress their citizens? Many on the left were surprised to see that far from coddling these autocratic regimes, the Reagan administration applied firm pressure on them to make the transition to democracy. Some on the right wondered what happened to Reagan's endorsement of the Kirkpatrick thesis, which seemed to imply that alliances with right-wing dictatorships were a necessary evil to resist the greater danger of communist totalitarianism. But Reagan believed that in the long run, these dictatorships tend to be surprisingly fragile, because they exhaust the patience of their citizens. Consequently, they sometimes provide fertile ground for Marxist resistance movements to take root and flourish.

Reagan's view, confirmed by the election outcome in Nicaragua, was that democracy provides the best bulwark against totalitarianism. In 1982 Reagan proposed an international initiative "to foster the infrastructure of democracy—the system of a free press, unions, political parties, universities—which allows a people to choose their own way, to develop their own culture, to reconcile their own differences through peaceful means." Reagan was proposing a single remedy—the ballot box—for both totalitarian and authoritarian regimes. He was not worried that some people might choose the path of communism. As Reagan himself put it, "Who would voluntarily choose not to have the right to vote; decide to purchase government propaganda handouts instead of independent newspapers; opt for land to be owned by the state instead of those who till it; want government repression instead of religious liberty; a single political party instead of free choice; a rigid cultural orthodoxy instead of democratic tolerance and diversity?"[23]

At Reagan's urging, Jeane Kirkpatrick became an eloquent advocate of American-style democratic capitalism at the United Nations. "It took everyone by surprise," Kirkpatrick told me. "Even diplomats from friendly countries told me to be careful how I spoke—no one at the U.N. talked like that. The prevailing dogmas were socialism and anti-Americanism." Some liberal Democrats who opposed Reagan's specific anticommunist measures were nevertheless willing to support the broad dissemination of democratic ideas. With bipartisan support, Congress in 1983 created the National Endowment for Democracy (NED), entrusted with the mission of strengthening indigenous democratic institutions such as a free press and unions both inside and outside the communist bloc. Under the leadership of Carl Gershman, NED programs in various countries bypassed government channels and worked with independent church groups, media, business, and voluntary organizations. For the first time, the United States had a global initiative to promote the infrastructure of democracy.

The Philippines provided a critical test for the Reagan administration's commitment to democracy. In February 1986 Reagan presided over a debate among his advisers on how the United States should handle the recalcitrant ruler, Ferdinand Marcos, who had been in power since the mid-1960s. A draconian ruler, Marcos was overshadowed in public by his wife, Imelda—the Philippines' answer to Marie Antoinette—whose extensive collection of imported shoes conveyed her attitude toward the nation's poor: "Let them wear Guccis."

For several years Marcos ruled by martial law, justifying his subversion of democratic pluralism by pointing to the communist insurgency attempting to seize power. The aims of the communists were not in dispute, but Marcos had developed the bad habit of calling anyone who disagreed with him a communist. In 1983 one of Marcos's political opponents, Benigno Aquino, returned from exile in order to organize popular resistance to the Marcos regime, only to be shot to death when he arrived at Manila airport. Marcos's soldiers, who were assigned to protect Aquino, became the main suspects in the assassination.

In 1984 and 1985, as protests against the Marcos regime escalated, President Reagan sent Nevada senator Paul Laxalt as his envoy to inform Marcos that he should hold an election to demonstrate whether he had a mandate to rule the country. Marcos procrastinated, then finally scheduled the election for January 1986. Several opposition parties united behind Corazon Aquino, the slain opposition leader's widow. Marcos prevailed, but the election was characterized by widespread voter intimidation and fraud. Reagan had sent a delegation under Senator Richard Lugar to monitor irregularities; Lugar concluded that Marcos had stolen the election. Demonstrators took to the streets. Two of Marcos's senior generals, his defense minister and acting chief of staff, resigned from the government and joined Aquino. Still, Marcos was determined to remain in office. A bloody showdown seemed imminent.

Reagan was reluctant to pressure Marcos to leave, because he viewed him as a longtime friend of the United States, yet he could not condone violence against the people. He sent a private message to Marcos that the United States would not tolerate his using force to stay in office. At an urgent meeting in Washington on February 23, 1986, Secretary of State George Shultz made the case for the United States to demand that Marcos resign. Marcos had lost support among the people, Shultz said. "He's had it," he told Reagan. Although chief of staff Donald Regan agreed with Shultz's assessment, he cautioned that there was a "distinct possibility" that, as in Iran, the Philippines could end up with a government unfriendly to the United States. Regan warned that an anti-American regime could endanger the future of two valuable American bases in the Philippines, Clark Air Force Base and Subic Bay Naval Station. Reagan listened carefully, then made his decision. "Marcos is clearly stubborn," he said. "He must go with dignity. We have asked him; now we need to tell him."[24]

This time Marcos got the message. The next day he left the Philippines on a plane bound for the United States. Unwilling to leave a former ally to a perilous fate, Reagan had offered him a safe exile. Aquino was sworn in as the duly elected president of the country. The United States recognized the new government, and Congress approved a generous aid package to assist the fledgling democracy. Aquino and her party proved to be staunchly anticommunist and—appreciative of America's role in promoting a peaceful transition—friendly to the United States.

In South Africa the Reagan administration, under the direction of Assistant Secretary of State for African Affairs Chester Crocker, pursued a policy of "constructive engagement" to promote reform in the political process and an end to the racist policy of apartheid. But the head of South Africa's ruling National party, P. W. Botha, responded with only cosmetic reforms that left the fundamental structure of apartheid and white-minority rule intact. As political resistance spread, the government in 1985 imposed a state of emergency in which all basic freedoms were curtailed. Still, the Reagan administration pursued a negotiated settlement between the ruling party and black leaders that would determine the country's future.

Here is a case where the pressure for economic sanctions, promoted by the liberal Democrats in Congress, proved to be the correct remedy. Reagan was concerned that sanctions would further destabilize the country and that political and economic chaos might endanger the United States's access to the vital mineral resources of that country. State Department officials raised the issue of who would succeed the National party, given that its opposition contained democratic elements like the African National Congress and nondemocratic elements like the South African Communist party.

Fortunately, Congress dictated the U.S. course of action. In 1985 Congress pressured the Reagan administration to impose limited economic and diplomatic sanctions against South Africa. The next year Reagan vetoed a more stringent sanctions bill, but Congress voted to override his veto. Somehow this "good cop, bad cop strategy" of friendly engagement on the part of the administration and tough threats on the part of Congress worked. Suffering from a growing crisis of legitimacy produced by external as well as internal pressure, the ruling National party agreed to hold free elections, and Nelson Mandela, who was for many years a political prisoner of the Afrikaner government, became the first black president of democratic South Africa.

The Reagan administration acquitted itself better in Chile, where it used diplomatic measures and supported indigenous groups in the country to pressure longtime dictator Augusto Pinochet to permit greater pluralism and respect basic civil liberties. As with Marcos, Reagan was reluctant for the United States to ask for the resignation of a U.S. ally who, in his words, had "saved Chile from Communism."[25] Reagan had no quarrel, however, with Shultz's recommendation that Pinochet should hold a referendum in October 1988 to test his popular support. Pinochet finally agreed, and to his amazement, a majority of Chileans gave him a vote of no confidence. Pinochet stepped down from power, Chile held free elections, and Patricio Aylwin, the candidate of the Coalition for Democracy, became the elected president in 1989.

In El Salvador, the Reagan administration was urged by the liberal Democrats in Congress to cut off all ties to the government. The Western media, led by Raymond Bonner of the *New York Times*, focused its attention on "death squads" roaming the country. Yet, instead of withdrawing and permitting the carnage to continue, the Reagan administration used its diplomatic and foreign aid leverage to ensure the monitoring of human rights abuses as well as the regular conduct of national elections.

Huge numbers of Salvadorans turned up at the polls even in the middle of a civil war in which Marxist guerrillas from the Farabundo Marti Liberation Front boycotted the elections and shot at the voters. Aides told me that Reagan was so impressed by the bravery of the Salvadoran peasants that he talked about it for weeks. José Napoleon Duarte, a social democrat, became the first freely elected president of the country, a position he held until 1989, when he was defeated by Alfredo Christiani, the candidate of the right-wing ARENA party. El Salvador remained a divided and war-torn country, but the Reagan administration ensured that El Salvador preserved at least the basic outlines of democratic self-government under the most difficult conditions.

Haiti's dictator, Jean-Claude Duvalier, also went into exile during Reagan's term in office. The Duvalier dynasty had ruled the country, with American economic and military backing, for three decades. Working through the U.S. embassy in Port-au-Prince, the Reagan administration pressured Duvalier to hold free elections or leave. It was popular resistance that was the main factor convincing Duvalier to board a plane for exile in southern France in February 1986. A few years later, Jean-Bertrand Aristide was elected president in the first free election in Haiti since the mid-1950s. The country remained unstable—Aristide himself was ousted by a coup, then restored to power by U.S. forces—but once again the Reagan administration had gone against precedent to put another dictator out of work.

Throughout the world, the pattern continued. South Korea held its first free election in 1987, and the next year General Chun Doo Hwan became the first leader to transfer power peacefully in the history of that country. In 1987 and 1988 the government of Taiwan eliminated several restrictions on political freedom and committed itself to a democratic system. In 1988 military rule in Pakistan ended, and Benazir Bhutto's opposition party came to power. The trend toward self-government was most dramatically evident in Central and South America. Dictatorships in Bolivia, Honduras, Argentina, Uruguay, Brazil, and Guatemala all moved toward democracy during the Reagan era. More than 90 percent of the region enjoyed some form of self-government by 1990.[26]

Problems of poverty and social inequality remained, but, for the first time in history, authoritarian regimes started to become an anomaly, and the majority of the world's people lived under democracy. The "democratic wave," as political scientist Samuel Huntington calls it, produced demands for liberalization and democratization even in remote places like Albania and Nepal.[27] China saw massive pro-democracy demonstrations in which students carried banners saying, "No Democratization, No Modernization" and "Government of the People, by the People, and for the People." Fang Lizhi, one of China's leading champions of democracy, told me, "We were inspired by the idea of the American revolution that Reagan championed. That's why the students built a Statue of Liberty in Tiananmen Square." No amount of force unleashed by the aging dictators of the world seems capable of stopping the contagion of the idea of freedom.

Only those with a sense of historical perspective will appreciate the magnitude of the change. As late as 1975, Daniel Patrick Moynihan conveyed the prevailing sentiment that Western-style democracy had no future outside Europe and America. "Increasingly," he wrote, "democracy is seen as an arrangement peculiar to a handful of North Atlantic countries."[28] Against the odds, the Reagan administration achieved a remarkable turnaround and a massive worldwide advance toward the idea of self-government. The democratic revolution boasts many heroes, but among them, Reagan's own role was paramount. "The world," Woodrow Wilson told a special session of Congress on April 2, 1917, "must be made safe for democracy."[29] It was Reagan who finally made it so.

Chapter 8

And the Wall Came Tumbling Down

To subdue the enemy without fighting
is the acme of skill.

Sun Tzu

"THERE WAS ONE VITAL factor in the ending of the Cold War," Margaret Thatcher recently said. "It was Ronald Reagan's decision to go ahead with the Strategic Defense Initiative."[1] Alexander Bessmertnykh, former foreign minister of the Soviet Union, agrees. He told a Princeton University audience in February 1993 that Reagan's SDI program accelerated the collapse of the Soviet Union. Other senior Soviet officials have made the same assessment.[2] Yet when Reagan announced his missile defense program, critics ridiculed the concept, which they traced to one of Reagan's films from the 1940s. Could the disintegration of the greatest empire of the twentieth century be attributed to an old movie script?

Of course not. Reagan didn't get his inspiration for SDI from Hollywood. He first became acquainted with the idea of missile defense in the late 1960s, while he was governor of California. In 1967, a few months after he was inaugurated, he visited the Lawrence Livermore laboratory in California, where Edward Teller, the inventor of the hydrogen bomb, showed Reagan the work that his students were doing on space-based lasers. These lasers, Teller said, would soon be powerful and accurate enough that they could be used to destroy nuclear missiles fired at the United States. Teller told me that

Reagan found the concept interesting and observed that history showed that all offensive weapons eventually met their match through defensive countermeasures. At some point, the sword invites the shield.[3]

On July 31, 1979, as he was preparing to run for the presidency, Reagan visited the North American Air Defense Command (NORAD) facility, the central control site for the launching of American nuclear weapons, buried deep in Cheyenne Mountain in Wyoming. The commander of NORAD, Air Force General James Hill, told Reagan about the latest advances in missile technology, which, he said, would enable the United States to hit targets in the Soviet Union with almost pinpoint precision. Reagan confessed that he was impressed, but asked what would happen if a single Soviet missile were launched against an American target: What could the United States do to prevent that? Hill replied: Nothing. Hill pointed out that the United States had the intelligence capability to track the incoming missile but added, "That's all we can do. We can't stop it." Does this mean, Reagan asked, that for all America spends annually on its defense budget, the nation is utterly defenseless against an enemy missile attack? Hill said yes. Aide Martin Anderson, who accompanied Reagan on this trip, told me that Reagan was struck by this exchange. He seems to have decided at that time that—the flaws of the SALT treaties aside—there was something profoundly wrong with the defense policy of the West.[4]

While Reagan may have been sold on the desirability of missile defense when he first came to Washington, it was not until 1983 that he became convinced it was the right time for the United States to begin a program to deploy it. His decision was influenced by Admiral James Watkins, chief of naval operations on the Joint Chiefs of Staff. Watkins, a committed Catholic, was offended by the political naiveté of a pastoral letter on nuclear weapons signed by the nation's Catholic bishops. Yet Watkins was moved by a section of the pastoral letter arguing that it was immoral for a nation to preserve its security by threatening the mass destruction of another nation's civilian population. Reagan wholeheartedly agreed with Watkins that the United States had a moral obligation to explore alternatives to existing policy.[5]

A second factor that propelled Reagan to go ahead was the conviction that U.S. advances in technology had made missile defense a realistic possibility worthy of serious exploration. Reagan met with Daniel

Graham, the former head of the Defense Intelligence Agency, who had published a study emphasizing the viability and cost-effectiveness of missile defenses. The president also consulted with Edward Teller, who assured him that the concept had scientific merit and should be advanced.

On March 23, 1983, Reagan gave a historic speech in which he called on American scientists to attempt to build a defense against intercontinental missiles that could ultimately "make nuclear weapons obsolete." This was not mere rhetoric. Reagan was announcing a major change in U.S. strategic policy, with far-reaching implications for the country's defenses and for arms control negotiations with the Soviet Union.

George Shultz remembers reading a draft of the speech only hours before it was delivered. His reaction was one of skepticism. "We don't have the technology to say this," he protested. Undersecretary of State Lawrence Eagleburger was equally aghast: "This changes the whole strategic doctrine of the United States."[6] Senior officials at the Defense Department were also opposed. Anticipating this reaction, Reagan had the concept of the Strategic Defense Initiative (SDI) developed only by the internal White House staff. At the last stage, a speechwriter was assigned to draft Reagan's remarks.

By the time other cabinet departments and agencies were shown the policy, it was a fait accompli. "SDI was entirely the president's idea," George Shultz told me, "and the way he went about it was also characteristic of him." Reagan solicited the reaction of his aides on how the program could be best structured and how it might be best presented to the public. But he was not interested in hearing objections to the concept itself. Kenneth Adelman, head of the Arms Control and Disarmament Agency, told me he received a call around that time from national security adviser William Clark. "Clark knew I had reservations about SDI," Adelman said, "but he made it clear to me that the president really liked the idea and that I should find a way to be constructive."

The Soviet Union reacted to SDI with hysterical denunciation. General Secretary Andropov was quoted in *Pravda* saying that the new

American program was "insane" and "a bid to disarm the Soviet Union." Reaction from the U.S. arms control establishment was equally apoplectic. Former Secretary of Defense Robert McNamara termed the concept of an effective missile defense a "pie in the sky."[7] Strobe Talbott, then of *Time* and eventually a State Department official in the Clinton administration, found that Reagan's new concept was less of a strategy and "more like an arcade video game."[8] The *New York Times* called SDI a "pipe dream, a projection of fantasy into policy."[9] The media promptly christened it "Star Wars," after the popular science-fiction movie.

Here was a peculiar situation. If strategic defense was indeed a science-fiction concept that could not possibly work, then the Soviet Union would have no reason to worry about the United States spending billions of dollars on a useless boondoggle. The intensity of Soviet objections to SDI suggested that Soviet scientists and strategists feared that it was not a pie in the sky but rather a technological feat that the United States was quite capable of pulling off. More than any other factor, Caspar Weinberger told me, the Soviet reaction confirmed Reagan's belief in the viability of missile defense.

Over the next few months, critics of Reagan's SDI program modified their original attack. They acknowledged that it might be possible, using existing technology, to develop lasers and projectiles that could shoot down incoming ICBMs, but they insisted that there was no way to build a leakproof defense. Reagan, they said, was foolishly trying to construct some kind of an Astrodome over the United States.[10] Some hawkish supporters of SDI conceded that a comprehensive defense was unlikely but argued that it would be sufficient if the United States could protect its own nuclear arsenal from destruction in a Soviet first strike. This would enable the United States to retaliate massively against the Soviet Union, and knowing this fact Moscow would be deterred from attacking in the first place.

Reagan never defended SDI in this way. He knew that a limited defense is better than no defense, for the same reason that a bulletproof vest is better than no protection. The fact that a bulletproof vest does not cover your entire body is hardly a justification for eschewing it when your life is in danger. At the same time, Reagan's science adviser George Keyworth told me, Reagan understood the political awkwardness of asking the American people to support a missile defense program that was aimed primarily at protecting missiles rather than people.

Reagan's main reason for supporting the concept of SDI was that he believed it was immoral for a nation to have an official policy of leaving its citizens defenseless against Soviet nuclear attack. Speechwriter Anthony Dolan told me Reagan never minded when critics called his program "Star Wars," a term that made conservative backers of SDI bristle. Reagan knew that the term "Star Wars" was used with the intention of making the very concept of missile defense seem fanciful. But Reagan was convinced that the American people wouldn't see it that way. Reagan cheerily pointed out that "Star Wars" reminded Americans of one of their favorite movies—one in which the forces of good conquer the forces of the dark side.

Reagan's SDI speech offered no guarantee, however, that a missile defense using current technology could offer full protection now. Reagan had offered the prospect of making nuclear weapons obsolete only as an aspiration for the future. He emphasized that he had initiated a research program; the issue of deployment would necessarily come later. Throughout the SDI debate, Reagan's own approach was refreshingly undogmatic. Aides told me that, after listening to a heated debate among his advisers on the feasibility of various defensive concepts—the "smart bullet," the electromagnetic railgun, neutral particle beams, the X-ray laser, and so on—Reagan simply said, "Why don't we go ahead with the research and see what works?"

The merits of this approach seem obvious, and yet the arms control establishment in the 1980s was strongly and explicitly in favor of the United States's having no defense at all. To understand this bizarre sentiment, we have to recall the prevailing doctrine of mutually assured destruction (MAD): if the United States and the Soviet Union had a large enough arsenal of nuclear weapons to annihilate the other country in the event of a war, then neither side would initiate an attack in the first place. Oddly enough, peace was to be guaranteed by both superpowers' agreeing to leave themselves entirely vulnerable to destruction by the other. This was the logic of the Anti-Ballistic Missile (ABM) Treaty of 1972, which outlawed all but token missile defenses on both sides.

The most serious objection launched by critics of Reagan's SDI program was that it was "destabilizing" because it upset the balance of mutual terror that the ABM Treaty sought to preserve. In its book *The Fallacy of Star Wars*, the Union of Concerned Scientists (UCS) argued that if one side believed that it could attack first and then protect itself against retaliation, nuclear war would be more likely. Moreover, if one side thought that the other was developing a defense that threatened to render its arsenal virtually harmless, perhaps it would launch a preemptive first strike against such a system. The UCS warned that if the United States abandoned MAD and proceeded with Reagan's missile defense program, the result would be an endless arms race in space.[11]

Reagan, by contrast, suggested that MAD was an insane policy that could have been developed only by intellectuals who were so immersed in the jargon of arms control—"throw weight," "fratricide," "circular error probability," "on-site verification," "cross-targeting," and so forth—that they had lost touch with the real world. Reagan asked, "Is there either logic or morality in believing that if one side threatens to kill tens of millions of our people, our only recourse is to threaten killing tens of millions of theirs?" He answered this question by posing another: "Wouldn't it be better to save lives than to avenge them?"[12] In a few sentences, Reagan decimated the logic of MAD and launched American strategic policy into a new era.

To those who warned that the Soviets would react to SDI by building their own missile defenses, Reagan replied, in effect: let them. What could be wrong, he implied, with a defensive arms race in which both sides put on ever-thicker coats of armor? Seeking to allay the fear that the Soviets might be provoked into a preemptive first strike, Reagan even suggested the possibility of sharing missile defense technology with Moscow. This was Reagan at his most audacious. "At first I thought Reagan was joking," arms control adviser Kenneth Adelman said in an interview. Only later did Adelman realize that whatever the military merits of Reagan's proposal, it was ingenious from a political point of view, because it neutralized the strongest Soviet objection to SDI. "Reagan wasn't a 'hidden hand' president who played his cards under the table," Adelman told me. "His true genius was that he put all his cards on the table and still managed to win most of the time."

The Soviets had walked out of the arms talks in Geneva as soon as the West began deploying its Pershing and cruise missiles. Reagan predicted that SDI would induce Moscow to resume negotiations. He also pointed out that missile defenses were themselves a form of arms control. If both the United States and the Soviet Union had a 50 percent defense, for example, that would be equivalent to both sides' abiding by an arms control agreement to dismantle half their nuclear arsenals. If the United States could use its superior technology to build a defense that was 75 percent effective and the Soviets had a 25 percent defense, this could be seen as a highly favorable arms control result from the American point of view. Even the most optimistic members of the arms control establishment did not envision treaties getting rid of thousands of warheads in the foreseeable future.

The SDI had two political consequences that Reagan's critics did not anticipate. It destroyed the base of the nuclear freeze movement, because Reagan showed himself to be more deeply committed than its leadership to reducing the danger to Americans posed by the Soviet nuclear arsenal. Reagan seemed to have found a more imaginative way that the United States could unilaterally move closer to eliminating the nuclear threat. SDI was disarmament through technology rather than diplomacy. Moreover, to the complete amazement of the arms control establishment, the mere concept of SDI did what Reagan said it would: it brought the Soviet Union back to the bargaining table.

What mattered most, it turned out, was not the perception of SDI on the part of Reagan's domestic critics but on the part of the Soviet leadership. Even if SDI was complete scientific nonsense, Moscow apparently was sufficiently impressed by U.S. technological capability—as previously demonstrated in programs such as the Manhattan Project and the moon landing—that it didn't want to take the risk of having its entire missile program rendered useless. Anatoly Dobrynin, Soviet ambassador to the United States from 1962 to 1986, recalls in his memoirs that the Soviet leadership treated SDI as a "real threat" because "our leadership was convinced that the great technical potential of the U.S. had scored again."[13]

The Soviets understood Reagan's political objectives very well. "They want to impose on us an even more ruinous arms race," *Izvestiya* protested.[14] The seasoned diplomat Andrei Gromyko charged that "behind all this lies the clear calculation that the USSR will exhaust its material resources . . . and therefore will finally be forced to surrender."[15] So the Soviets in no uncertain terms proclaimed that they would be willing to resume arms talks with the specific objective of restricting missile defense programs.

Reagan's critics saw that the immediate consequence of SDI was not a celestial arms race but rather renewed interest in a superpower summit. Even by their criterion, Reagan's program had justified itself. Finally, grudgingly, the gurus like Strobe Talbott were forced to acknowledge that they were wrong: "SDI was a factor in luring the Soviets back to the bargaining table . . . for that Reagan deserves credit."[16] Reagan's vision proved to be superior to all the strategic machinations of the arms control establishment.

Mikhail Gorbachev became general secretary of the Soviet Union in 1985, after three of his predecessors—Leonid Brezhnev, Yuri Andropov, and Konstantin Chernenko—had passed away in rapid succession. "They keep dying on me," Reagan had quipped in the beginning of his first term, when he was pressed about why he hadn't yet met with a Soviet leader. Gorbachev was a new breed of communist, utterly unlike any of his predecessors, so why was he appointed by the Old Guard? Gorbachev himself supplies the answer in his writings. He got the job over other candidates of comparable experience because past strategies had failed and the Politburo had come to recognize this.

It is important to note that Gorbachev is not merely discussing economic failure. True, life in the Soviet Union was characterized by high rates of infant mortality and low rates of life expectancy. True, many of the stores were empty. Yet economic and medical hardship had not produced any sign of a popular revolution brewing against the ruling party. So the Soviet ruling elite—the *nomenklatura*—had no reason to believe that its lifestyle of luxury would be seriously threatened by the fact that many people were having trouble getting their provisions and many were dying in their fifties. These problems were not new.

In the 1970s, the Politburo had found a promising strategy to cope with them, which was to invest its primary resources in the projection of Soviet power abroad. Far from being an unorthodox approach, this is the natural recourse of empires that are suffering domestic strains. Moreover, this strategy paid such rich dividends during the Carter administration that Moscow seems to have confidently established as its goal for the 1980s the political neutralization of Western Europe and the nuclear intimidation of the United States. The objective apparently was to extract political and economic concessions from the West that would continue to sustain the power and privileges of the *nomenklatura* and sustain its drive for global hegemony.

A review of statements by Soviet officials and the Soviet press shows how Moscow reacted to Reagan's new counteroffensive. Not surprisingly, when the Politburo first heard about Reagan's plans for a defense buildup, it expected the new president's rhetoric to outdistance the reality. Thus when Reagan actually proceeded with rearmament, the scale and rapidity of the process seems to have stunned Moscow. The Pershing and cruise deployments were, to the Soviets, an unnerving demonstration of the unity and resolve of the Western alliance. Through the Reagan doctrine, the United States also halted Soviet advances in the Third World: since Reagan assumed office, no more real estate had fallen into Moscow's hands, and one small nation, Grenada, had moved back into the democratic camp. Thanks to the Stinger missiles supplied by the United States, Afghanistan was rapidly becoming what the Soviets would later call "a bleeding wound." Then there was Reagan's Strategic Defense Initiative, which invited the Soviets into a new kind of arms race that they could scarcely afford and one that they would probably lose. "The Soviet leadership seems to have realized that the momentum of the cold war had dramatically shifted," Sovietologist Richard Pipes, one of Reagan's defense advisers, told me. "None of their previous techniques were working any more." Pipes's view is confirmed by a close reading of the memoirs of senior Soviet officials such as Andrei Gromyko and Anatoly Dobrynin, as well as by the actions of the Politburo. Clearly the Soviets felt that after Chernenko's death in 1985 it was time to try something different.

It was Reagan, in other words, who seems to have been largely responsible for neutralizing the Soviet strategy of the 1970s and inducing a loss of nerve that caused the Politburo to seek a new approach in the mid-1980s. Gorbachev's assignment was not merely to find a way to deal with the country's economic problems but also to figure out how to cope with the empire's reversals abroad. *Glasnost* ("openness") and *perestroika* ("restructuring") were Gorbachev's responses to circumstances that he did not create—circumstances that were to a large extent determined by the effectiveness of the Reagan administration in thwarting the Soviet strategy of the previous era. For this reason, Ilya Zaslavsky, who served in the Soviet Congress of People's Deputies, said later that the true originator of *perestroika* and *glasnost* was not Mikhail Gorbachev but Ronald Reagan.[17]

To understand Gorbachev, we must be very skeptical about his writings after the fall of the Soviet empire because they are self-servingly revisionist: Gorbachev recreates himself as a Western-style liberal democrat. Rather, his statements and actions while he was general secretary are the best clues to his motives and objectives. How little Gorbachev understood the nature of the changes necessary to solve his country's problems can be seen in his first move, a crackdown on alcoholism, absenteeism, and corruption.

Gorbachev's initial insight was that the Soviet economy did not work because people drank too much vodka, lacked the work ethic, and traded in the black market. He apparently did not see that these were symptoms of the failure of the political and economic system. The black market was the closest thing to free enterprise, and it was vodka that made life under communism bearable. In a September 1985 interview with *Time*, Gorbachev disclosed his plans for "greater discipline and order, demanding more from everyone" together with "a drive against irresponsibility and red tape." Gorbachev remarked that "to improve the functioning of the national economy it will be necessary to further strengthen centralization."[18] So they rounded up some drunks and arrested some slackers who didn't meet their production quotas. Nothing changed.

Gorbachev finally realized that the problem went deeper. Still, he had no clear idea how the country should proceed. His early statements were little more than slogans. "Everyone has got to restructure things," Gorbachev frequently said. Another of his favorite lines was that "everyone has got to develop a new way of thinking and acting." There was no point in asking him to be more specific. Gorbachev himself didn't seem to know what he meant, and his policies reflected this intellectual confusion. They were tentative and frequently contradictory.

For example, Gorbachev wanted greater economic efficiency, so he increased the autonomy of the local management of collective farms, but he also wanted political accountability, so he gave the Central Committee greater supervisory authority.

Given the magnitude of his challenge to reform both the economic and political system, we should not be too hard on Gorbachev. Yet, in order to judge whether he succeeded or failed, it is important to recognize what he was trying to accomplish. He tells us himself in his 1987 book, *Perestroika,* as well as in his public statements as general secretary. Far from seeking to destroy the Soviet system, Gorbachev's objective was to save it: "We are not retreating from socialism, but are moving toward it." He was a communist true believer, perhaps one of the few who took seriously the promises of the bolshevik revolution. He writes that he wanted to prove that Leninist principles, which had been distorted in the Soviet Union over the years, could still be made to work. He did not seek to eliminate the Party but to enhance its privileges and consolidate its power. That's why the Politburo supported his reforms: he promised "regained confidence . . . in the Party." He was able to win the support of the Soviet military by promising that his economic reforms would lead to more money and better technology for the armed forces. "The need to accelerate our socioeconomic development," he said, "is dictated by external circumstances. We are forced to put the necessary resources into the country's defense." Gorbachev had no intention of presiding over the destruction of the Soviet empire.[19]

Gorbachev inspired wild enthusiasm on the political left and in the Western media. Not only did he have a solution for his country, columnist Mary McGrory wrote, he had a "blueprint for saving the planet." It was "cosmic stuff" as far as McGrory was concerned.[20] Author Gail Sheehy was dazzled by Gorbachev's "luminous presence" and struck by his talent "for reaching out to people of all social levels."[21] In 1990, *Time* proclaimed Gorbachev a "political genius" who had "staked out the political center" and was highly popular with the Soviet people. "He travels the country like an ebullient ward boss, pressing the flesh, listening to complaints." The magazine even compared its Man of the Decade to Franklin Roosevelt. Just as Roosevelt during the 1930s had to transform capitalism in order to save it, so Gorbachev was credited with reinventing socialism during the 1980s in order to rescue it.[22]

The reason for these "Gorbasms," which make embarrassing reading today, was that Gorbachev was a model for the kind of leader that Western intellectuals admire. He was a top-down reformer who portrayed himself as a progressive. He was a technocrat who gave three-hour speeches on how the agriculture program was coming along. He talked a lot about "global interdependence" and the need to avoid "simplistic solutions" in an "increasingly complex world." He flattered the intellectuals and the media and sought their accolades. He was an aficionado of the ballet, which suggested cultural sophistication. Most of all, the new Soviet leader was attempting to achieve the great twentieth-century hope of the Western intelligentsia: communism with a human face! A socialism that works!

Yet, as Gorbachev discovered, and the rest of us now know, it cannot be done. The vices that Gorbachev sought to eradicate from the system turned out to be the essential features of the system. For all his theoretical training, Gorbachev's understanding of the economic and political underpinnings of the Soviet regime turned out to be sorely defective. Nor did Gorbachev understand that ethnic nationalism is a potent political force and that liberty is contagious. Gorbachev really believed that the Soviet people shared his aspiration to make communism and socialism work.

If Reagan was the Great Communicator, then Gorbachev turned out to be, as Zbigniew Brzezinski puts it, the Grand Miscalculator.[23] To the degree that he had a Western counterpart, it was not FDR but Jimmy Carter. The hard-liners in the Kremlin who warned Gorbachev that his reforms would cause the entire system to blow up turned out to be right. In a sense, conservatives in the West were also vindicated: communism *was* immutable and irreversible, in the sense that the system could only be reformed by destroying it.

Gorbachev, like Jimmy Carter, had one redeeming quality: he was a decent and relatively open-minded fellow. Gorbachev was the first Soviet leader who came from the post-Stalin generation. Not having participated in Stalin's purges, he didn't have to climb over bodies to get to the top. He wasn't a thoroughly hardened cynic. He had vacationed in Europe and knew about the West. His cosmopolitan demeanor contrasted sharply with the provincialism of previous Soviet leaders. None of this meant that Gorbachev was not a card-carrying communist, but he recognized that the promises of Lenin were not being fulfilled, and he was humane enough to be troubled about the gap between Marxist theory and contemporary Soviet reality.

Margaret Thatcher recognized at once the human qualities that made Gorbachev different. "I like Mr. Gorbachev," she said, after their first meeting at Chequers House in Britain in December 1984. "We can do business together." Coming from a dove, this would have been nothing more than the tiresome syndrome of declaring every Soviet leader a brave new reformer. But when Thatcher said it, Reagan listened. And upon meeting Gorbachev for the first time, Reagan found that he shared Thatcher's assessment. Caspar Weinberger was chagrined and, he now admits, more than a little concerned, when Reagan returned from his 1985 meeting with Gorbachev and urged Weinberger to tone down his anti-Soviet rhetoric. In 1988, as he walked through Red Square during the time of the Moscow summit, Reagan was asked whether he still considered the Soviet Union an evil empire. He replied that he did not: "I was talking about another time, another era."[24]

Many conservatives were alarmed and even outraged at Reagan's apparent change of stance toward the Soviet Union in his second term. Reagan's reasons for changing his mind about Gorbachev were "ignorant and pathetic," columnist Charles Krauthammer wrote. He added that no one should be surprised that Reagan had lost his head because "it was never weighted down with too many ideas to begin with."[25] More charitably, William F. Buckley urged Reagan to reconsider his more positive assessment of the Gorbachev regime: "To greet it as if it were no longer evil is on the order of changing our entire position toward Adolf Hitler."[26] George Will mourned that "Reagan has accelerated the moral disarmament of the West by elevating wishful thinking to the status of political philosophy."[27] Paul Weyrich of the Free Congress Foundation recalled for me an incident in which he got into a "shouting match" with Reagan: "I told him that he had totally changed his position. I told him to read his earlier speeches. I told him that nothing that he was saying made any sense."

The charge of inconsistency against a leader is very damaging if it reveals incoherence of purpose and uncertainty of approach. Yet for a statesman whose ultimate objectives are not in doubt and who moves resolutely to achieve them, adapting himself to the situation as it develops, inconsistency of word and even action is not a vice. Attempting to explain an apparent inconsistency in Edmund Burke, who detested the French Revolution, while defending the American Revolution, Winston Churchill wrote: "A statesman in contact with the moving current of events and anxious to keep the ship on an even keel and steer a steady course may lean all his weight now on one side and now on the other. His arguments in each case, when contrasted, can be shown to be not only very different in character, but contradictory in spirit and opposite in direction. . . . We cannot call this inconsistency. The only way a man can remain consistent amid changing circumstances is to change with them while preserving the same dominating purpose."[28]

What began to change Reagan's mind about Gorbachev was the little things. Reagan discovered that Gorbachev was curious about the West and showed a particular interest in anything that Reagan could tell him about Hollywood. Also he had a sense of humor and could even laugh at himself. "Maybe there was a little of Tip O'Neill in him," Reagan wrote in his autobiography.[29] Reagan did not believe that these personal qualities could be easily feigned. "I think I'm a good judge of acting," he once said of Gorbachev. "I don't think he's acting."[30]

In one case Reagan told Gorbachev about the American and the Russian who were arguing about their two countries. The American said, "Look, I can go into the Oval Office, pound the president's desk, and say: Mr. President, I don't like the way you're running our country." And the Russian responded, "I can do that." The American said, "You can?" The Russian replied, "Sure. I can go into the Kremlin, into the general secretary's office, and say: Mr. General Secretary, I don't like the way that President Reagan is running his country." Gorbachev laughed heartily.

Gorbachev's favorite Reagan joke concerned his own crackdown on lawlessness in the Soviet Union, which resulted in an edict that anyone caught speeding, no matter what his position, should get a ticket. According to the story, one day Gorbachev came out of his dacha—his country home—and was late in getting to the Kremlin. He told his limousine driver to get in the backseat; he would drive. And down the road he raced. They passed two motorcycle cops. One took after him, and soon he returned to his buddy. His partner said, "Well, did you give him a ticket?" And the cop said, "No, I couldn't. He was too important." His partner asked, "Who was it?" The cop replied, "I couldn't recognize him. But his driver was Gorbachev."

Reagan believed in personal diplomacy. He studied people while his defense analysts studied data. He believed that ultimately individuals are the ones who shape events. Instead of having superpower relations conducted exclusively through official communiqués, Reagan preferred private exchanges in which he could meet Soviet leaders face to face. With Gorbachev, Reagan finally had his chance. As we saw earlier, Reagan was eager that Gorbachev accompany him on a trip across the United States, so that the Soviet leader could see how Americans lived and decide for himself which system worked better. Reagan never got to realize this aspiration, but he did propose the idea and found Gorbachev intrigued by it.

Reagan also discovered that Gorbachev was troubled by Reagan's earlier reference to the Soviet Union as an "evil empire." Gorbachev raised the subject when Tip O'Neill led a congressional delegation to Moscow in 1985. O'Neill reported that "it seemed to upset him more than anything else."[31] To Reagan, Gorbachev's reaction was significant because it showed that Gorbachev had a sense of conscience. The concept of presiding over an evil regime bothered him. He did not seem to be another Stalin who could kill large numbers of people in the afternoon and sleep well at night.

Reagan was struck by the fact that Gorbachev routinely referred to God and Jesus Christ in his public statements and interviews. When asked how *glasnost* and *perestroika* were likely to turn out, he would say, "Only Jesus Christ knows the answer to that." This could be dismissed as merely a rhetorical device to make a point, but Reagan didn't think so. Although Reagan never asked Gorbachev about his religious beliefs, he believed it was significant that Gorbachev had a grandmother who was a Christian and read the Bible to Gorbachev in his childhood.

Moreover, Reagan believed in the truth of a Russian saying he liked to quote: *dovorey no provorey*, which means, "Trust, but verify." Reagan tested the Soviet leader in various ways. In one case he asked Gorbachev to free a group of religious dissidents who were being held as political prisoners. "Do what you can," Reagan said. "I'll never mention these names to the press and I'll never take credit for it if you let them go." Subsequently, Reagan found out that many of the people on his list had been released.

As they sat across the negotiating table, however, Reagan saw that Gorbachev was a tough negotiator and that he would need all the skills he learned at the Screen Actors Guild to deal with him. Aides told me of one exchange in which Gorbachev responded to U.S. concerns about Afghanistan with a lengthy account of American interventions in Third World countries over the past decades. "Mike," Reagan interrupted him, not shy to use the Western form of Gorbachev's name, "what you are doing in Afghanistan is burning villages and killing children. It's genocide, and you are the one who has to stop it." At this point, Kenneth Adelman told me, "Gorbachev looked at Reagan with a stunned expression. Apparently no one had confronted him in that way before, and he didn't know what to say."

In another exchange, Reagan described America as a nation of immigrants. People in the United States, he said, have the right to travel and live where they wish. He appreciated the recent relaxation of Soviet restrictions on Jewish emigration, but he thought many more people should be permitted to leave. How could a nation justify imposing quotas? Reagan asked. Why not just release them? Gorbachev replied by attacking the United States for its immigration policy. He pointed out that the United States had armed patrols on the Mexican border and was even then discussing plans to build a fence to limit the number of immigrants who could enter. Without pausing Reagan pointed out the flaw in Gorbachev's analogy. "There's a big difference," Reagan responded, "between wanting out and wanting in."[32]

At their first meeting in Geneva in November 1985, Reagan and Gorbachev took a break from the formal negotiations and walked to a nearby boathouse, where they sat by the fireplace and had a frank exchange. Gorbachev insisted that the United States had to shelve SDI if there was to be hope on a broader agreement to reduce nuclear arsenals. He said the Soviet people felt threatened by the prospect of an American missile defense. Reagan was reassuring at first; he told Gorbachev the Russians had nothing to fear. The only advantage the Soviets stood to lose if the United States deployed such a defense, he said, was the opportunity to engage in nuclear intimidation. When Gorbachev warned that the Soviets would have to expand their offensive and defensive systems to meet the American threat, Reagan responded with equal firmness, saying, "We won't stand by and let you maintain weapon superiority over us. We can agree to reduce arms, or we can continue the arms race, which I think you know you can't win."[33]

The extent to which Gorbachev took Reagan's remarks to heart became obvious at the October 1986 Reykjavik summit. There Gorbachev agreed in principle with Reagan's zero option that would eliminate intermediate-range nuclear missiles from the European theater. The Soviets also pledged to reduce their strategic arsenal virtually by half, basically endorsing the outlines of Reagan's START proposal. Gorbachev and Reagan even expressed general support for the concept of getting rid of nuclear weapons altogether. Arms control advocates in the West, who less than five years ago had regarded it as their most ambitious goal to freeze U.S. and Soviet arsenals at current levels, could not believe that the superpowers were discussing deep reductions and even contemplating the wholesale destruction of their stockpiles.

Yet Gorbachev had one condition, which he unveiled at the very end: the United States must agree not to deploy missile defenses. Gorbachev conceded that SDI research could continue as long as it was confined to the laboratory, but he was adamant that the program not proceed beyond that stage. George Shultz and the State Department advised Reagan that this was a bargain he could not refuse. Think about the global outcry, Reagan's advisers said, if it gets out that you had the opportunity to secure arms agreements of historic significance and turned them down in order to go ahead with a missile defense program that is still in the research stage. They pleaded with Reagan to consider Gorbachev's terms. But Reagan flat-out refused. "The Soviets are trying to blackmail us," he explained. The next day he told Gorbachev, "The meeting is over. We're leaving." Even Gorbachev was stunned, yet he stood his ground. The next day Gorbachev apologetically said to Reagan, "I don't know what else I could have done." Reagan coldly replied, "You could have said yes."

On the plane back to the United States, Reagan's aides were in a panic. The big question was what to say to the world. A heated debate ensued about how the complex aspects of U.S. negotiating strategy could be explained to the media and the American people. The specialists went into a huddle to produce a draft press release. All this time Reagan sat in a corner, scribbling away on a yellow legal pad. He didn't want State Department legalese; he was writing a draft of what he intended to say to the American people. A copy of Reagan's original exists, and we can see that he wrote his remarks virtually without correction. When speechwriter Josh Gilder saw Reagan's written text, he distributed it to his colleagues. "We were utterly amazed," Gilder told me. "This man had made the case for his actions better than any of us could have done it. He converted all the complexity of the negotiations into clear language that people could understand. Yet he didn't distort or misrepresent anything. All this time we had been writing for him, and it turned out that he was the best writer in the house. Suddenly I felt very humble, very superfluous."

Immediately the press went on the attack. "Reagan-Gorbachev Summit Talks Collapse as Deadlock on SDI Wipes Out Other Gains," read the banner headline in the *Washington Post*.[34] "Sunk by Star Wars," *Time*'s cover declared.[35] The consensus of the pundits was that he blew it. The critics had a point. Measured purely in terms of offensive arsenals, the Soviets had offered a very good deal, and it seemed a small price to pay to relinquish a space defense program that was in the early research stage.

To Reagan, however, SDI was a point of principle. As he said in a televised speech the day after he returned from Iceland, "There was no way I could tell our people their government would not protect them against nuclear destruction. . . . I went to Reykjavik determined that everything was negotiable except two things: our freedom and our future." Reagan advanced a case for missile defense that was not tactical but moral. The American people listened, and they supported Reagan's stance. Polls showed that three out of four people now backed SDI, a sharp increase from previous levels of support, and the same proportion of Americans endorsed the way Reagan was handling negotiations with the Soviet Union.[36]

Reykjavik, Margaret Thatcher says, was the turning point in the cold war. Finally Gorbachev realized that he had a choice: continue a no-win arms race, which would utterly cripple the Soviet economy, or give up the struggle for global hegemony and establish peaceful relations with the West. If he did the latter, he could save the huge sums the Soviets were spending to maintain their nuclear arsenal and their conventional forces, as well as the billions of rubles in aid to surrogate regimes like Cuba and Nicaragua. Gorbachev could then pursue Western investment and technology, which, with structural reform, could enable the Soviet economy to become prosperous like the economies of the West. After Reykjavik, Gorbachev seems to have resolved on this latter course.

In December 1987, Gorbachev abandoned his previous "nonnegotiable" demand that the United States give up SDI and visited Washington, D.C., to sign the INF Treaty in which the superpowers agreed to reduce their intermediate-range nuclear missiles to zero. For the first time in history, the United States and the Soviet Union had agreed to eliminate an entire class of nuclear weapons. Since the treaty involved the destruction of four times as many warheads on the Soviet as on the American side, experts agreed that the INF Treaty constituted the most favorable terms ever obtained by the United States in an arms agreement. Moscow even agreed to on-site verification, a condition that it had resisted in the past. Once again the doves, who said Reagan's zero option was unrealistic and that he had blown it at Reykjavik, were proved wrong. Reagan's vision and consistency of purpose had altered the realm of the possible.

The hawks were suspicious from the outset. Gorbachev is a masterful chess player, they said; he might sacrifice a pawn, but only to gain an overall positional advantage. "Reagan is walking into a trap," conservative columnist Tom Bethell warned in the *American Spectator* in 1985, as discussions with the Soviet Union got under way. "The only way he can get success in negotiation is by doing what the Soviets want."[37] Some of the hawks had championed the zero option in the firm belief that Moscow would never agree to it; now their clever maneuver had backfired. Republican senators like Steven Symms and Jesse Helms planned "killer amendments" designed to sink the treaty. In 1986, a coalition of right-wing groups purchased a full-page ad in several newspapers comparing Reagan to Neville Chamberlain and warning of the dangers of appeasement. Howard Phillips of the Conservative Caucus even charged Reagan with "fronting as a useful idiot for Soviet propaganda."[38]

Yet, as at least some hawks like Bethell now admit, these criticisms missed the larger current of events that Reagan alone understood. They were the ones who turned out to be naive. Gorbachev wasn't sacrificing a pawn; he was giving up his major pieces on the board. The INF Treaty was in fact the first stage of Gorbachev's surrender in the cold war. It set the stage for negotiations on the reduction of strategic missiles—the so-called START Treaty, finally signed in 1991. This treaty produced deep cuts in strategic missiles in almost exactly the ratios that Reagan had advocated, and effectively ended the Soviet nuclear threat whose elimination Reagan had made the top priority of his presidency.

Reagan knew that the cold war was over as early as 1987, when Gorbachev came to Washington. Gorbachev was a media celebrity in the United States, and the crowds cheered when he jumped out of his limousine and shook hands with people on the street. Out of the limelight, Reagan had dinner with a group of conservative friends, including Ben Wattenberg, Georgie Geyer, and Robert Tyrrell. As Wattenberg recounted the incident for me, the group complained to Reagan that Gorbachev was getting all the favorable publicity and the media credit for essentially reaching an agreement on Reagan's terms. Reagan smiled. Wattenberg asked, "Have we won the cold war?" Reagan hedged. Tyrrell persisted. "Well, have we?" Reagan finally said yes. Then his dinner companions understood: he wanted Gorbachev to have his day in the sun. Reagan was being magnanimous in victory, a principle of statesmanship endorsed by Winston Churchill. Asked by the press if he felt overshadowed by Gorbachev, Reagan replied, "I don't resent his popularity. Good Lord, I co-starred with Errol Flynn once."

To appreciate Reagan's diplomatic acumen, it is important to recall that he was pursuing his own distinctive course, rejecting the recommendations of both the hawks and the doves. The hawks urged him to view Gorbachev as a typical Soviet leader, who was making tactical concessions in order to lull the West into complacency; then the trap would be sprung. Reagan, in contrast, supported Gorbachev. He knew that the movement for reform was fragile, Gorbachev's own position in Moscow was becoming increasingly insecure, and hard-liners in the Kremlin were looking for U.S. statements and actions that they could use to undermine his initiatives. Thus Reagan recognized the importance of permitting Gorbachev a zone of comfort in which to pursue his program of reform.

Gorbachev needed this, and he appreciated Reagan's support. In later years, he never endorsed the condescending view of Reagan held by the Western elite. In the summer of 1997, I wrote Gorbachev to ask him his assessment of Reagan's leadership, and he replied, "Reagan was a man adhering to conservative values. But in real life, he was not dogmatic, but a person ready to compromise. Reagan's merit is this, that he responded to our first step together toward . . . real disarmament, and—very important—he did not retreat from this agreement and secured its ratification. . . . I know that Reagan was criticized as having a superficial style, an unwillingness to analyze details. With a leader of such large scale, several stylistic peculiarities are permissible. It did not prevent us from finding a common language."

As Reagan resisted hawkish pressure to stop dealing with Gorbachev, he also spurned the counsel of the doves, who wanted him to encourage Gorbachev by making good-faith gestures. When Gorbachev in 1988 announced that Soviet troops would pull out of Afghanistan, for example, doves in the State Department implored Reagan to "reward" the Soviet leader with economic concessions and trade benefits. Reagan recognized that this approach ran the risk of restoring the health of the sick bear—Gorbachev's goal, of course. But Reagan never forgot that it was not his goal. Rather, his goal was—as Gorbachev himself once joked—to take the Soviet Union to the edge of the abyss and then induce the regime to take "one step forward."

Thus Reagan judiciously encouraged Gorbachev's reform efforts while applying constant pressure on him to move faster and further. This was the significance of Reagan's trip to the Brandenburg Gate on June 12, 1987. President Kennedy had visited Berlin a quarter of a century earlier and won the favor of the locals by proclaiming in German that he too was a Berliner. This was uplifting rhetoric, but it was only rhetoric. Reagan, by contrast, used his speech to drive Gorbachev into an awkward political position, to compel him to prove his sincerity before the world. Reagan said, "General Secretary Gorbachev, if you seek peace, if you seek prosperity for the Soviet Union and Eastern Europe, if you seek liberalization: Come here to this gate! Mr. Gorbachev, open this gate! Mr. Gorbachev, tear down this wall!"

As with Reagan's reference to the Soviets as an "evil empire," the State Department kept deleting from Reagan's speech the reference to dismantling the Berlin Wall. Even the more hawkish National Security Council was opposed. But Reagan kept putting it back in. "That wall has to come down," he told speechwriter Peter Robinson. "That's what I'd like to say."[39] Reagan kept up the drumbeat of pressure. A year later, in May 1988, Reagan stood beneath a giant white bust of Lenin at Moscow State University where in front of an audience of Russian students he gave the most ringing defense of a free society ever offered in the Soviet Union. On that trip he visited the ancient Danilov Monastery, which had been recently returned to the Russian Orthodox church, and preached about the importance of religious freedom and a spiritual revival. At the U.S. ambassador's residence, he hosted a highly publicized meeting with dissidents and "refuseniks" and told them to take heart because the day of freedom was coming soon. All of these measures were calibrated to force Gorbachev's hand.

First, Gorbachev agreed to deep unilateral cuts in Soviet armed forces stationed on the border of Western Europe. Between May 1988 and early 1989, Soviet troops pulled out of Afghanistan, the first time the Soviets had voluntarily withdrawn from a puppet regime. The Soviets also supported efforts to end civil conflicts in Angola, Ethiopia, and Southeast Asia. Soviet advisers left Ethiopia and returned home. With Gorbachev's approval, Cuba recalled its troops from Angola. Toward the end of Reagan's second term, Moscow consented to have Vietnam withdraw 50,000 troops from Cambodia. These actions set the stage for negotiated settlements that did not remove underlying discontent but at least brought peace and a greater measure of self-determination to some of the world's most bloodstained societies.

The collapse of the Soviet empire in Eastern Europe occurred shortly after Reagan left office. The revolt began in Poland, where Premier Jaruzelski finally consented to hold elections. The communists were routed, and Lech Walesa became president of Poland. Next, Hungary dismantled its barbed-wire fence to the West and soon after proclaimed itself a free republic. Demonstrators in East German cities stormed the Communist party headquarters and toppled longtime despot Erich Honecker; on November 9, 1989, they pulled down the Berlin Wall. East Germany was free and could now be reunited with West Germany. In Czechoslovakia, as mobs stormed the capital, the Communist party surrendered, free elections were held, and Václav Havel became president. In Romania, Nicolae Ceausescu and his wife were captured and executed. Observers formulated an epigram to capture the rapidity of these developments. In the race toward freedom, they said, Poland took ten years, Hungary ten months, East Germany ten weeks, Czechoslovakia ten days, and Romania ten hours.

During this period of ferment, Gorbachev's great achievement, for which he will be credited by history, was to abstain from the use of force—the response of his predecessors to popular uprisings in Hungary in 1956 and Czechoslovakia in 1968. Yet by now Gorbachev and his team seemed to have become converts to the Reagan approach. Not only were they permitting the empire to disintegrate, as Reagan had predicted and intended; they even adopted Reagan's way of talking. In October 1989 Soviet foreign ministry spokesman Gennadi Gerasimov announced that the Soviet Union would not intervene in the internal affairs of Eastern bloc nations, allowing the people there to determine their own destiny. "The Brezhnev Doctrine is dead," Gerasimov said. Reporters asked him what would take its place, and he replied, "You know the Frank Sinatra song *My Way?* Hungary and Poland are doing it their way. We now have the Sinatra Doctrine."[40] The Gipper could not have said it better himself.

In 1990, shortly before the end, Gorbachev visited Reagan in California. Reagan had completed two successful terms and retired a contented man. Gorbachev had become one of the most unpopular figures in the Soviet Union, and his regime was on the edge of collapse. Gorbachev asked Reagan whether he had any advice. Reagan simply told him, "Stay the course."[41] And Gorbachev did, consigning himself to political oblivion but establishing his place in history.

Finally the revolution made its way into the Soviet Union. Gorbachev, who had completely lost control of events, found himself ousted from power in a coup. The usurpers were apprehended, but the loyalty of the people was clearly not with Gorbachev but with Boris Yeltsin, who earlier that year had become the first legitimately elected president of Russia. The Soviet Union voted to abolish itself. Leningrad changed its name back to St. Petersburg. Republics like Estonia, Latvia, Lithuania, and the Ukraine gained their independence. Serious problems of adjustment to new conditions would remain, but emancipated people know that such difficulties are infinitely preferable to living under slavery. In the former Soviet Union, as in Eastern Europe, the politics of normalcy began to be restored.

The tears of joy with which millions of people greeted the collapse of the Soviet Union proved that Reagan was entirely justified in calling it an "evil empire." Even officials of newly independent Russia began to use that phrase. Andrei Kozyrev, a minister in the Yeltsin government, said that it had always been a mistake to use the term "Union of Soviet Socialist Republics." He added, "It was, rather, as was once put, an evil empire."[42] The doves who proclaimed that the Soviets were "just like us" were exposed as naive and insensitive to totalitarian repression.

Reagan proved correct not only in his moral condemnation of communism but also in his analysis of the Soviet threat and the policies he devised to counter it. Events bore out the accuracy of Reagan's conviction that the real danger to America came not from nuclear weapons themselves but from the nature of the Soviet regime that possessed them. Reagan's strategy of rolling back the Soviet empire, which the elites identified with the wild-eyed aspirations of the far right, proved to be both sensible and viable. On one of the most important political questions of our time, the far right turned out to be exactly right.

Even some who were previously skeptical of Reagan were forced to admit that his policies had been thoroughly vindicated. Reagan's old nemesis, Henry Kissinger, observed that while it was Bush who presided over the final disintegration of the Soviet empire, "it was Ronald Reagan's presidency which marked the turning point."[43] Cardinal Casaroli, the Vatican secretary of state, remarked publicly that the Reagan military buildup, which he opposed at the time, placed unsustainable demands on the Soviet economy and thus precipitated the events that led to the disintegration of communism.[44]

These conclusions are widely accepted in the former Soviet Union and in Eastern Europe. During his visit to Washington, D.C., in May

1997, I asked Czech president Václav Havel whether Reagan's defense strategy and his diplomacy were vital factors in ending the cold war. Of course, Havel said, adding that "both Reagan and Gorbachev deserve credit" because without them, communism might have collapsed eventually, but "it would have taken a lot longer."

Havel's point is incontestable: no two other men could have produced the same result. Yet Reagan won and Gorbachev lost. If Gorbachev was the trigger, Reagan was the one who pulled it. Now that the dust has settled, we can see that the triumph over Soviet communism ranks with the defeat of the Nazis as one of the most important achievements of the West in the modern era. Indeed for the third time in this century, the United States has fought and prevailed in a world war. In the cold war, Reagan turned out to be our Churchill; it was his vision and leadership that led us to victory.

Chapter 9

The Man Behind the Mask

I BEGAN THIS BOOK BY noting that Reagan's character is defined by the concept of paradox. Frustrated by the paradoxes of Reagan's personality, some who worked with him for years have given up trying to understand him.

One can sympathize with their bafflement. Reagan was an intensely ambitious person who was, at the same time, very modest. Even in the face of tragedy, he remained upbeat and optimistic. He was a realist who had a low view of human nature; at the same time, he was an optimist who had a high view of human possibility. He was a tolerant man who nevertheless had fixed and unalterable convictions. He was gregarious and liked people, yet he was a loner who seemed happiest by himself. He spent short hours at work but accomplished a great deal.

Although he was genuine and almost mystical in his religious beliefs, he didn't go to church and took a sardonic view of organized religion and clergy. He was an advocate of family values who had a deeply fulfilling relationship with his second wife, but difficult relationships with his children and virtually none with his grandchildren.

At first glance there seems to be no way to resolve these paradoxes.

A paradox, however, is not a contradiction. It is an apparent contradiction that, upon closer examination, turns out to display a deeper coherence. Let us examine how Reagan's seemingly opposed traits can be reconciled, revealing a personality that appears obvious and transparent on the surface and yet proves rich and complex for those who are willing to look beyond appearances.

———

Both Reagan's allies and his critics were mystified and a little annoyed at the cool confidence with which he handled the toughest job in the world. He made it look a bit too easy. He arrived in Washington after a series of failed presidencies, when there was open speculation about whether any single individual could do the job. "Reagan proved that he could be president, address the country's problems, and still go riding once a week," his former campaign manager, John Sears, remarks. Reagan's predecessors had visibly aged in the White House. He, by contrast, went in older than any of them and came out looking not much older than the day he was inaugurated. For him, the presidency wasn't a crippling burden; it was just another day at the office.

Reagan was once introduced at a dinner by Clare Boothe Luce, who read passages from the memoirs of previous presidents that ruminated about the awesome responsibility, the anguish of decision making, and the toll that the job took on a single individual. "Well, Clare, I must be doing something wrong," Reagan quipped. "I'm kind of enjoying myself." From his lack of stress, everyone concluded that he must be leaving major tasks undone. Friend and adversary alike worried that he was in it for the show. He was accused of being too fond of the pomp of the presidency while neglecting the complexity of its daily responsibilities.

Reagan indeed loved the ceremonial aspects of the presidency. Nothing inspired him more than hearing the Marine Band. He enjoyed saluting those men. "Hail to the Chief" was a melody he never tired of hearing. Yet this should not be ascribed to vanity. Reagan had an elevated opinion of the presidency, not of himself as president. He approached his office with humble respect. Michael Deaver once noticed the president was perspiring in the Oval Office and asked him to take off his coat, as he had frequently done as governor of California. "Oh no," Reagan replied. "I could never take my coat off in this office." And except for the few occasions when he returned from an event in which he was casually attired, Reagan always dressed formally and never took off his jacket.[1] Unlike Jimmy Carter, he never conducted office business in slacks and a sweater. Reviewing state papers in a jogging suit or shorts and t-shirt, as Bill Clinton does, would have struck Reagan as appallingly arrogant.

Even as leader of the United States and head of the Western Alliance, Reagan remained unfailingly modest. "He had very little personal ego," George Shultz told me. Reagan often began public remarks by saying, "When I got this job . . ." Of the White House he frequently observed, recalling his childhood, "I'm back living above the store again." To a group of visitors touring the residence he would say, "Welcome here to your house, which you're letting me live in for a while." Commenting on the commonly held notion that he was the most powerful man in the world, Reagan replied, "I don't believe that. Over there at the White House someplace there's a fellow who puts a piece of paper on my desk every day that tells me what I'm going to do every 15 minutes. *He's* the most powerful man in the world."[2]

Reagan's daily schedule was the centerpiece of his life as president. On a typical day, Reagan arose at 7:30 with a wake-up call from the White House operator. He began the day with the newspapers, usually skimming the front page and then turning to the comics. Martin Anderson, Reagan's domestic adviser during his first term, points out that he was fairly serious about his favorite comics and followed the unfolding adventures of the characters, sometimes recalling for his wife's sake their previous exploits. Reagan enjoyed the comics because they reveal the ironies of life in a light and entertaining way.

When he finished the comics, he would return to the rest of the newspapers or, more likely, go directly to his daily packet of press clips, a compilation of important news items prepared by the White House staff. Then the Reagans, together with their cocker spaniel, Rex, a gift from William F. Buckley, Jr., and his wife, Pat, would have their standard breakfast of juice, toast, and decaffeinated coffee and watch the morning news shows. Occasionally the staff taped a particular segment that they thought Reagan should see.

Reagan arrived at the Oval Office exactly at 9:00 A.M. for his daily meeting with the chief of staff and Vice President Bush. He never returned to the residence until the end of the day. His critics said he was "prone to nodding off" during the afternoon,[3] but contrary to the popular rumor, there is no evidence that he took naps in his office. "I never saw him do it," says Ed Meese, who served as counselor to the president. All those who worked with Reagan confirm that he worked a full day without interruption.

This is not to fault the Coolidge approach; what better symbol of limited government than the president's taking an afternoon siesta in his pajamas? The only time Reagan dozed during the day was after a cross-country journey or an international flight. On one hectic European trip, Reagan almost fell asleep in a meeting with the pope, an embarrassing episode that was probably due to overscheduling. Aides say that Reagan always worked when he traveled. Others on Air Force One might be chatting or having a drink, but Reagan would sit by himself, reading or putting the finishing touches on his next speech. Larry Speakes, his press secretary, writes that Reagan had enormous stamina and could keep working when his much younger staff was thoroughly exhausted.[4]

Reagan's day was mainly made up of meetings. At 9:30 A.M., he met with his national security adviser, who briefed him on problems around the world. Following were conferences with cabinet members, staff, congressmen, representatives of various groups, and foreign visitors. His schedulers would try to allow him an hour in the late morning to catch up on his reading or answer correspondence. During this time, aides would often see him going through his favorite magazine, the conservative weekly *Human Events,* highlighting articles that offered a different perspective on the news than was reflected in the major newspapers or on the television networks. Reagan once complained that he couldn't clip out a story from *Human Events* without ruining the page on the other side, provoking aide Richard Darman to suggest jokingly that he be given two subscriptions. *National Review* was another favorite source for Reagan's midmorning reflections. Usually Reagan ate a light lunch of fruit and a bowl of soup at his desk; once a week he dined with George Bush.

In the afternoon were more meetings. When these sessions became too monotonous, Reagan sometimes would doodle on a blank sheet of paper. Ed Meese once glanced over at Reagan's yellow pad, only to see caricatures of a series of heads wearing large cowboy hats. He looked more closely and noticed that Reagan had sketched all the people in the room with an unsparing eye. Yet, as Meese points out, aides who were convinced that Reagan was not paying attention—that his mind was in cartoon land—were frequently surprised when the president plunged right back into the discussion, showing that he had absorbed everything that was said.

Occasionally in the middle of a meeting, Reagan would reach over to a jar and pop a few jellybeans into his mouth. This could be an entirely casual gesture, but his aides soon learned that it sometimes conveyed Reagan's impression that the participants were getting overly heated or technical. It could also be a signal that the topic at hand was exhausted, and it was time to move on.

Reagan adopted the jellybean habit when he gave up smoking in 1969, after hearing the news that his friend Robert Taylor had died of lung cancer. Jellybeans became a kind of trademark of the Reagan administration. "Everywhere I go," economist Milton Friedman sighed, "I see jellybeans." Reagan himself had a philosophical take on the subject. "You can tell a lot about a man's character," he said, "by whether he picks out all of one color or just grabs a handful." Presumably neurotics belonged to the first group, whereas Reagan himself belonged to the second, a reflection, perhaps, of his easygoing nature. Jellybeans were Reagan's favorite candy, but he didn't eat them in large quantities. He rarely snacked between meals and only occasionally permitted himself a glass of wine, usually at public events.

Reagan was punctilious in the way he approached his daily schedule. He went down the list of his appointments, printed on green stationery with the presidential seal at the top, checking each one off with a pencil after it ended and putting an arrow pointing to the next. He would conclude each meeting a few minutes before the time was up, clear off his desk, and prepare for the next one. He did everything on time; he hated to keep people waiting. Aides observed that the president took evident satisfaction in the regularity of his regimen and the brisk thoroughness with which he discharged his responsibilities. Chief of staff Donald Regan wrote in his memoirs, "I cannot remember a single case in which he changed a time or canceled an appointment or even complained about an item on his schedule."[5] Yet he also enjoyed the occasional change of pace, when he got to leave the White House to give a speech or attend a function.

Around 5:00 P.M., when Reagan had concluded his appointments, he cleaned his desk and assembled a pile of reading material to take home. Then he changed and returned to a bedroom in the White House that had been converted into an exercise gym and worked out with weights for thirty to forty-five minutes. Reagan even took along portable equipment when he was traveling. He was a great believer in regularity and rarely missed a workout session.

Many evenings the Reagans were expected at state dinners or other events. They were impeccable hosts, yet neither approached these events with breathless excitement. The Reagans had seen Hollywood in its glory days; they were no strangers to opulent entertainment. At his age, Reagan once joked, "When you're faced with two temptations you choose the one that will get you home at 9:30." Absent a function, the Reagans were just as happy to eat an early dinner from portable tables—meat loaf or chopped steak and mashed potatoes, and macaroni and cheese were Reagan's favorites—while watching the evening news simultaneously on all three networks.

Once a week or so he and Nancy would watch an old movie. She liked romantic comedies; his favorites were war films and westerns. They took turns at choosing what to see, but it was rare for either of them to select a film made after the 1960s. Reagan frequently complained about the vulgarity and sexual explicitness of contemporary films, which leave nothing to the imagination. "I have always thought it was more suggestive," he told Michael Deaver, "to see a hand reach out and hang the 'Do Not Disturb' sign on the door."[6]

Most days, however, Reagan had dinner and then worked for a couple of hours in his study. He trusted his subordinates to include everything that he needed to read and never stopped until he had gone through it all. During this time he could not be disturbed. When he finished with his briefing papers, Reagan did some casual reading in bed—a magazine about horses or a novel by Tom Clancy or Louis L'Amour—before falling asleep around 11:00 P.M.

Reagan's daily schedule revealed his "less is more" approach to the presidency. "He had an extremely moderate lifestyle—unusual for a man in his position," remarks domestic aide Martin Anderson. "He paced himself in a very disciplined way. He was incredibly organized. I have never seen a man so totally focused." Anderson notes that it was Reagan's well-regulated regimen and concentrated decision making that allowed him to stay healthy and get more done than most other modern presidents while putting in fewer hours at the office.

Sometimes the inner character of a leader remains forever concealed from those he leads. The reason is that public figures wear a kind of mask, which comes off only in unguarded moments. If the leader is a seasoned performer, as Reagan was, those moments can be quite rare. Yet these occasions can provide a clearer insight into the leader than countless hours of staged appearances. Fortunately the American people were able to see Reagan's true nature early in his presidency because of an event he could not anticipate: John Hinckley's assassination attempt. "As for dying," Montaigne writes, "practice can give us no assistance. A man may by experience fortify himself against pain, shame, want and other such accidents, but as for death, we can essay it but once: we are all apprentices when we come to it."

On March 30, 1981, just nine weeks after assuming office, Reagan was leaving the banquet room of the Washington Hilton Hotel when six shots rang out, fired in rapid succession. Press secretary James Brady collapsed with a bullet in his head. Secret Service agent Timothy McCarthy and policeman Thomas Delahanty were also hit. Agent Jerry Parr shoved the president into his limousine while other agents rushed the gunman. Reagan, who did not know he had been shot, felt an acute pain in his chest. Parr noticed that blood was coming out of the president's mouth and ordered the limousine to George Washington Hospital, where doctors discovered a bullet lodged less than an inch from Reagan's heart. Benjamin Aaron, the surgeon who operated on him, said he was "right on the margin" of death.

Reagan survived the barrage of his assailant, a troubled drifter named John Hinckley, and in the process showed the American people that he had the right stuff. On his arrival at the hospital, he quipped to the doctors, "Please tell me you're Republicans." When he opened his eyes again and they asked him how he was feeling, he replied by scribbling on a notepad the old W. C. Fields line, "All in all, I'd rather be in Philadelphia." He probed the hospital staff about the man who had tried to kill him: "Does anybody know what that guy's beef was?" He explained what had happened to Nancy Reagan: "Honey, I forgot to duck," the words boxer Jack Dempsey told his wife when he lost the heavyweight title to Gene Tunney in 1926. In a telephone conversation he told his daughter Maureen that "this fellow Hinckley" had ruined one of his favorite suits, and he was obligated to buy a new one.

To a solicitous nurse who held his hand, Reagan cautioned, "Does Nancy know about us?" When the hospital staff told him about the progress being made by the others who had been wounded in the assassination attempt, Reagan said, "That's great news. We'll have to get four bedpans and have a reunion." To three White House staffers who came to see him, Reagan mumbled, "Hi fellas. I should have known I wasn't going to avoid a staff meeting." His first question to Michael Deaver was, "Who's minding the store?" Deaver told him everything was going smoothly in his absence, and he chuckled, "What makes you think I'd be happy to hear *that?*" Before Reagan left, he told the doctors and nurses, "If I had this much attention in Hollywood, I'd have stayed there." A year later, Reagan spoke again before the same group he had addressed when he was shot. Reporters asked him if he was afraid, and he replied, "No, but I'm wearing my oldest suit today." To the audience he said, "I know you all understand how happy I am to be back," he said, "but if it's all the same to you, when I finish speaking, I think I'll slip out the back door this time."

When has a man taken a bullet in his chest with greater élan? Many Americans who were deeply shocked by the assassination attempt were relieved and comforted to hear how well Reagan was doing. Almost subconsciously, Reagan was performing a valuable task of psychological leadership. By his own example, he was helping the country recover its balance after a traumatic national event.

Reagan was the first president to survive a wound in an assassination attempt. Andrew Jackson, Harry Truman, and Gerald Ford were all targets of botched attempts. Other presidents, like Lincoln and

Kennedy, were killed in office. In Lincoln's case the manner of his death only enhanced the aura of his greatness, which, even in life, arose out of tragedy. Kennedy's assassination, which ended his brief presidency, validated the truth of the saying that immortality is chiefly a matter of dying at the right moment.

Two of the great presidents of this century, the Roosevelts, were also the targets of would-be assassins. During his 1912 bid to return to the presidency, Teddy Roosevelt was shot and injured by a political enemy and—being Teddy Roosevelt—elected to give his campaign speech anyway, with blood on his shirt. In 1933 an assailant fired five times at Franklin Roosevelt, but he missed, hitting Chicago mayor Anton Cermak instead. Roosevelt showed calm command of the situation, revealing a steely interior. Yet for sublime grace and wit, even the two Roosevelts' conduct under fire could not compare with that of Reagan.

Suddenly it could no longer be said of Reagan that he was the giddy optimist, that he lacked gravitas because he had not experienced tragedy. Courage, Reagan demonstrated, is more than the lack of fear. The president had been shot, but he had stayed in the saddle and lived to laugh about it later. John Wayne, in his best performance, could have done no better. The assassination attempt showed Americans that even when Reagan's body was wounded, his spirit remained intact. It gave the president an almost mythic dimension in the eyes of his countrymen.

It also infused Reagan with a sense of mortality and mission. He was convinced when he returned from the hospital that he had a limited amount of time to achieve his ambitious agenda. Yet his goals were not only political but also personal. With Cardinal Cooke, who came to visit him, Reagan struck a spiritual note: "I have decided that whatever time I have left is for Him." The late Mother Teresa, who visited the White House that June, told Reagan, "You have suffered the passion of the cross and have received grace. There is a purpose to this. Because of your suffering and pain you will now understand the suffering and pain of the world. This has happened to you at this time because your country and the world need you." Reagan was speechless. Nancy Reagan wept.[7]

It is always striking to see a man remain good-natured and optimistic in the face of the greatest possible danger. We are impressed because such serenity is rare. Confronted with pain and tragedy, most of us become bitter and vengeful. Reagan was capable of fits of anger: he sometimes hurled his glasses on the floor or across the room. Senator Robert Dole saw Reagan do this in early 1983, after Reagan exploded that he had "had it up to my keister" with the banking industry for making distorted claims about his social security reform legislation.[8] Yet these occasions were infrequent. So how can we make sense of Reagan's everyday optimism, which seemed mysteriously immune to refutation by the travails of life and the vagaries of fate? We can answer this question by once again turning to that invaluable reference source, Reagan's jokes.

Reagan was perhaps the wittiest occupant of the White House in American history. Few other presidents can boast a comparable inventory of jokes and one-liners. Speechwriter Aram Bakshian recalls, "I used to spend a lot of time writing funny lines in the President's speeches. Then I'd see them taken out by the President in favor of better lines that he would add."[9] Reagan frequently asked his aides if they had any new ones for him. George Bush and Michael Deaver actually collected jokes in a file to share with the president. Senator Paul Laxalt told me that some of his fondest memories are those in which he listened to Reagan trade humorous stories with Charles Wick, a California buddy who had worked in Hollywood before serving as head of the U.S. Information Agency in the Reagan administration. "Those two were like a professional routine," Laxalt says. "They could go at it for hours."

Many of Reagan's best lines were unscripted and uttered on the spur of the moment with perfect timing. In a question-and-answer session with reporters in 1983, he was asked how he felt about being seventy-two years old. "I think that it's fine," he said, "when you consider the alternative." Toward the end of his second term, Reagan attended a pro-life dinner at which businessman Peter Grace, who headed the Grace Commission on government waste, mistakenly spoke of the urgent need for laws that protect the life of "feces." The audience gasped, but Grace didn't catch on. "I was once a feces," he said. "You were feces." And so on. After the dinner Reagan was apologetically approached by the organizers of the dinner, who asked him whether he was embarrassed. "Oh no," he said. "But I'm afraid the feces really hit the fan tonight."

For Reagan, jokes were parables that reflected his view of the world. He used humor to communicate some of his most fundamental beliefs. He also found that wit, especially of the self-deprecating sort, is a wonderful way to open a speech or get people to relax during a conversation or to diffuse tension during a negotiation. Reagan was not shy about sharing his anecdotes with world leaders and in the process demonstrated that humor has the capacity to cross national and cultural boundaries. Caspar Weinberger, his defense secretary, testifies that Reagan's humor helped to "produce some vital agreements that neither logic nor table pounding nor cajoling could bring about."[10]

The only people who did not always enjoy Reagan's one-liners were his debating opponents and political adversaries who were on the receiving end. Reagan delivered the most crushing witticism of his career during his 1984 debate with Walter Mondale. When Henry Trewhit of the *Baltimore Sun* bluntly asked Reagan whether he was too old to be president, Reagan replied, "I will not make age an issue in this campaign. I am not going to exploit, for political purposes, my opponent's youth and inexperience."

In private, Reagan also told somewhat bawdy and politically incorrect jokes, which he knew would get him into trouble if he uttered them in public. He liked the story about Winston Churchill, who is said to have arrived at a London hotel for a function when he decided to stop by the men's room. No sooner did he find a position to relieve himself than who should enter the men's room but his old political rival Clement Attlee. To Churchill's surprise, Attlee came and stood right next to him, so Churchill nervously moved a few places away. "My, my, Winston," Attlee exclaimed. "Are we being modest?" Churchill replied, "Not at all Clement. It's just that whenever you see something that is large, privately owned, and working well, you want to nationalize it."

Before he became president, Reagan enjoyed ethnic humor, which he delivered in a variety of accents, but once he entered the White House, he realized that such humor was taboo and he was under careful scrutiny. Reagan stopped telling jokes about the scams of welfare queens. He limited himself to Irish jokes, which, given his Irish descent, he felt entitled to share, especially in the company of other Irish

Americans like Tip O'Neill and Donald Regan. Yet occasionally Reagan permitted himself a naughty quip that would find its way into the media and generate indignation and protests. Those who fancy themselves protectors of minority sensibilities were appropriately outraged, for example, when Reagan joked about the fellow at the Bureau of Indian Affairs who was seen sobbing at his desk because he had just discovered that "my Indian died." While many people might regard this as a racial joke, it is worth noting that the butt of Reagan's ridicule is not the American Indian but the bureaucrat.

Reagan's favorite jokes were about human nature. He liked to tell the one about the farmer and the lawyer who got into a bad traffic accident—a head-on collision. They both staggered out of their cars. The farmer took one look at the lawyer, walked back to his car, took out a package, and brought it back. There was a bottle inside, and he said, "Here, you look pretty shaken up. I think you ought to take a nip of this; it'll steady your nerves." So the lawyer did. Then the farmer said, "You still look a little bit pale. How about another?" And the lawyer took another swallow. At the farmer's urging, he took another and another and another. Finally he said he was feeling pretty good, and asked the farmer if he didn't think that he ought to have a little nip too. The farmer said, "Not me. I'm waiting for the state trooper."

Another Reagan story concerned two campers who were hiking in the woods when they spotted a grizzly bear lumbering over the hill, headed right for them. One of them reached into his backpack and quickly began to put on his tennis shoes. "What are you doing?" his friend said. "You can't possibly outrun a grizzly." The fellow with the tennis shoes replied, "I don't have to outrun the grizzly. I just have to outrun you."

These jokes reveal a mordant and even wicked side to Reagan's humor. They demonstrate that Reagan was not naive or sentimental about life. He shrewdly recognized that human beings have a dark side and believed in the Christian concept of original sin. Anthony Dolan, the president's chief speechwriter, once told me that in his conversations with Reagan he was surprised to encounter what he called Reagan's "philosophical disposition." Reagan understood, according to Dolan, that evil is not simply a characteristic of political systems such as communism, but is inherent in human nature itself. Yet it was precisely this pessimistic premise that seems to have contributed to Reagan's everyday bonhomie and good cheer. He operated on the assumption that nature can be cruel and that human beings are flawed; as a result, he didn't expect perfection and was always pleasantly surprised when events turned out for the better. Also he never ceased to be impressed when people rose above selfishness and vulgarity and faced their challenges with a smile. He cultivated this quality in himself.

Reagan's indulgent attitude toward human failings enabled him to be tolerant of what he considered weakness and vice while at the same time upholding an objective standard of truth and virtue. I vividly remember a remark columnist Joseph Sobran once made to me: "If Reagan led a life of conspicuous religious fervor, there might be some plausibility in the idea that he was bent on enforcing conformity. But his personal style, with its mix of conventional piety and relaxed practice, is reassuring, even endearing. It makes him like most Americans. He respects certain norms, even when he does not live up to them. He would rather appear to be a sinner, than abolish the idea of sin." The accuracy of this analysis can be verified by examining Reagan's religious convictions, as well as his attitude toward two controversial social issues, homosexuality and abortion.

Reagan's views on homosexuality were not entirely compatible with those of his evangelical Christian supporters or with those of the gay rights community. Before he became president, he once confessed his belief that homosexuality is a "tragic illness."[11] He was quite capable of making gay jokes and would put on a squeaky voice and a limp wrist for dramatic effect. Yet, as we might expect, Reagan knew lots of gays in Hollywood, and he and his wife socialized with people who were avowedly homosexual. Reagan himself did not support state-sponsored discrimination against homosexuals as a group. As governor, he opposed a bill that would have prohibited gays from teaching in public schools and serving in other government jobs that involved interaction with children. When the subject of homosexuals came up, Reagan once quoted the remark attributed to Mrs. Patrick Campbell from the trial of

Oscar Wilde: "I have no objection to anyone's sex life as long as they don't practice it in the street and frighten the horses."[12]

Although Reagan would never have put it this way, he was essentially in favor of a civic compromise: homosexuals agree to be discreet, and the community agrees to leave them alone. Essentially Reagan was endorsing tolerance as a political settlement between vice and virtue. He sought to preserve moral standards while recognizing the need for society to permit human behavior that frequently falls short.

On abortion, however, Reagan would not be flexible, because he firmly believed that millions of lives were at stake. His pollster Richard Wirthlin informed him that most Americans did not agree with him, and even Republicans were divided on the issue. Many of his aides begged him to stay away from the subject. But Reagan refused to modify his views, and throughout his presidency he publicly advocated the cause of the unborn. He took the unusual step as president of writing a book about his pro-life convictions, *Abortion and the Conscience of the Nation*.[13] He even had the controversial film *The Silent Scream*, which seeks to demonstrate that the unborn fetus feels pain during an abortion, shown at the White House.

Although Reagan supported legislation and court rulings that would overturn the *Roe v. Wade* decision legalizing abortion nationwide, Reagan knew that the political configuration of the courts and the Congress in the 1980s was such that abortion could not be outlawed. The best that pro-life supporters could do was the Hyde Amendment, a measure that restricted public funding for abortion, which Reagan willingly signed into law. A few days before he left office, he remarked that his greatest regret was that he was unable to do more as president to protect the lives of the unborn and that America would never be "completely civilized" as long as abortion on demand was legal.[14]

As many Americans saw, it was possible to disagree with Reagan on abortion while respecting the depth of his convictions and the eloquence of his appeal to moral reason. In his 1986 State of the Union address, Reagan called abortion "a wound in our national conscience." He was not interested in a technical debate about when life begins. "If you don't know whether a body is alive or dead, you would never bury it," he argued in one of his speeches. "Until someone can prove the unborn child is not a life, shouldn't we give it the benefit of the doubt and assume that it is?" He meditated on the cumulative effect of more than a million abortions a year: "These children, over tenfold the number of Americans lost in all our nation's wars, will never laugh, never sing, never experience the joy of human love; nor will they strive to heal the sick, or feed the poor, or make peace among nations. Abortion has denied them the first and most basic of human rights, and we are infinitely poorer for their loss."

Reagan's religiosity was, like that of Abraham Lincoln, generic and a little bit suspect. His churchgoing over the years was irregular. As governor he occasionally attended Bel Air Presbyterian Church but stopped going to church while he was president, citing Secret Service concerns about security. It must be noted that such concerns did not stop either of Reagan's successors, George Bush or Bill Clinton, from attending church services outside the White House. Reagan resumed regular church attendance when he returned to California. His aides noticed that he was a superstitious man who knocked on wood and carried a good-luck penny. His humor displayed a distinctly wry view of ostentatious piety and an irreverent approach to the pretensions of the clergy.

One of his jokes concerned a fellow who fell off a cliff. As he was hurtling down, he grabbed a protruding limb and looked down into the canyon hundreds of feet below. Then he looked up and said, "Lord, if there's anyone up there, give me faith. Tell me what to do." And a voice from the heavens said, "If you have faith, let go." He looked down to the canyon floor and then took another look up and asked, "Is there anyone else up there?"

Yet this sardonic humorist is the same man who was not abashed to conclude his acceptance speech at the Republican National Convention in 1980 by setting aside a minute for everyone to say a silent prayer. Nor was Reagan simply posturing in public. Aides who worked with him daily told me that on several occasions he got down on his knees in the Oval Office and prayed with people who came to see him. Pastors sometimes offered to lay their hands on his head and pray for him, and he was visibly moved and sometimes wept. These displays frequently embarrassed Reagan's aides and invited the scorn of secular intellectuals and the media when they became public.

He dabbled in religious prophecy and was fascinated by predictions about the end of the world. Billy Graham visited Reagan in the hospital while he was recuperating from minor surgery, and they discussed whether the next great event of world history would be the second coming of Christ. Reagan believed that the founding of the State of Israel in 1948 was one of the biblical signs that we are entering the last period of history. He did not believe that history consists of one random event after another; rather, he was firmly convinced that providence operates through the actions of people.

He frequently expressed his view that America's destiny, and his own, were guided by a providential hand. His critics professed to be outraged at this grotesque violation of the church-state barrier, but Lincoln believed the same thing. Moreover, in his October 21, 1984, debate with Walter Mondale, Reagan replied to a reporter's question by acknowledging that "no one knows" when the end will come and "I have never seriously warned and said we must plan according to Armageddon."[15] He simply believed that as a leader he should pray for guidance so that he could act in harmony with God's plan and, in a truly spiritual sense, make history.

He was reserved and understated about his personal beliefs because he didn't want to sound self-righteous or exhibitionistic. When he did speak of God, it was often in casual terms, as in "the man upstairs." Yet there is no doubt about the sincerity of his deep faith in God and his acceptance of the fundamental truths of Christianity. On more than one occasion he was asked whom he admired most, and he always answered, "the man from Galilee."

Reagan's private beliefs can best be gauged from his personal correspondence, published in a collection edited by his former secretary Helene von Damm. In 1978 a Methodist minister wrote to Reagan to say that he admired Christ's teachings but could not accept that he was the son of God. In a rebuttal apparently borrowed from C. S. Lewis's *Mere Christianity,* Reagan wrote back that Christ's own statements "foreclose, in my opinion, any questions as to his divinity. It doesn't seem to me that he gave us any choice: either he was what he said he was, or he was the world's greatest liar. It is impossible for me to believe that a liar or charlatan could have had the effect on mankind that he has for 2,000 years. We could ask: would even the greatest of liars carry his lie through the crucifixion when a simple confession would have saved him?"[16]

Americans who saw Reagan on TV or encountered him on the campaign trail recognized at once his affection for people, which revealed itself in his warm personality and affable sociability. "His good nature was a valuable political asset," political scientist William Schneider told me. "While the right has traditionally suffered the charge of being mean and lacking compassion, Reagan came across as a nice conservative."

A true egalitarian, Reagan seemed to relate to everyone, regardless of their position in life, and he fit comfortably into any group. He would engage in good-natured banter with the governor of a large state, and a few minutes later would have an equally amiable exchange with a hotel doorman or one of his Secret Service agents. "He was indifferent to class differences," remarks Ed Meese. When I worked in the White House, I noticed that Reagan seemed to have a special affection for the unfashionable folk—the cops and nuns and refuseniks and Sons of Italy. However incongruous they seemed in corridors lined with dapper professionals, all these people could be seen around the White House during the Reagan years.

He treated heads of state with an almost embarrassing informality. When he first met Japanese prime minister Yasuhiro Nakasone, Reagan asked him, "What does your wife call you at home?" Nakasone replied, "Yasu." Reagan said, "Well, Yasu, my name's Ron."[17] Although Nakasone may have been initially nonplussed by Reagan's familiarity, over time the two developed a genuine liking for one another, and in Japan Nakasone boasted of his "special relationship" with the man he called Ron. Reagan also captivated Gorbachev by telling him about an article he read in *People* magazine in which a man weighing over a thousand pounds got stuck in the doorway on his way to the bathroom and became so frightened that he went on a diet. When the interpreter conveyed Reagan's story Gorbachev incredulously asked, "Is this a real fact?" Reagan eagerly proceeded to give him further details about the case.[18]

In the presence of ladies, Reagan's personal conduct was always gentlemanly and chivalric. Margaret Thatcher, his close political ally, whom he described as "the other woman in my life," once called to harangue him over some disagreement. Reagan took the telephone away from his ear, placed his hand over the speaker, and said to his aides, "Isn't she *marvelous?*" National security adviser Frank Carlucci recalls that on more than one occasion he warned Reagan, "Mr. President, if you do that, Margaret Thatcher is going to be on the phone in an instant." And inevitably Reagan replied, "Oh, I don't want that."[19]

Reagan's graciousness extended even to his critics and political opponents. He once asked the White House switchboard, which has the capacity to locate just about anyone, anywhere in the world, to put his telephone call through to a Democratic congressman. What he didn't know was that the congressman was then on a trip in Australia, and his phone was ringing at three in the morning. The moment Reagan realized this, he apologized and said, "You know, it's not really me. It's an impostor. I'm sure the real president will call you back at a decent hour." When Jimmy Carter invited Reagan to speak at the dedication of the Carter Center in Atlanta, Reagan delivered such a magnanimous tribute to his former adversary that Carter told him, "I think I now understand more clearly why you won in November 1980 and I lost."[20]

Each day Reagan set aside some time to review fifty or so personal letters that were selected for him to read by Anne Higgins, who headed the White House correspondence office. Senior staffers tried to dissuade him from this habit, considering it a waste of the president's time, but Reagan never saw it that way. He liked meeting people and hearing about their circumstances through letters that conveyed a naive assurance that letters to the president were going to be personally read by the president. People considered him their friend. They sent pictures of themselves and their families. In many cases Reagan rewarded the expectations of writers and amazed their families and friends by answering them in his own hand.

Frequently Reagan would be moved by someone's tale of distress and, without checking to verify the circumstances, would send a care package or write a personal check. He did this back in his days as governor too. He once mailed one of his suits to a man who wrote him to say he was getting married but had nothing appropriate to wear. A soldier from Sacramento wanted Reagan to send his wife flowers for their anniversary; Reagan ordered a big bouquet and delivered it in person. Yet even philanthropy is a bit more complicated when you are the president of the United States. In more than one case, his check could not be cashed because the local bank teller would not believe it was Reagan's own signature, or because his personally autographed check was considered to be more valuable than the amount it was made out for. So someone from the White House had to call the bank.[21]

Speechwriter Peggy Noonan recalls the story of eighty-three-year-old Frances Green, who lived by herself on social security in Dale City, California. She was a woman of modest means, but every year she had sent a contribution of one dollar to the Republican National Committee. One day she received an invitation from the RNC inviting her to the White House to meet President Reagan, so she got her best outfit laundered and then rode the train cross-country from California to Washington, D.C. She didn't notice the reply card, which clarified that the event was a fund-raiser and those who came were expected to make a large donation.

When she arrived at the White House at the appointed date and time, the guards told her that her name was not on the list and she could not enter with the group. She was heartbroken. But her story was transmitted to a White House aide, who relayed it to the president's secretary, who took it to Reagan. He asked them to bring her to see him, but his schedule was crowded that day. His aides were sympathetic, but they didn't see how he could fit her in. They did the best they could and arranged a tour of the White House for her. It ended at the Oval Office, where she hoped to get a glimpse of the president. A National Security Council meeting was concluding. As the military brass walked out, Frances Green suddenly heard her name called, and it was the president speaking. "Frances! If I had known you were coming, I would have come out there to get you myself." They sat down in the Oval Office and chatted like old friends. We can be sure Reagan did not consider a minute of that time to be wasted.[22]

Despite his gregarious magnanimity, Reagan was also a naturally diffident man. Except on the campaign trail, he was reluctant to approach strangers or ask questions of people he didn't know. He also hated to cause anyone inconvenience or embarrassment. "I've almost never heard him complain," Nancy Reagan writes. "If something is bothering

Ronnie, he'll rarely mention it. And he never tells anyone, not even me, if he's not feeling well."[23] Vice President Bush once visited him in the hospital and was surprised to see Reagan on his knees in the bathroom, mopping the floor. Against doctor's orders, he had given himself a sponge bath and he didn't want the nurse to have to clean up. If one of her supervisors saw her doing that, Reagan worried she would be in trouble.[24]

He had countless acquaintances, but few close friends. Bush had a gift for friendship; Reagan didn't. Political consultant Ed Rollins says, "You could walk away from a dinner with Ronald Reagan believing he was your new friend for life, and you'd never hear from him again."[25] In both California and Washington, the Reagans as a couple stayed in touch with people, but they were mainly friends of Nancy. She spent a great deal of time on the phone, often confessing her worries and frustrations; he would say hello, exchange a few pleasantries, and then hand the receiver to her.

None of the millionaire entrepreneurs who backed Reagan over the years ever developed a genuine personal relationship with him. He returned their phone calls, sometimes took their advice, and that was it. Ed Meese, considered one of Reagan's most trusted friends, says that even when Reagan was governor, the two of them never socialized together. Theirs was entirely a business relationship. Meese told me, "I always called him 'Governor' or 'Mr. President,' never by his first name." Paul Laxalt, often described as the President's closest friend in the Senate, had a similarly cordial but distant relationship with Reagan.

Patti Davis writes that to her knowledge, her father had only one close friend, the actor Robert Taylor. In the 1960s Robert Taylor and his wife, Ursula, lived in the same Pacific Palisades neighborhood as the Reagans. Taylor and Reagan frequently went riding together, and the two couples enjoyed sitting around the yard swapping stories about horses and Hollywood. Reagan is said to have broken down as he gave the eulogy at Taylor's funeral; if so, it is one of the very few times he is known to have become emotional over a personal matter.

Like the hero of a thousand Westerns, Reagan was, at bottom, a solitary man. He didn't mind company but preferred to ride by himself. Even as president, there was a part of him that was exiled from the business of politics. Recognizing this, the Secret Service gave him a suitable code name: Rawhide. When I took friends on a tour of the White House, they frequently observed that Reagan had given the place a distinctly western aura. There were Remington paintings and sculptures everywhere, and Reagan had special shelves built into the Oval Office so that he could display a collection of miniature saddles, loaned to him by the publisher Walter Annenberg and his wife, Lee.

Despite his enthusiasm for the job, Reagan felt a bit claustrophobic in the White House, where for security reasons all the windows are sealed shut. He also found the atmosphere in the nation's capital stultifying. He once described Washington, D.C., as "an island, surrounded on all sides by reality." He found himself seeking a refuge from the madhouse of political wheeling and dealing. He yearned for the solitude of the open country.

Reagan enjoyed making a getaway to Camp David, the rustic presidential retreat in Catoctin Mountain Park, a thirty-minute helicopter ride from the White House. Even more, he loved his vacation time so he could return to his 688-acre retreat in the Santa Ynez mountains near Santa Barbara, which he called Rancho del Cielo—"ranch in the sky." It was a large plot with spectacular views on all sides, but the old adobe house itself had just two bedrooms and suggested a frontier simplicity, with its Indian blankets and hatrack by the door. A large part of the house the Reagans had rebuilt with their own hands.

At the ranch Reagan rode every morning, and in the afternoon he chopped wood, cleared brush, and did other chores. Comfortably attired in jeans and plaid shirt, he was always building or repairing something. Like that other outdoor individualist, Teddy Roosevelt, Reagan seemed to draw strength from his connection with nature. It helped to give Reagan a sense of wholeness and serenity. "Somehow," Reagan writes in his autobiography, "it just seems a lot easier to sort out a problem when I'm on a horse."[26]

He took great pride in his physique and outdoor labors. He grumbled when the Secret Service insisted that he wear his bulletproof jacket, "Everybody will think I'm getting fat." ABC News White House correspondent Sam Donaldson once suggested that Reagan's rustic enthusiasm was a bit of a publicity stunt and that he probably stopped cutting wood when the cameras were turned off. Reagan was clearly miffed by the report. He took photographs from several angles of a huge pile of logs that he had just shredded and sent them to Donaldson, who confessed to me, "I must say, it was an impressive sight."

Doctors who examined Reagan were frequently astonished at his condition. When he emerged from the operating room where doctors removed part of his intestine to extract a cancerous growth, one of the surgeons exclaimed, "This man has the insides of a forty-year-old."[27] Reagan was then seventy-four. Not long after his hospital stays, Reagan was usually back working outdoors and doing exercises. Whenever anyone raised the question of his health, he asked them to feel the muscles on his arms and chest. Author Tom Clancy was struck just by the firmness of his grip: "The guy has a handshake like a lumberjack."[28] Education Secretary William Bennett, who bumped into Reagan a couple of times, discovered that despite his own large physique, "I moved him not at all." Reagan was just as sturdy on the outside, Bennett noted, as he was on the inside.[29]

If Reagan had a single close friend in the world, it was Nancy. "Sometimes I think my life really began when I met Nancy," Reagan remarked. "From the start, our marriage was like an adolescent's dream of what a marriage should be."[30] Evangelist Billy Graham said that one of the greatest gifts the Reagans gave America was that, through their example, they taught us about true marital love and companionship. They were very different people, but they suited each other. They did not seem to need anyone else; they were a self-contained unit. "Ronald and Nancy Reagan are two halves of a circle," writes their daughter Patti Davis. "Together, they are complete."[31]

She called him "Ronnie"; he called her "Mommy." He was ever the uxorious husband, doting on her with a zeal that the media and the American public admired but did not entirely share. The press was highly critical of Nancy Reagan's expensive taste in clothes. Her acquisition of new china for the White House seemed ostentatious at a time when the country was going through hard times. At the summits, she seemed to be carrying on her own cold war with Raisa Gorbachev. Her reputation was not helped by Donald Regan's disclosure that she regularly consulted an astrologer. Some Americans saw Nancy as high-strung, manipulative, and a bit strange. Nancy was even suspected of exercising sinister control over the Reagan household, like Mrs. Danvers in *Rebecca*.

These criticisms were mostly unfair. A former Hollywood actress who once dated Clark Gable, Nancy Reagan was elegant and stylish. She had exquisite taste, although her spending habits were no more lavish than those of Jacqueline Kennedy. The White House china was purchased with funds donated by a private foundation; it didn't cost the taxpayers anything. She apparently began her astrological consultations after the attempt on Reagan's life, in a desperate but understandable attempt to prevent a similar occurrence. Her astrological projections had no effect on policy. She sometimes inconvenienced his schedule by insisting that he travel during an auspicious time, but he regarded these concessions as a small price to pay if they helped her sleep better at night. By all indications, she tried to make friends with Raisa Gorbachev but was put off when she found herself at the receiving end of stentorian lectures from this former professor of Marxist-Leninist thought at Moscow University about the deficiencies of American capitalism.

Nor is there any truth to the rumor that Nancy Reagan was the real power behind the throne. Nancy Reagan was a socialite whose main concern was with the world of movies and high fashion. Bob Hope captured the essential difference between the Reagans when he quipped that "Ronnie's hero is Calvin Coolidge and Nancy's is Calvin Klein."[29] Her main political involvements—the "Just Say No" campaign against drugs and the Foster Grandparents' Program—were initially devised by the White House staff to give her a favorable public image, although over time she became genuinely dedicated to those causes.

This is not to suggest that Nancy Reagan stayed out of her husband's business. She was a politician's wife and understood that role very well. To some she seemed wide-eyed and gullible, yet she had a shrewdness that was both personal and political. At a 1984 reception, the Soviet diplomat Andrei Gromyko drew her aside and whispered to her, "Does your husband believe in peace?" She replied, "Of course." He said, "Then whisper 'peace' in your husband's ear every night." She said, "I will, and I'll also whisper it in your ear." And leaning over with a smile she softly whispered, "Peace."[33]

Reporters sneered at her rapt and adoring glance at the president, which they nicknamed The Gaze. Yet they overlooked the fact that she too was an actor. In public, she played the part of the supportive spouse; in private she demonstrated to all who didn't know that she had a mind of her own and the resolve to see her intentions carried out. She had one overriding cause: Ronald Reagan. In an environment where everyone had an agenda—personal advancement, or the welfare of the party, or an ideological perspective—she alone had the sole interests of her husband in mind. She ministered to his personal needs—watching out for his health and making sure he was not overscheduled—and protected the president from what she considered harsh and unfair criticism.

The only time she involved herself in policy issues was when she felt that Reagan was getting a bad reputation in the press and the public eye. If she thought that this was because he was taking a hard-line stance, she tried to convince him to soften it. He always listened to her, but on substantive policies he usually rejected her counsel. She urged him to moderate his position on abortion; he refused. She protested what she considered the harshness of his "evil empire" rhetoric; he didn't modify it until the circumstances warranted. She felt that strategic defense would take money away from the poor and needy; he pressed on with the program. During the recession of 1982, she proposed he support new spending initiatives that would refute the charge that he lacked compassion. He ignored her advice.

The one area in which Reagan appreciated his wife's protectiveness and trusted her intervention was on personnel matters. He relied heavily on her because he knew that he had an administrative weakness: he tended to trust people on the assumption that they were being straightforward with him and had his best interests at heart. Nancy Reagan knew this wasn't always so. He also eschewed personal confrontation because he hated pettiness. She, on the other hand, was willing to take harsh measures on her husband's behalf.

Nancy didn't care if one of Reagan's aides, like national security adviser Richard Allen, had known the president for years. It mattered little that Interior Secretary James Watt was fanatically loyal to Reagan and his principles. She was indifferent to whether chief of staff Donald Regan's problems were partly due to unfair press coverage. If they made her husband look bad, she wanted them gone. Reagan was sometimes slow to take her advice; he was especially resistant to firing people who in his opinion had done no wrong but were being smeared in the media.

In cases where her husband did not cooperate, Nancy recruited others in the administration to help her get rid of the millstone around the president's neck. In one case she urged Vice President Bush to go to Reagan and demand that Regan be fired. "It's not my role," Bush protested. Nancy insisted, "It's exactly your role."[34] Bush did not oblige, but Nancy persisted relentlessly. The rivalry between her and Regan reached such proportions that in 1986 Reagan joked at the White House Gridiron Dinner, "Nancy and Don tried to patch things up the other day. They met privately over lunch—just the two of them and their food tasters." Yet eventually she got her way: Regan was out. When Nancy decided that someone had to go, that person might as well have started packing. "Your chances for survival were always better if Nancy Reagan didn't know who you were," remarked Ed Rollins, who directed Reagan's 1984 reelection campaign.[35] My impression was that everyone in the White House was a little scared of her.

Their children were a problem. Three of them have written memoirs emphasizing the flaws of their parents, especially Nancy. Only Ron has kept his silence. Yet it is clear from the children's own accounts that they were a difficult lot. Michael Reagan confessed that since his family was rich and famous, he adopted the attitude that no matter what he did, he could get away with it because his parents would "clean up the mess after me."[36] While Reagan was considering a career in conservative politics, his daughter Patti Davis says she fantasized about becoming a hippie and a radical activist who could spend her time "throwing rocks through the windows of ROTC buildings." She rejected the name "Reagan" in favor of her mother's maiden name because she was embarrassed to be identified with her father's political views.[37]

"Disagreements with my daughter are nothing new," Reagan once said of Maureen. He jokingly added, "I just can't take her over my knee for a good spanking anymore." Even when his children were young, Reagan gave them a great deal of independence. Once when Maureen threatened to run away, he gave her a dollar and told her that she should write if she got a job, but if she wanted to return, she could give him a call.[38] Michael's early expectations of being a rich man's son were frustrated when his circumstances compelled him to take a minimum wage job at a car wash and then in a hotel. His friends were puzzled that he had to struggle to make ends meet when his father was a famous actor, but the Reagans didn't feel that they should help him out financially. Later Michael Reagan became a successful talk show host and joked to callers who protested the do-it-yourself philosophy implied by Reaganomics. "Don't complain to me," Michael would say. "I've been living under it all of my life."[39]

Reagan did try to teach his children how to use their freedom. On the eve of his son Michael's wedding, Reagan wrote him a letter of advice: "Some men feel their masculinity can only be proven if they play out in their own life all the locker-room stories, smugly confident that what a wife doesn't know won't hurt her. The truth is, somehow, way down inside, without her ever finding lipstick on the collar or catching a man in the flimsy excuse of where he was till 3 A.M., a wife does know, and with that knowing, some of the magic of this relationship disappears. There are more men griping about marriage who kicked the whole thing away themselves than there can ever be wives deserving of blame. . . . If you truly love a girl, you shouldn't ever want her to feel, when she sees you greet a secretary or a girl you both know, that humiliation of wondering if she was someone who caused you to be late coming home, nor should you want any other woman to be able to meet your wife and know she was smiling behind her eyes as she looked at her, the woman you love, remembering that this was the woman you rejected even momentarily for her favors."[40] As this letter shows, despite his Hollywood background, Reagan had traditional views about marital fidelity, which he sought to convey to his children.

It was not easy to do this across the generational chasm. Moreover, Reagan's main shortcoming as a father was that, as a consequence of his political commitments, he was seldom around to spend time with his children. Patti Davis remarked that she did not feel she knew her father any better than the countless Americans who knew him as a public figure. As a consequence, he became estranged from the way his children felt and lived. When Patti moved in with a rock singer from the group the Eagles, Reagan told her, "This young man will not be welcome in our house. This is just immoral, what you are doing." Patti demanded to know what was wrong with living together, and Reagan replied, "God wrote that men and women should get married. It's a sin in the eyes of God. It's in the Bible." Reagan was being perfectly sincere, but what he didn't recognize was that, like many others in her generation, Patti had long since ceased to regard the Bible as a source of moral authority; indeed she considered her father's appeals to be "outside the parameters of logic."[41]

Eventually the Reagans understood that their children had chosen a different path and stopped trying to mold them. When their younger son, Ron, decided to become a dancer, the Reagans initially were nervous, not because they objected to that particular career but because they suspected that his choice of profession might suggest that he was a homosexual. When Ron moved in with his girlfriend Doria Palmieri, a woman he subsequently married, Michael Reagan broke the news to his father on the telephone: "Well, dad, there's good news and bad news." Reagan asked, "What do you mean?" Michael said that the bad news was that Ron was living with a woman. "The good news is that we know he isn't gay." And Reagan chuckled and replied, "I hadn't thought of it that way."[42]

Reagan's two sons and two daughters rarely visited him in the White House, nor did the Reagans typically stop by to see their children if they were in town for a function. Their grandson Cameron was once asked by a reporter if he ever saw his grandfather. "Sure," he replied. "On TV." Yet when Patti Davis confronted her father with the charge that "we've never exactly been a close family," Reagan pulled out an old photograph with everyone smiling and said, "Look, we were a happy family." He wanted it to be so and never understood why Nancy and he could not connect better with their children. For most of his life, the Great Communicator experienced a breakdown of communication with his own sons and daughters.

The American people knew that Reagan had family problems that made his pro-family rhetoric more of an aspiration than a domestic reality, yet Reagan's household headaches only made him seem more normal—just another guy who cherished an ideal of family bliss even while he was divorced and had strained relationships with the children. In this respect, as in many others, an extraordinary man like Reagan never seemed more ordinary to his fellow citizens.

Chapter 10

Spirit of a Leader

HAVING SURVEYED BOTH the man and his achievements, we are now in a position to solve the mystery of Ronald Reagan. The puzzle can be summarized in this way. Remarkable events occurred during the 1980s: the restoration of economic growth, the curbing of inflation, the end of the gasoline crisis, the technological boom, the beginning of the collapse of Soviet communism, the spread of freedom and democracy around the world. Reagan was a guiding force behind these events. Yet even his ideological allies have difficulty crediting him with these accomplishments because, judging by his film background and nonintellectual style, he was such an implausible statesman. He was a political outsider who, even after years in public office, retained the style of the naive amateur. He saw the world in simple terms of good and evil. He didn't bother to familiarize himself with the complex details of public policy. His governing style was unorthodox: he delegated a lot and spent much of his time "acting the role" of president, giving speeches and making jokes. How, despite these peculiar qualities, was he so successful?

The key to understanding Reagan is that he was not successful in spite of these traits but because of them. We are slow to acknowledge his greatness because we expect our leaders to be deeply reflective people who take their responsibilities seriously, downplay the ceremonial aspects of government, and work diligently to master the complex details of public policy. Richard Nixon and Jimmy Carter fit this description; they have been failed or only mediocre presidents. The case of Reagan, who was vastly more successful, compels us to rethink our views about what makes a good leader.

Some who were previously skeptical about Reagan have undergone precisely such a reexamination. When François Mitterand was elected president of France as a socialist, he was both ideologically hostile and personally contemptuous of Reagan. By 1986, however, Mitterand was thoroughly impressed by Reagan's effectiveness, and described his power as "primal: like a rock in the Morvan, like plain truth, like the wilderness of Nevada."[1] Even Senator Edward Kennedy, who opposed virtually every Reagan initiative during the 1980s, told a Yale University audience in March 1989, "Whether we agree with him or not, Ronald Reagan was an effective president. He stood for a set of ideas . . . he meant them, and he wrote most of them not only into public law but into the national consciousness."[2]

Reagan himself once defined the challenge of statesmanship in this way: "to have the vision to dream of a better, safer world, and the courage, persistence and patience to turn that dream into a reality."[3] Based on Reagan's understanding, as well as his example, we can now summarize the three basic elements of leadership. The first is *vision*, which gives the leader conviction as well as a destination. It is impossible to lead if you are unsure about where you want to go. Vision is a function of perceptive power, but it relies less on academic intelligence than on moral imagination. The most dramatic example of Reagan's vision is his foresight into the vulnerability of Soviet communism and his confidence that freedom and democracy would leave totalitarianism on the ash heap of history.

In addition to vision, leadership requires *action*—the ability to get from here to there. The successful leader must be willing to act, even in the absence of full information, in order to achieve as much of his or her agenda as possible under the circumstances. Courage, resourcefulness, and motivational skills are often necessary for a leader to implement the vision. The final element of leadership is *consent*. Leaders must be able to articulate their vision in order to rally the people behind it and build lasting support for their policies. Genuine leaders are hard to find because this combination of abilities in a single individual is rare. Let us examine more closely how Reagan exercised his leadership, and contrast his approach with that of other politicians.

Many politicians today allow their positions to be shaped by pollsters. The pollster conducts opinion surveys to determine what the American people think about a particular issue. Taking this into account, the politician then develops a proposed course of action, and submits it to be test-marketed to "focus groups" to see if they approve. If not, the politician abandons the idea or choreographs his stance and rhetoric to conform more closely to the prevailing sentiment of the voters. This modus operandi, which is standard practice on the part of both the Clinton administration and the Republican congressional leadership, seems warranted in a democratic society, where the people are the rulers and thus entitled to determine the course of public policy.

Yet true leaders do not operate in this way because they know that public opinion on any issue is usually inchoate and unformed. Moreover, we do not live in a direct democracy, where citizens are expected to formulate the particulars of domestic and foreign policy. Rather, ours is a representative democracy; the people choose presidents and members of Congress to make and carry out public policy. At the same time, citizens reserve the right to react to what their elected representatives are doing. Leadership in a modern democracy does not require continuing subservience to the whim of the people, but it is ultimately accountable to the considered judgment of the electorate.

Reagan knew this. His philosophy was based on the premise, "Trust the people." Yet he was not unnerved by news reports during the 1982 recession that showed his popularity had plummeted. "Well," he joked to his aides, "I could always get shot again." Reagan knew that if he took a poll and asked Americans, "Should I invade Grenada?" they would probably say no. His approach was not to consult the electorate on what to do in every situation but rather to presume that he reflected the shared values of the people. Given the facts, he made his best judgment and acted. Then he made his case to the public, confident that once they were in possession of the relevant information and his policies had time to work, they would approve his course of action.

This is not to say that Reagan eschewed opinion surveys, which were regularly assembled for him by his pollster Richard Wirthlin. But Wirthlin told me that instead of using these surveys to determine what he should do, Reagan used them to prepare the public for an anticipated course of action. "He consulted the polls to identify areas where a majority of his fellow citizens disagreed with him," Wirthlin said, "so that he could use his power of persuasion to change their minds."

Aides recounted for me an incident during the first few weeks of Reagan's presidency that demonstrates Reagan's attitude toward public opinion. Reagan was asked by Alexander Haig, his new secretary of state, to approve continuing negotiations for the Law of the Sea treaty. The treaty was based on the premise that the mineral and natural resources of the oceans do not belong to the country that extracts them from the seabed; rather, they are the common property of all nations and should be shared according to some agreed-on formula.

Reagan said he would not support the treaty and asked that negotiations be suspended. Incredulous at what he took to be the president's naive and reflexive opposition, Haig tried to make him see the light by pointing out that discussions had been going on for years and that every recent president and virtually all leading figures in both parties accepted the general framework of the treaty. "Well, yes," Reagan said, "but you see, Al, that's what the last election was all about."

"What?" Haig sneered. "About the Law of the Sea treaty?"

"No," Reagan replied. "It was about not doing things just because that's the way they've been done before."

Reagan's leadership approach was tested in his first year in office when the 12,000 members of the Professional Air Traffic Controllers Organization (PATCO) decided to go on strike until their demands for reduced workloads and higher salaries were met. Reagan was in an awkward position, because PATCO was one of the few unions that had supported his candidacy. Further, some of its complaints, such as the need to modernize the nation's air traffic control system, were legitimate. Political calculation might dictate that a new president should work out an amicable settlement rather than alienate a powerful union that supported him and risk paralyzing the country's civil aviation system.

The decisive fact for Reagan was that PATCO workers were public employees and had taken an oath not to strike against the U.S. government. What the strikers were threatening was, in Reagan's view, illegal and immoral. Confronted with a similar situation in 1919, Reagan's role model Calvin Coolidge famously declared, "There is no right to strike against the public safety by anybody, anywhere, any time." Reagan gave the air traffic controllers forty-eight hours to show up for work. When they didn't, he fired them and ordered Transportation Secretary Drew Lewis to hire replacements.

Union leaders predicted that planes would crash if they were being directed by inexperienced staff. If there had been an accident, the political consequences for Reagan might have been catastrophic. But he took the risk, and this did not happen. The aviation industry survived; it was PATCO that lost its certification and crashed into bankruptcy. Reagan adopted his stern course of action without consulting pollsters, yet he was strongly supported by the country because he convinced most people that he was standing firm and upholding the law in the face of threats and intimidation. In the PATCO incident, which set the tone for his presidency, Reagan proved that the right thing to do can also be politically advantageous.

Another case where Reagan acted first and then sought popular approval involved the man Reagan called the "mad dog of the Middle East," Muammar Qaddafi. Shortly after he became president, Reagan was notified that Libyan planes were harassing U.S. aircraft conducting training exercises in the Mediterranean. The American planes were in international airspace, but Qaddafi insisted that the sky above the Gulf of Sidra was Libyan territory. Reagan told the navy not to provoke a conflict, but if the Libyans opened fire, they should shoot back. Conscious of the complicated engagement rules that burdened U.S. forces in Vietnam, Reagan was asked, "What about hot pursuit?" He replied unhesitatingly, "All the way into the hangar."

In August 1981 Libyan planes fired at two American F-14s from the carrier *USS Nimitz*. In keeping with Reagan's orders, the U.S. planes shot the Libyans down. The attack took place in the early morning, and Reagan was asleep at the time. His critics faulted the White House staff for not waking him immediately, but Reagan was unruffled. With his trademark grin, he told the press he had given Ed Meese explicit instructions: "If we shoot down their jets, let me sleep. If they shoot down ours, wake me up."

Five years later, in April 1986, a bomb exploded in a West Berlin discotheque, killing and injuring several Americans. U.S. intelligence intercepted communication from the Libyan embassy to Tripoli, taking credit for the attack. Here was a rare case in which the United States had concrete proof of Libya's involvement in an act of state-sponsored terrorism. Reagan met with the Joint Chiefs of Staff and congressional leaders, who were unanimous that some response was necessary. Reagan ordered an attack, which took place the next morning. U.S. planes bombarded military targets in Tripoli and Benghazi, including sites where Qaddafi was reputed to hide out.

Reagan's action was harshly criticized in the United States. Senator Lowell Weicker said that it was "no different than what Qaddafi had done" in mounting terrorist operations. Senator Robert Byrd predicted an escalation of Qaddafi's terrorist activities. These themes echoed in the national media. Columnist Pete Hamill spoke for many in the press in proclaiming a moral equivalence between Reagan and Qaddafi.[4] With his usual hyperbolic panache, left-wing columnist Alexander Cockburn condemned Reagan for "tossing aside elementary dictates of law, evidence, morality, compassion, common sense, logic, self-interest and proportion."[5]

Reagan was undeterred. The day of the attack he went on national television and said, "Today we have done what we had to do. If necessary, we shall do it again." His approval ratings soared,[6] yet it was not clear at the time that the people's confidence was justified. Reagan never promised an end to Libyan terrorism. He couldn't, since there was no way of knowing in advance how a "mad dog" would react. Reagan ordered the Libyan air strike because he believed that Qaddafi deserved it and was convinced that only the threat of punishment was likely to deter a maniac like Qaddafi. Once again, Reagan turned out to be right. The escalation of Libyan terrorism that his critics predicted proved to be imaginary. Qaddafi seems to have been subdued by the knowledge that his actions would produce a severe response. After U.S. jets bombed his compound, his provocations and attacks on American targets ceased.

In the case of PATCO and Libya, Reagan acted decisively and then won the endorsement of the American people. There are times, however, when a leader must pursue a course of action that he considers in the long-term interest of his country but is extremely unpopular at the time. One such case involved Reagan's controversial decision to visit the Bitburg cemetery in Germany in April 1985.

The Bitburg incident began benignly enough. German chancellor Helmut Kohl suggested that as part of the commemoration of the fortieth anniversary of the end of World War II, Reagan visit a German grave site to show how the two countries had overcome their former hostilities and become allies. When presidential advance man Michael Deaver scouted the Bitburg cemetery, the ground was covered with snow, and he did not think to inquire who was buried there. Soon it became clear that of the 2,000 German soldiers interred at Bitburg, there were nearly 50 graves that contained the corpses of Hitler's notorious Waffen SS.

Suddenly Reagan's visit assumed a vast moral significance. Jewish groups, led by Nobel laureate Elie Wiesel, said that if Reagan visited Bitburg, he would confer legitimacy on the Nazis. "Your place," Wiesel said, "is with the victims." The American Legion, the largest veterans' group, pointed out that Bitburg contained the bodies of many Germans who were responsible for summary executions of American troops. Church groups urged Reagan to cancel his visit out of recognition that the Holocaust was the greatest moral crime of this century. Fifty-three senators and almost four hundred congressmen signed petitions asking Reagan not to go. Polls showed that a majority of Americans, both Democrats and Republicans, opposed Reagan's scheduled trip. Responding to this gathering storm, chief of staff Don Regan asked the White House advance team in Germany to come up with an alternate site. Nancy Reagan pleaded with her husband to yield to the public outcry that seemed to be issuing from all sides.

Still, Reagan went to Bitburg. Out of deference to American Jews, he also visited the Bergen-Belsen concentration camp. There he honored the victims of Nazi atrocities, while emphasizing that the lesson of the Holocaust was not the despair but the triumph of the human spirit.

"Here, death ruled. But we have learned something as well. Because of what happened, we found that death cannot rule forever. . . . We are here because humanity refuses to accept that freedom, or the spirit of man, can ever be extinguished. . . . Out of the ashes—hope; and from all the pain—promise."[7]

Reagan's Bitburg stop was a brief one, and he was careful to make the visit in the company of ninety-year-old General Matthew Ridgway, who had led the U.S. Eighty-second Airborne Division in the war against Nazi Germany. Yet the question remains: Why, in the face of universal resistance, did the president persist in going to Bitburg, risking what the *New York Times* called "the biggest fiasco of Reagan's presidency"? The conventional explanation is that he had told Chancellor Kohl he would come, and Kohl was very insistent. Yet presidents cancel engagements all the time, and there is no particular reason that Reagan should have weighed Kohl's demands so heavily that they displaced all other considerations.

Reagan's own statements offer a much clearer explanation. "We do not believe in collective guilt," he said, adding that most of the graves at Bitburg were those of young German soldiers who had been forced to enlist in Hitler's army. "They were victims," Reagan said, "just as surely as the victims in the concentration camps." If some of the men had committed serious offenses, Reagan said, "all of those in that cemetery have long since met the Supreme Judge of right and wrong." His main concern was not with the past but with the future. "I didn't feel that we could ask new generations of Germans to live with this guilt forever without any hope of redemption. This should be a time of healing."[8]

Reagan's attempt to equate the circumstances of the slain combatants of Hitler's army with those of Jews killed in the Holocaust was utterly unconvincing. As moral agents, those who served in the German military bear a measure of responsibility for their actions on behalf of that "evil empire." This remains true whether or not they acted under compulsion, because they had the option of refusing, even in the face of punishment or execution, to carry out Hitler's orders. By contrast, the Jews who were killed in the camps were complete innocents. Reagan made this comparison in a spontaneous exchange at a news conference, yet it was a flawed analogy that supported his critics' charge of insensitivity.

On the other hand, Reagan's broader argument is more compelling. Reagan believed it was unjust and corrosive for the guilt of the Holocaust to be transmitted to generations of Germans who were not even born during that time. They cannot be held responsible for the crimes of others simply by virtue of their German descent. Reagan sought to vindicate a spiritual insight, which is the destructiveness of forcing a nation to bear a perpetual, collective guilt complex. He understood the harmful effects of compelling successive generations of Germans, who had come a long way in building a free and democratic society, to wallow in the psychosis produced by the accusation of complicity in mass murder.

"We who were enemies are now friends," Reagan said in his speech at Bitburg Air Base. "Out of the ruins of war has blossomed an enduring peace. . . . We cannot undo the crimes and wars of yesterday, nor call the millions back to life. . . . The one lesson of World War II, the lesson of Nazism, is that freedom must always be stronger than totalitarianism and that good must always be stronger than evil. The moral measure of our two nations will be found in the resolve we show to preserve liberty."[9] Reagan's argument was both an ethical and a practical case for reconciliation. His contention was that the West was in a better position to resist the contemporary evil of totalitarianism by permitting postwar Germany to outlive its Nazi past, recover its national pride, and join the fraternity of free nations on an equal basis. That's why he went to Bitburg, and why many Americans who disagreed with his visit nevertheless respected him for standing up for his convictions.

The Bitburg incident, like many others, reveals one of Reagan's most remarkable leadership qualities: his ability to maintain his course and not to be deterred even in the face of intense opposition. Previous presidents, like Nixon, were obsessed with the antagonism of political and social elites. It is hard to think of a politician today who does not care deeply about his or her image as portrayed by *Time* and the *Washington Post*. For a politician, this trait is a serious weakness, because it makes the person vulnerable to manipulation through the techniques of abuse and flattery. It is a measure of Reagan's complete self-assurance that he was totally indifferent to what the elites thought and said about him.

Where did he get that kind of confidence? Partly it was his Hollywood background. Reagan was a bona fide celebrity. He had starred with beautiful actresses like Ann Sheridan, Barbara Stanwyck, Ginger Rogers, and Doris Day. His professional and social circle included Humphrey Bogart, Bette Davis, Errol Flynn, Shirley Temple, James Cagney, and Claude Rains. What did he care what some assistant editor at *Time* thought of him? If Reagan had regarded himself as an intellectual, he might be expected to crave the accolades of the intellectual class, but he didn't, and this indifference gave him an immunity to the judgment of the wise men. As far as he was concerned, their views were entitled to the same consideration as those of anybody else.

The most important source of Reagan's self-assurance, however, was his unshakable faith in his convictions that he developed in his early childhood largely through his mother's influence. Reagan never lost this moral serenity. He believed that he knew just as much as the experts about the things that mattered most. He didn't mind the scorn of intellectual elites because he was sure that he was right and they were wrong. From his point of view, when they railed against his free market and anticommunist policies, they might as well be raging against the force of gravity. He once observed that one of his professorial critics seemed to be "trying to repeal the laws of supply and demand." Even when they called him vile names, it did not matter. Reagan's personal detachment—the wall that he constructed around his inner self—insulated him from vicious ad hominem insults.

Consider the suave indifference with which Reagan responded to his harshest critics. When Reagan was governor of California, he was asked if he was familiar with the unremitting stream of vituperation directed against him by the influential columnist Herb Caen. His reaction was: "What's that guy's problem?" It never occurred to Reagan that Caen's criticisms might have some foundation. His instinctive reaction was to wonder what was wrong with Herb Caen.

Reagan brought this same attitude to the White House. On the rare occasions when his actions were praised by the *New York Times*, he would say, "I don't know what's gotten into them. They must be having a bad day." Confronted with unbalanced treatment of his administration in the press, Reagan responded with good-natured humor. At a White House Gridiron dinner in the mid-1980s Reagan was confronted with the charge that he read important briefing papers during commercial breaks, while perched in front of the television set. "That's not true," Reagan protested. "I *watch* the commercials. I read my papers while the news is on."

The president took an equally jocular attitude to the criticism unleashed against his policies by the nation's leading economists. He was reminded, he said, of the three gentlemen who had just died and were standing at the gates of heaven to be admitted. One was a surgeon, the other an engineer, and the third an economist. They had all fulfilled the entrance requirements, but it developed that there was room for only one at that time. So St. Peter said, "I'll tell you what. I'll pick the one who comes from the oldest profession." The surgeon stepped forward and said, "I'm your man. Right after God created Adam, he operated. He took a rib and created Eve. So surgery has to be the oldest profession." The engineer said, "No. You see, before God created Adam and Eve, he took the chaos that prevailed and built the earth in six days. So engineering had to precede surgery." The economist finally spoke up and said, "Just a minute. Who do you think created all that chaos?"

Prominent journalists and pundits had developed the image of Reagan as a slacker who didn't work very hard and lacked the power of concentration. Far from disputing these characterizations, he encouraged them. He was an actor, and he knew how to play the part of Shakespeare's fool. When a reporter reminded him, "You said that you'd resign if ever your memory started to go," he responded, "When did I say that?" Asked about his "short attention span" Reagan said, "I was going to reply to that, but what the hell, let's move on to something else." Even though there are no known instances of Reagan's napping during a cabinet meeting, he joked that after he left office, his cabinet chair would bear the label, "Ronald Reagan Slept Here." Reagan recognized that the less his adversaries expected of him, the more he was likely to accomplish. Reagan understood, as his critics did not, that the fool is often the smartest fellow in the play.

Journalists loved to expose Reagan's rhetorical outrages, which they called "gaffes." Lou Cannon devoted a weekly *Washington Post* item to the subject, which he called "Reaganism of the Week." Strangely enough, Reagan had no objection and frequently turned to the column to discover his own gaffes. Reagan's advisers soon discovered what the boss already knew: that Americans didn't mind his gaffes and were even entertained by them. Reporters who were confident that they had exposed Reagan as ignorant and incompetent could not figure out why they were unable to discredit their target. "He's a very frustrating quarry," Steven Weisman of the *New York Times* confessed.[10]

Columnist Michael Kinsley once defined a gaffe as one of those infrequent occasions when a politician tells the truth. When we recall Reagan's gaffes, we see that he sometimes used them as a kind of code to transmit important political messages that would be incomprehensible to a hostile media. Some of Reagan's gaffes seem designed to be interpreted as blunders by the media but recognized as valid points by the people whom Reagan was trying to reach. Moreover, he chose this particular mode of communication because he understood the political value of outraging liberal sensibility.

For instance, Reagan once said that historically women were responsible for civilizing men, and that were it not for female influence, men might still be living in caves and running around in skin tights carrying clubs. Feminists were suitably appalled, but in living rooms and bars across America, most people probably enjoyed a private chuckle that Reagan had dared to utter this anthropologically sound but politically incorrect statement in public.

In his dealings with the press, Reagan was never surprised to encounter ideological bias; he expected it. He instinctively understood the futility of railing against media distortion. Whenever possible, he used television addresses to communicate directly with the American people. Michael Deaver and Richard Darman choreographed Reagan's public appearances so that whatever journalists said about him on the evening news, Americans would see for themselves that he looked confident and in charge. Several Reagan aides told me of the occasion when TV reporter Lesley Stahl was doing a profile of Reagan that emphasized the harsh social effects of his domestic policy. The White House permitted lots of footage of the president, and in every image he smiled and appeared entirely at ease. When Darman next saw Stahl, he thanked her for her "commercial" on the president's behalf. Outraged, she said, "Didn't you hear the things we said about him?" Darman replied, "Oh yes, but nobody paid any attention to what you said. Those shots of Reagan were absolutely priceless."[11]

Even Reagan's famous confrontations with ABC White House correspondent Sam Donaldson were, to some extent, staged to place Reagan in the most favorable light. In his memoirs, Donaldson complains that he received hundreds of letters from indignant viewers who berated him for being rude and shouting questions at Reagan. The general sentiment of the letters was, "Lay off the president. Give the man a break." Yet Donaldson points out that he had no alternative but to raise his voice because the White House would not let him or anyone else in the press get close to the president.[12] Reagan and his handlers wanted the American people to see the image of a president being harassed by the media. Donaldson never understood the degree to which he was playing a part in Reagan's script. He kept trying to expose Reagan, and ended up exposing himself. Yet he couldn't stop; he was like the toy soldier who walks into a wall and keeps going. Eventually his journalistic aggression took on a comic aspect. Reagan immensely enjoyed these exchanges, because he knew who came out the winner every time.

Looking back on the Reagan presidency, Donaldson admitted to me that he has been forced to reconsider the merits of the man. "We thought he was a lightweight, and maybe he didn't know everything, but he was a tenacious fellow who knew what he wanted. He reminds me of the Gila monster: when it grabs you, you can't get away. He came to Washington to change the world for the better, and for the most part, he did. I didn't think I would say this, but I miss him. There is no one like him on the scene today."

If the press didn't understand Reagan very well and condescended to a man who was actually their better, the president's aides had the same problem. Reagan's aides generally fell into two camps: the conservative true believers and the moderate pragmatists. True believers were the ones who wore Adam Smith ties and showed up for conferences at the Heritage Foundation. This group included Attorney General Ed Meese, CIA director William Casey, national security adviser William Clark, Defense Secretary Caspar Weinberger, United Nations ambassador

Jeane Kirkpatrick, budget director Jim Miller, and Interior Secretary James Watt. The true believers shared Reagan's philosophy and trusted his political instincts. Their motto was: "Let Reagan be Reagan."

The pragmatists came from the moderate wing of the Republican party. They were "inhabitants of the more temperate zones," as one of their number, White House aide Richard Darman, put it. This camp included chief of staff James Baker, deputy chief of staff Michael Deaver, communications director David Gergen, Secretary of State George Shultz, Labor Secretary William Brock, and Education Secretary Terrel Bell. The pragmatists liked Reagan as a man and admired his rapport with the American people, but they viewed him as far too dogmatic, and sometimes inclined to be his own worst enemy, so they tried to moderate his agenda, and coaxed him to follow a script rather than say what was really on his mind. Their motto, in effect, was "Save Reagan from Reagan."

For eight years, true believers and their allies in the think tanks and the conservative press tried to get Reagan to fire the pragmatists. Political strategist Clifton White once said to the president, "You can't win a revolution with mercenaries." Edwin Feulner, president of the Heritage Foundation, told me he regularly reminded Reagan of the axiom, "People are policy," and urged him to take measures to ensure that the administration was filled with true believers from the conservative ranks. True believer William Casey urged Reagan to get rid of pragmatist George Shultz and replace him with the more hawkish Jeane Kirkpatrick. But Reagan never listened to this advice, even when it came from people whom he knew for a long time and trusted to reflect his own philosophy.

In fact, Reagan didn't seem to mind having people on his team who did not share his views. Richard Perle, an assistant secretary of defense and a true believer, once told the president at a dinner that a majority of people in the department did not agree with Reagan and were actively working to undermine his policies for dealing with the Soviet Union. Recalling the incident, Perle told me, "I thought he would be shocked. But instead he laughed and asked me to keep up the fight, and not to let them wear me down." Mystified at his tolerance for the pragmatists, many true believers concluded that Reagan was a well-meaning but ineffective chief executive who was unable to keep control of the government.

Reagan did not share this pessimism. He had an inclusive style that he was confident would enable him to reach his goals. A weak-minded man or an inflexible ideologue would have surrounded himself exclusively with like-minded people. Reagan, by contrast, valued multiple channels of information. During the first term, the Reagan White House was run by the triumvirate of James Baker, Ed Meese, and Michael Deaver. These were very different men with competing agendas in some cases, but Reagan appreciated having diverse sources and a wide range of options before him. "He really believed in the free market of ideas," David Gergen told me. Reagan also understood that he needed both pragmatists and true believers to unify the two wings of the Republican party. During his second term, he had no hesitation in appointing as his chief of staff Howard Baker, who had fought him on the Panama Canal issue and opposed him when he ran for president.

His heart was with the true believers, but he also knew their limitations. Some of them, like Weinberger, Casey, and Jim Miller, were highly competent. Others, like James Watt and John Poindexter, were Manichean in their worldview and lacked the virtue of prudence. "I never use the words *Republicans* and *Democrats*," Watt liked to say. "It's liberals and Americans." Poindexter took great pride in the fact that he didn't read either the *New York Times* or the *Washington Post*, thus ensuring his ignorance of the political ramifications of his foreign policy ventures.[13] These stances would no doubt have amused Reagan, but he knew that the true believers could become so blinded by ideology that they were more likely to step on a land mine and blow themselves up than to reach their political destination. Some of them preferred to go up in flames rather than compromise and live to fight another day. This is precisely what happened in a number of cases. Reagan did not share these suicidal tendencies.

The pragmatists in the Reagan administration had their own problems. Their attitude may be conveyed by a story that Reagan himself liked to tell about an accident on the street, with the victim lying there and bystanders all around. An elderly fellow was bending over the victim, trying to help, but another man elbowed his way through the bystanders, shoved the old guy aside, and said, "Let me at him. I have first aid training." The elderly fellow obliged, and the man began carrying out the steps he had learned in first aid class. At one point the old guy tapped him on the shoulder and said, "When you get to the part about calling the doctor, I'm right here."

Like the man in the story, the pragmatists were a self-satisfied lot; many did not recognize either Reagan's remarkable ability or their own limitations. The problem with pragmatism as a philosophy, G. K. Chesterton once said, is that it doesn't work. The reason is that pragmatism supplies only the means, not the destination. The pragmatists in the Reagan administration knew how to get there but had no real idea of where to go. Their skills were operational: they understood the administrative machinery of government; they knew how to build congressional support; they were skilled at handling the media. By themselves, these things count for little, as the pragmatists discovered after the Reagan era, when they tried to stand on their own. Nevertheless, Reagan realized that if he supplied the ideological rudder and gave the pragmatists a set of goals and broad direction, they would be effective in helping him to achieve his agenda.

Yet the presence of the rival factions was a formula for continual infighting. The true believers regarded the pragmatists as the enemy within, and the pragmatists viewed the true believers as dangerous loonies. Each side conspired to reduce the influence of the other. Reagan was aware of the division in his administration—he once joked that "my right hand does not always know what my far-right hand is doing"—but he didn't seem to care about the internecine hostilities. Frequently true believers in the administration were ousted in power struggles with pragmatists, who were more adept at this sort of hand-to-hand combat. Yet conservatives who viewed their tribulations as the result of fighting for the president's agenda soon found out that it was useless to appeal these matters to Reagan himself. He seemed quite willing to accept that his revolution would involve political casualties and was not interested in helping the wounded. If someone lost his job, that was it; he was off the stage; Reagan never contacted him again. Reagan kept his eye on the big picture, seeking to realize his major objectives.

Aides were flummoxed and sometimes frustrated by Reagan's elusive governing technique. Donald Regan, Frank Carlucci, Robert McFarlane, and others complained that Reagan did not give them specific directions, and, confronted with elaborate blueprints for future action, he sometimes responded with a vague "let's go ahead," a noncommittal "uh-huh," or Sphinx-like silence. Alexander Haig, who served briefly as secretary of state, confessed that to him the Reagan White House was "as mysterious as a ghost ship—you heard the creak of the rigging and groan of the timbers and sometimes even glimpsed the crew on deck. But which of the crew had the helm? It was impossible to know for sure."[14]

The reason for Haig's confusion was his assumption that someone other than Reagan must be piloting the ship. His condescending view of Reagan was complemented by Haig's high regard for his own ability. He wanted to be the vicar of foreign policy, forgetting that this is the president's domain. Though he considered himself irreplaceable to the Reagan administration, he soon found out how replaceable he was. Yet Haig was not entirely to blame for his bewilderment. Reagan was a visionary whose gaze was so firmly fixed on the future that he moved in a way that was incomprehensible to those who did not share his vision. Like a quarterback putting into motion a critical play, Reagan concentrated on the long pass; all that Haig and many others could see was the apparent chaos of players running in different directions.

Reagan refused to get bogged down in the day-to-day running of the government. He understood that the federal government is such a gargantuan enterprise that if you immerse yourself in its minutiae, you will soon be buried in it. This is not to say that Reagan was never detail oriented. On issues Reagan cared about, such as arms control and tax policy, he insisted on personally reviewing the fine print. Yet on most issues Reagan formulated a broad agenda and relied on competent subordinates to carry it out. He summarized his management philosophy in an interview with *Fortune:* "You surround yourself with the best people you can find, delegate authority, and don't interfere."[15]

I attended meetings at the White House in which Reagan permitted his senior advisers to argue for various courses of action. During these discussions he rarely said much. He seemed to understand that when the president reveals what he is thinking, everyone in the room is likely to modify his stance to accommodate the chief executive. Reagan apparently wanted to encourage his advisers to debate policy options vigorously and candidly without feeling intimidated. Then he would step in at the end, summarize the issue as he saw it, and decide on a course of action. Having permitted all to be heard, he now expected them to support his final decision, even if they disagreed with it. I remember thinking at the time, and I still do, that this was a very intelligent way to lead a discussion.

Those who attended Reagan's staff meetings will testify that the president had no problem making decisions and made all the major ones himself. Critics who credit the Reagan administration's policies to the generic influences of his aides do not seem to realize that his aides were perennially quarreling with each other over what should be done. James Baker in his memoirs complains of a "witches' brew of intrigue . . . and separate agendas."[16]

Baker and Stockman wanted tax increases to reduce the deficit; Regan and Meese were opposed. Weinberger sought to boost defense spending; Stockman wanted to put a leash on the military. Casey and Weinberger were determined to overthrow the Sandinistas, Baker and Shultz favored a negotiated settlement between the Nicaraguan government and the contras. Shultz, who proposed that the United States trade the SDI for deep cuts in the Soviet offensive arsenal, was opposed by Weinberger, who preferred to deploy missile defenses even if this meant no arms reduction treaty. Both Shultz and Weinberger opposed the idea of trading arms for Iranian hostages, whereas McFarlane and Casey supported the idea. In each case, according to the testimony of those involved, it was Reagan who made the final decision. Sometimes, as when he proposed the complete elimination of nuclear weapons, Reagan stood alone against everyone else. On that issue, U.S. arms control negotiator Max Kampelman writes, "I do not know of a single adviser to the President who agreed with him."[17]

On smaller matters, however, Reagan let his aides operate with a great deal of discretion. As Peggy Noonan puts it, when Reagan himself did not act, "the idea of Reagan ruled." Reagan's public philosophy, elaborated over two decades, was so well known that any competent person could say with a high degree of accuracy how the president would respond to a particular initiative. Ed Meese notes that Don

Regan himself seems to have figured this out. "Don says that Reagan never told him what to do," Meese told me, "but as secretary of the treasury Don ended up doing exactly what Reagan wanted him to do." What Reagan seems to have discovered is that when you give subordinates full responsibility for the results they produce, they demonstrate far greater motivation and creativity than when they are merely carrying out instructions.

Yet, on some issues, Reagan's administrative style did not work well. For example, although his criticism of race and gender preferences was well known, when Attorney General Edwin Meese sought to restrict the administration's affirmative action programs Labor Secretary William Brock strongly opposed him. Reagan never arbitrated the dispute, leaving an unresolved polarization in the ranks of the administration that persisted for several years. Many smaller but by no means unimportant matters languished in this manner. Delegation works well when there are good people to assume the responsibility and no conflicts of jurisdiction among subordinates. On issues that were not central to his vision, Reagan was a good motivator but a poor administrator.

When he did make decisions, however, Reagan showed shrewd insight in the way he approved one man's recommended course of action without making the other man feel like a loser. Brock, who was overruled several times in this manner, comments that Reagan was so gracious in deciding against him that Brock never felt a sense of personal rejection or humiliation. Yet at times Reagan's psychological techniques were too subtle for even his brightest subordinates to comprehend. Elliott Abrams, an assistant secretary at the State Department, told me that during Reagan's second term, he and George Shultz repeatedly urged the president to consider military action to capture the Panamanian dictator Manuel Noriega and bring him to the United States to face drug trafficking charges. Caspar Weinberger was strongly opposed to such an operation. Every few days Abrams would ask, "Has the president decided?" and would discover that there was no answer from the White House. Finally in exasperation Abrams erupted to Shultz, "Why doesn't Reagan decide? The man is being paid two hundred thousand dollars to make decisions." Shultz replied, "Boy, are you naive! The President *has* decided. He has decided to go with Weinberger. But I went out on a limb on this one, and he wants to decide in such a way as to cause me the least amount of embarrassment."

Shultz is one of the few pragmatists who ended up with a keen appreciation for Reagan's vision and leadership, yet virtually all of his senior aides found themselves emotionally unsatisfied by their personal dealing with the president. Despite his easygoing affability, he never established a close relationship with any of them. Caspar Weinberger once remarked that however hard he worked for the president, Reagan never showed that he was personally touched. "Gratitude does not come easily to him."[18] Reagan seems to have assumed that, like him, his aides were doing this to honor a higher commitment, and that should be its own reward. He never said, "I couldn't have done it without you," because it wasn't true. Reagan's senior officials also saw that they were all dispensable, pawns of the president's global vision. Aides came and went, but Reagan maintained his steady course. Proud men find this treatment hard to take, and many who were strongly committed to Reagan's public philosophy ended up deeply disappointed in their relationship with the man. This personal bitterness is evident in a number of the memoirs of former Reagan staffers.

The conventional wisdom is that the Iran-contra scandal revealed the breakdown of Reagan's management style, which is thought to have relied too heavily on delegation. In his book *Revolution,* Martin Anderson writes that the Iran-contra affair showed that when Reagan's management worked well the results were spectacular; when it failed, the results were also spectacular.[19] What this viewpoint misses is that in the first part of the scandal—the selling of arms to Iran in the hopes of securing the return of American hostages—Reagan was personally involved at every stage. The second part of the scandal—the deflection of money from the arms sales to the Nicaraguan contras—did not involve delegation at all. Reagan did not give John Poindexter and Oliver North the authority to deflect money from the Iranian arms sale to the Nicaraguan contras. Independent counsel Lawrence Walsh has acknowledged that after years of inquiry, he found no proof that Reagan directed or even knew about the transfer of funds.[20]

From what we know of his politics, Reagan would have loved the outcome. But from what we know of his character, he is not likely to have approved the means. Probably Reagan's aides took his general plea, "I want you to do what you can to keep the contras together," as a carte blanche to use virtually any means necessary to achieve that end. Undoubtedly the people involved thought they had devised a scheme of Machiavellian ingenuity. In its attempt to circumvent the normal channels of democratic accountability, the Iran-contra operation was a Nixonian caper, even in the way it backfired in the end.

Unlike Watergate, the Iran-contra scandal may become a historical footnote that future generations will not even remember. By the time the various congressional investigations had been concluded, the American public had already lost interest in the affair. When the scandal broke in late 1986, however, it had a devastating impact. Reagan's approval ratings dropped precipitously from nearly 70 percent to around 35 percent, the sharpest drop ever recorded in a matter of weeks. The skepticism of the American people was entirely justified: here was a president doing business with a regime he himself called "Murder Inc."

Even this mistake would not be catastrophic if committed by an ordinary politician. Reagan, however, was a leader of conviction; this was an important source of his power. And in this case, his actions were entirely at odds with the public's image of him. One observer noted that for the American people, learning that Reagan had traded arms for hostages was "like suddenly discovering that John Wayne had secretly been selling liquor and firearms to the Indians."

Reagan made a grave error of judgment in carrying on a covert policy that directly contradicted his public policy. His secret arms deal with Iran was the most serious blunder of his presidency. Yet unlike Nixon, Reagan didn't violate the public trust in the pursuit of personal power. He did it because he empathized with the suffering of the hostages and their families. Consequently he refused to listen to Shultz and Weinberger's prudent recommendations that he avoid the foolish enterprise altogether. Reagan was willing to try virtually anything to secure the hostages' release. His empathy made him gullible.

When the Iran policy turned into a debacle, Reagan was badly shaken. He was a visceral politician who had trusted his instincts in approving this high-risk operation. As it turned out, his inner compass, which had proved so reliable in the past, failed him this time. He was unsure whether he could rely on it again. Without his source of strength, Reagan suddenly seemed befuddled and vulnerable, like Samson without his locks.

He tried to maintain his usual good cheer in the face of calamity. At the White House Gridiron dinner in 1987, Reagan joked, "Do you remember the flap when I said the bombing would begin in five minutes? Remember when I fell asleep during my audience with the pope? Remember Bitburg? Boy, those were the good old days." On another occasion Reagan permitted himself more grim humor when a member of his staff asked him, "How are you going to go about rebuilding the Reagan presidency when this is all over?" Reagan replied, "Who the hell wants to rebuild when I'm quitting in two years anyway?"[21] Yet for all this bravado, aides testify that privately Reagan was deeply distraught that many Americans did not believe he was telling the truth. The scandal also paralyzed the administration for months and even raised the prospect of an ignoble end to Reagan's presidency.

Reagan's critics were gleeful. "Ha, ha, ha . . . it turns out that you can't fool all the people all of the time," columnist Michael Kinsley exulted.[22] Benjamin Bradlee, executive editor of the *Washington Post,* was convinced that Reagan was close to impeachment and proclaimed that he was having the most fun he'd had since Watergate. Reagan's supporters feared the worst. Conservative columnist Fred Barnes even observed that the public revelation of the transfer of funds to the contras represented the "de facto end of the Reagan presidency."[23]

Once again the pundits of left and right proved to be mistaken. Reagan survived. The Iran-contra scandal was the one chance his enemies had to destroy his presidency, and they tried. But Reagan once again showed himself to be a political Houdini. To everyone's amazement, he wriggled out of his shackles and escaped. Not only that, but his greatest foreign policy achievements came after the Iran-contra scandal. With the signing of the Intermediate Range Nuclear Forces (INF) Treaty with Gorbachev in 1987, Reagan won back his earlier renown and finished his second term more popular than ever.

How did he manage this feat? Partly it was his infectious good nature. However seriously Americans felt he had erred, they retained their fondness for Reagan the man. Moreover, most Americans didn't want to see another president fail. They appreciated what Reagan had done to restore America's self-confidence. As long as there was no evidence that Reagan deliberately lied about his participation in the transfer of funds to the contras, the country seemed willing to forgive the administration's blunder and move on.

The reason Reagan received the benefit of the doubt was that, over the previous decade, he had established a powerful bond of trust, affection, and intimacy with the American people. His TV addresses from the Oval Office echoed, for those old enough to remember, Franklin Roosevelt's fireside chats, in which FDR gave Americans the impression that he was speaking to them personally, confiding his views and seeking their reaction. Like Roosevelt, Reagan had the ability to reach a wide range of people in different spheres of life. "He did not sound like a politician," author Richard Reeves observed, "which made him a great politician."[24]

Reagan's speeches are not heroic, like those of Lincoln, or grandiose, like those of Kennedy. Although several of his addresses are justly famous, he did not utter many unforgettable lines. His style was conversational, not oratorical. In his autobiography, *An American Life*, Reagan says that in preparing for a speech, he would picture a group of people, the kind of regular folk he grew up with, gathered in a bar or barbershop, and he would speak directly to them.[25] His trademark as a speaker was the pause, the slow smile, the slight tilt of the head. He often began a sentence with the word *well* as in, "Well, I just don't believe . . ." He prepared his remarks for people to listen to them, not to read them in print. He used the classic techniques of rhythm, repetition, and alliteration to set his words to music.

His speeches are notable for their simplicity and clarity. He loved the telling statistic, but mostly his rhetoric focused on simple concepts and striking images. Frequently he drew on themes from the movies and popular culture, as when he challenged Congress to raise taxes, in the words of Clint Eastwood: "Go ahead—make my day." He emphasized a clear statement of basic principle and eschewed abstruse and technical argument. His rhetoric was aimed at the heart rather than the head. As one of his former aides put it, he didn't want people to react to a speech by saying, "That's an interesting idea." He wanted them to say, "Damn right!"

His speechwriters said that it was easy to draft remarks for him because his public philosophy was so consistent. Reagan had wonderfully talented writers, yet his speeches bear his own unmistakable imprint. Pat Buchanan was his White House communications director, but Reagan's rhetoric shows none of Buchanan's truculence. The president didn't give Buchanan-speeches; he gave Reagan-speeches. One of the president's writers, Peter Robinson, told me his research for a forthcoming speech on defense or tax cuts often involved reviewing Reagan's public statements on the issue going back to the 1970s. "He didn't steal from us," Robinson said. "We stole from him." Speechwriter Mari Maseng calls Reagan "the best editor I ever had." She was struck by the president's ability to inject a personal touch into otherwise formal prose and to communicate complex ideas in a straightforward way.[26]

Even as president, Reagan sometimes penned his own speeches. White House communications director David Gergen remembers that he drafted his first inaugural address on an airplane from Washington, D.C. to California "and when we examined his note pad afterward, we found that he had written it straightaway, crossing out only a handful of words."[27] When Reagan delivered the speech in his inimitable style, it inspired continuous outbreaks of applause and a thunderous ovation at the end.

He also wrote many of his own best lines. The speechwriter's draft of the "Star Wars" speech said, "I call upon the nation—our men and women in uniform, our scientists and engineers, our entrepreneurs and industrial leaders, and all our citizens—to join with me in taking a bold new step forward in defense to ensure a more peaceful and stable world of the future." Reagan eliminated the bombast, focused his appeal to the scientific and technological community, and eloquently described his vision for a nuclear-free world: "I call upon the scientific community in our country, those who gave us nuclear weapons, to turn their great talents now to the cause of mankind and world peace, to give us the means of rendering these nuclear weapons impotent and obsolete."

Speechwriter Anthony Dolan's draft of the "evil empire" speech said, "Surely, those historians will find in the councils of the Marxist-

Leninists, who preached the supremacy of the state, who declared its omnipotence over individual man, who predicted its eventual domination of all peoples of the earth—surely historians will see there the focus of evil in the modern world." Reagan removed the academic reference to historians, changed the past to the present tense, and clarified the moral context of the argument. In the final version, Reagan expressed the hope to his evangelical audience that the Soviet communists would abandon their ideology and "discover the joy of knowing God. But until they do, let us be aware that while they preach the supremacy of the state, declare its omnipotence over individual men, predict its eventual domination of all peoples of the earth, they are the focus of evil in the modern world."[28]

The press called him the Great Communicator, but Reagan saw himself as a communicator of great American ideals. The pundits believed he had a charmed way of saying things, but how effective would his speeches be if he were promoting yoga or Zen Buddhism? Undoubtedly the power of his rhetoric derived from both how he expressed himself and the content of his message. His critics and even some of his aides regarded his rhetoric as a symbolic device for manipulating constituencies, thus revealing a contempt for the intelligence of the American people, who were seen as easily duped or misled by Reagan's appeal to their passions and prejudices.

Reagan, however, worked hard on his speeches because he knew that a democratic leader must also be a teacher. He regarded his didactic role as one of the most important functions of a president. He had a deeper instinctive understanding of American ideals and aspirations than most people who had studied the Constitution and *The Federalist* over a lifetime. Reagan offered citizens a noble vision of a free and great country that would give meaning to their lives and allow them to realize their dreams. Ultimately he sought not just to change the laws but also to change the hearts and minds of his countrymen.

The central theme of Reagan's rhetoric was patriotism. He portrayed a vision of America as a city on a hill, a beacon to the nations of the world. "In my mind," he said, "it was a tall proud city built on rocks stronger than oceans, wind-swept, God-blessed, and teeming with people of all kinds living in harmony and peace, a city with free ports that hummed with commerce and creativity, and if there had to be city walls, the walls had doors and the doors were open to anyone with the will and the heart to get there."[29] As these images suggest, Reagan's conception of America was inclusive. He saw the United States as a land of immigrants, where one's origins matter less than one's destination. He sought to export the American ideal to other countries in the firm conviction that it reflected global aspirations. His "American exceptionalism" was inextricably united with American universalism.

Many intellectuals take a sardonic view of such rhetoric, so it is worth asking what in Reagan's view made America such a great country. Unlike many of his critics on the left, Reagan never despised the materialistic accomplishments of a free society. He did not mind when Senator Howard Baker defended his policies in purely bourgeois terms: "People can buy cars and houses and take vacations again." Like Tocqueville, Reagan seemed to accept that self-interest is a necessary foundation for liberal democratic regimes.

Yet unlike many traditional conservatives, Reagan saw no necessary conflict between self-interest and civic virtue. He believed that people get the greatest satisfaction by doing good for their families and communities. Reagan was confident that if Americans were given greater political and economic freedom, they would use it productively and decently. Freedom, in Reagan's view, promotes not just the good life but also the life that is good. He insisted that when we place confidence in people, we bring out the best in them. Thus, Reagan's optimism provided a link between his belief in freedom and his belief in virtue.

At the same time, he considered it the responsibility of political leaders to use example and encouragement to instruct citizens in the highest uses of liberty. Reagan believed that freedom creates the conditions for heroism and urged Americans to use their freedom to perform noble deeds for their communities and their country. This was the significance of the "hero in the balcony" that he frequently recognized in his speeches. Reagan invented that tradition.

Reagan's heroes were men like Lenny Skutnik, who threw himself into the Potomac River to rescue the drowning survivors of an airline crash, and Martin Treptow, who was killed in action in World War I after fighting "as if the whole struggle depended on me alone." Reagan delivered perhaps his most moving paean to heroism in June 1984 when he addressed sixty-two Rangers on a windswept beach in Normandy on the fortieth anniversary of their death-defying landing: "These are the boys of Point du Hoc. These are the men who took the cliffs." Lou Cannon reports that tough and jaded men wept when they heard Reagan's words—not just the Rangers themselves, but also Secret Service agents and American journalists.[30]

The people Reagan held up as role models weren't Horatio Alger figures—men who started with nothing and became business tycoons. Reagan admired entrepreneurs and scientists, whom he saw as explorers crossing new frontiers of knowledge in order to expand human possibilities. But his real heroes were common folk who performed uncommon feats of self-denial and courage. Mostly he admired soldiers, firefighters, and police who place their lives in danger to preserve freedom and allow Americans to sleep safely at night. No one can reasonably argue that it is in a person's self-interest to do this. Moreover Reagan believed that human worth is tested, and greatness emerges, from the crucible of conflict.

The Republican party consistently won national elections during the 1980s because Reagan defined it as the party of liberty as well as virtue. While the GOP had previously been the party of business, Reagan helped to make it the party of taxpayers and religious believers, with its base in the South and West. His tough stance in foreign policy and his advocacy of traditional values won the support of many blue-collar ethnics, the so-called Reagan Democrats. "He was FDR's true successor," political analyst William Schneider told me. "He destroyed the New Deal coalition and laid the groundwork for the Republicans to become the majority party for the first time in half a century."

Yet Reagan differed from FDR in at least one crucial respect. Roosevelt believed that in order to produce a lasting shift in people's allegiances, you have to demonize your opposition. Roosevelt blamed the "Hoover Republicans" for the depression and took credit for getting the country out of it. FDR portrayed his opponents as "monopolists" and "war profiteers," motivated by greed and selfishness. He called them "economic royalists" and "Tories," implying that they were un-American. In his 1936 address in Madison Square Garden, Roosevelt said of his critics, "They are unanimous in their hatred of me—and I welcome their hatred."[31]

Reagan would never say that. His view was that the Democrats are well meaning but mistaken. Reagan appealed to a shared American identity that transcended partisan politics. Consequently he gave people a good reason to vote for him but did not give them a good reason to switch parties. Reagan's 1980 election helped the Republicans win the Senate, but his huge landslide in 1984 did little to advance the GOP in Congress. Two years later, the Senate fell to the Democrats. By the time Reagan left office, the Republicans had closed the gap with Democrats in party self-identification, but the Democrats were still in the majority.[32]

What Reagan did achieve was an ideological realignment. He shifted the political center by changing the terms of the debate. He made "liberal" a term of embarrassment, so that in 1988 the Democratic presidential candidate, Michael Dukakis, fled from the "L-word." The true test of a political revolutionary is the effect that he has on the other party. Reagan forced liberalism as an ideology and the Democrats as a political party to transform themselves in order to survive. Thus Reagan ensured that the effects of his revolution would endure for the long term, because even his opponents adopted his rhetoric and swore their fidelity to his main objectives. Of all his victories, this triumph may have been the one that Reagan found the sweetest.

———

Shortly before he left office in January 1989, Reagan met with a group of us at a reception in the White House. "We have had a revolution," he said, "and the revolution has been a success." He listed the data showing how much the country and the rest of the world had changed for the better in the preceding eight years and ended on a characteristically light note: "All in all, I must say, not bad for a fellow who couldn't get his facts straight and worked four hours a day." Then I heard him murmur, almost apologetically, "They tell me I have to go."

I reflected for a moment on that phrase, which conveyed the message that Reagan didn't want to say good-bye; he would rather spend more time with us, but his aides—the bad guys—were making him leave. Even in the little things, Reagan revealed his political genius. Then it occurred to me that this was the end. He was returning to California, and I would probably never see him again. A few days later, amid much fanfare, the Reagans boarded a plane and departed. But I like to think of him riding off into the sunset, a lone horseman silhouetted against an open sky.

Epilogue

———

The Road Not Taken

Since Reagan made his exit from the scene, American politics has been dominated by the search for his successor. Great leaders are a hard act to follow. George Washington was succeeded by a series of intellectually distinguished men—Madison, Adams, and Jefferson—who proved far less effective than he was as a national leader. Upon his death Abraham Lincoln was replaced by the mediocre Andrew Johnson and the even less impressive Ulysses S. Grant. Franklin Roosevelt found a more worthy successor in Harry Truman. Reagan has yet to find his true political heir. What we have witnessed, over the last decade, are the antics of a series of would-be Reagans: George Bush, Newt Gingrich, Pat Buchanan, and (surprisingly) Bill Clinton.

Bush was the anointed beneficiary of Reagan who, immediately after the 1988 election, seemed to forget the man to whom he owed his success. Even after working closely with Reagan for eight years, Bush seemed to have learned surprisingly little from him. After running a tough, ideological campaign against Michael Dukakis—one in which Bush placed himself in the Reagan mold by pledging, "Read my lips, no new taxes"—Bush entered the White House, distanced himself from Reagan's agenda, and began his own search for what he called "the vision thing." Americans eventually discovered that Bush's campaign rhetoric was an act, and that his real purpose in seeking the presidency, after serving in a series of high-level government jobs, was scarcely more than to complete his resume.

Bush's presidency was not a total failure. He deserves credit for presiding over the final collapse of the Soviet empire and for his success in the Gulf War, which was made possible by the Reagan military buildup. But when Bush agreed to raise taxes in flagrant violation of his pledge, his domestic policy lost all credibility. Ironically the man who pressed him to do it was a Reagan aide, Richard Darman, whose "responsible" counsel turned out to be a disaster. Unlike Reagan, who led Americans through the recession of 1982 with a forthright appeal to "stay the course," Bush seemed unable to cope with the much milder recession of 1991. His denial that the country was even in a recession convinced many Americans that, far from being another Reagan, Bush was out of touch with reality. His failure demonstrated the truth of the maxim that you can take the country-club Republican out of the golf course, but you cannot take the golf course out of the Republican.

Probably no one was more surprised at the results of the unusual three-way 1992 election than the ultimate winner, Bill Clinton. Despite his background as a draft-dodger and war resister, Clinton was elected because the cold war was over and foreign policy was no longer a dominant issue. Moreover, Americans were weary of Bush and believed Clinton's earnest promise to cut taxes for the middle class and govern from the center as a "new Democrat." Yet Clinton, like Bush, abandoned his campaign rhetoric after the election. He seems to have regarded his 1992 victory as evidence that the Reagan era was over.

Clinton's health care plan, devised in large part by his wife, Hillary, was an effort to restore the Great Society vision of government supervising the welfare of citizens, in this case by taking over one-seventh of the private economy. The prospect of another national entitlement, with a gargantuan bureaucracy to administer it, appalled most Americans, and the health care plan was soundly defeated. Then came the 1994 election, a stunning rebuke to Clinton. The Republican party seized control of both houses of Congress. If Clinton had been up for reelection that year he almost certainly would have been ousted.

Since 1994 Clinton appears to have realized that Reagan had permanently shifted the goalposts of American politics, creating new parameters within which others must now operate. Abandoning all hope of undoing the Reagan revolution, Clinton adroitly reconciled himself to it, conceding that "the era of Big Government is over." He adopted a centrist course more in line with his original promise to govern as a new kind of Democrat. While continuing to promote Lilliputian initiatives to restore the credibility of government (like preventing deadbeat dads from owning guns and promoting the use of school uniforms), Clinton frequently sounds Reaganite themes of economic growth, personal responsibility, and traditional family values.

Bill Clinton, of course, is no Ronald Reagan. His character flaws and naked pursuit of power and self-aggrandizement have led to numerous scandals—Whitewater, Travelgate, Paula Jones, the use of the Lincoln Bedroom for campaign fund-raising—which have demeaned the presidency and demonstrated Clinton's unworthiness to be the leader of a great country. Contemplating Clinton's well-known debaucheries, columnist P. J. O'Rourke remarked, "We nostalgically recall the days when sleeping with the president meant attending a cabinet meeting." Yet the electorate seems mostly indifferent to Clinton's indulgences because, under his watch, the peace and prosperity of the 1980s have so far continued. Self-indulgent to the end, Clinton and his advisers routinely sit around the White House discussing their place in history.

Applying Clare Boothe Luce's standard, what is the one line for which Clinton will be remembered? Since his health care initiative was a failure, it is hard to credit Clinton with a single achievement that is distinctively his own. Most likely he will be recalled by future generations as the reluctant custodian of the Reagan revolution, and the man who reconciled the Democratic party to the new political landscape created by Reagan.

Newt Gingrich came to power as Speaker of the House in 1994 in one of the most remarkable political convulsions in American history. Promising to complete the Reagan Revolution, the Republicans won an additional 52 seats in the House of Representatives, gaining control for the first time in four decades, and eight seats in the Senate, winning a majority there as well. The GOP also gained 11 governorships and won control of many state legislatures. Although 1994 was not a presidential year, the result was widely considered the sign of a profound political realignment, comparable to the elections of 1828, 1896, and 1932, which all signaled an enduring transfer of power from one majority party to another.

Many conservatives hailed Gingrich as Reagan's true heir. Indeed several right-wing pundits were convinced that as an intellectual who showed a detailed familiarity with the workings of government, Gingrich would prove a far more effective leader than Reagan, and would complete the tasks that Reagan left unfinished. Gingrich not only summoned the can-do optimism of Reagan, but he electrified the conservative ranks with his clarion calls for revolution and his self-description as an ideological revolutionary.

Gingrich's manifesto was the Contract With America, which was billed as a signed agreement with the American people, in contrast with the usual promises of politicians that are routinely broken. The premise of the Contract was that since Reagan had been successful in ending the cold war and cutting taxes, it was now up to the Gingrich team to finish the job by reducing the growth of domestic spending and balancing the budget. The Republicans did manage one major achievement: they pressured a reluctant Clinton to sign a comprehensive welfare reform bill that ended welfare as an entitlement and for the first time introduced time limits on benefits and work requirements for able-bodied recipients. Already the welfare rolls have dropped sharply in states across the country, a result in which the Republican leadership can take justifiable pride.

Despite this victory, after a series of showdowns with President Clinton, Gingrich's personal popularity plummeted, making him one of the most detested figures in American politics. One Republican policy proposal after another was defeated, and the GOP surge of 1994 seemed halted in its tracks. In 1996 the Republican candidate, Robert Dole, contested the presidency while never seriously threatening Clinton. If Bush had been a terrible candidate in 1992, Dole was even worse. In the wake of his ignominious defeat, the Republican party and the conservative intellectual movement are now aimless and frustrated.

The GOP leadership now seems utterly bereft of either the vision or the resolution to pursue any major new initiatives. Instead, the emasculated Republicans seem obsessed with preserving their fragile congressional majority by testing their ideas against public opinion surveys and focus groups. Meanwhile, bitter internecine warfare has broken out, and the plots and backbiting among the Republican leaders seem to become more Byzantine and murderous every day.

Conservative intellectuals and activists are no less divided, with tensions erupting between free market libertarians who want government to leave them alone and social conservatives who seek to use government to promote public morality and character formation. A nationalist wing, led by Pat Buchanan, blames America's problems on free trade and immigration. Conservatives like Richard John Neuhaus raise the question of whether the American regime is constitutionally and morally legitimate, and whether civil disobedience is called for on the part of religious conservatives. From the point of view of an outside observer, the right seems to be returning to the fever swamps from which it first arose.

What went wrong? Many Republicans seem to have concluded that, since their efforts to reduce the growth of Medicare and other spending programs proved unsuccessful, the American people have been manifestly corrupted by big government and are now willing to surrender their liberty in exchange for a secure dependency.

In that same vein, cultural conservatives like Robert Bork argue that the American people have been corrupted by liberal permissiveness and are, in his phrase, "slouching towards Gomorrah." Bork, who advocates both censorship and congressional restrictions on the courts, is joined by some religious conservatives who hold Reagan partly to blame for not doing more to reduce pornography, abortion, and illegitimacy.

Other conservatives argue against looking to government for answers. If the American people are now the problem, changing their minds and behavior is the only solution. What is needed, argues neoconservative Gertrude Himmelfarb, is a "remoralization" of America. William Bennett and others now promote cultural renewal through public moralizing and support for local initiatives like church programs to teach parental responsibility.

The new approach to politics on the right could not be further from that of Reagan and is meeting with spectacular defeat for precisely that reason. Reagan offered a unifying moral vision for America; today's leaders have given us no comparable ideal. At most, politicians like Pat Buchanan court the votes of the blue-collar Reagan Democrats by telling them what and whom they should oppose. But Buchanan's appeal has proven brittle and unattractive, and has failed to broaden the Republican base. Reagan's America was a generous and inclusive place, far different from Buchanan's narrower and more xenophobic vision.

Furthermore, while Reagan offered a few simply outlined proposals to reform the tax code and build up the nation's defenses, the Contract With America was a legalistic document containing a melange of initiatives—term limits for politicians, capital gains tax cuts, criminal sentencing reform and so on—with little or no connecting theme. Reagan's substantive emphasis was always on lowering taxes with a view to accelerating growth and limiting the spending capacity of the federal government. By contrast, the Contract With America emphasized the goal of balancing the budget and represented a return to the conservative strategy of "fiscal responsibility" that has proved a consistent political loser since the New Deal.

Unlike Reagan, who understood the importance of compromise, the Gingrich team refused to meet Clinton halfway and thus came across as rigid ideologues. With a precision as fastidious as it was inexplicable, they insisted that the federal budget should be balanced in seven years. When Clinton demurred the Republicans threatened to shut down the government, and did. Americans seem to have been stunned by Gingrich's inflexible obstinacy. His rhetoric of revolution, which had been effectively used for years by Reagan, sounded extremist and a bit frightening.

Reagan was always more concerned with results than with personal glory, whereas the Republican leadership has shown itself to be a battleground of gigantic egos. Moreover, Reagan would have heartily disapproved of the vacillation and back-pedaling that now characterizes the Republicans. Far from letting polls and focus groups set his agenda, Reagan was willing to endure short-term unpopularity in the firm confidence that his policies would be vindicated by the next election.

Most important, Reagan possessed the faith in ordinary people without which no democratic leader deserves to be in office. Unlike many Republican politicians and conservative intellectuals, Reagan did not condescend to the American people or regard them as foolish or depraved. Instead, he believed that with the right leadership Americans could always be trusted to seek the upward path, and he saw it as his role to provide that sort of leadership. Today's politicians, by contrast, refuse to lead and then blame the American people for going in the wrong direction.

Reagan believed in cultural reform—indeed he often spoke of the need for a spiritual renewal in America—but he would not have endorsed the right's effort to achieve this end by abjuring the use of state power. Congressman Steven Largent recently remarked that his most important public involvement was with his church. That's good news for Largent on Judgment Day, but is this why he was elected to serve in the Congress? Reagan understood that the way to change the culture is to change law and public policy.

Reagan's approach has been vindicated by recent reductions in crime rates and the welfare rolls, which are not the consequences of best-selling moral compendia like William Bennett's *Book of Virtues* but of new laws that discourage unproductive and harmful behavior. As Reagan himself might have put it: If you want to reduce crime, toughen the penalties so that crime doesn't pay. Likewise, if you want to strengthen the work ethic, stop paying people not to work.

Admittedly, judged against the standard that he set for himself, Reagan made limited progress on social issues like abortion, welfare, and affirmative action. By necessity, he had to focus on the Soviet threat and the economic crisis facing the country. He did, however, appoint more than half the federal judiciary that, during the 1990s, has scaled back race and gender preferences and permitted modest restrictions on abortion. Reagan's rhetoric also laid the groundwork for sweeping changes in public attitudes that led to welfare reform.

Reagan would certainly not have approved of the way in which many Republican politicians have fled from the social issues, fearing that they will scare away libertarians and women and splinter the majority coalition. Reagan believed that the conflict between the economic and social conservatives could best be settled by what he termed his "new federalism." He favored letting the moral issues be settled by communities governing themselves at the local level. If the people of Tupelo, Mississippi, want to outlaw obscene rap lyrics and keep *Penthouse* out of the school library, let them. And if you happen to live in Tupelo and don't like the new restrictions, move.

At the same time, Reagan would have been appalled at the schoolmarm tone in which the pundits of the right lecture the American people. Like Lincoln, Reagan saw the depth of human frailty but appealed to the better angels of our nature. He spoke of achievement rather than indolence, triumph instead of failure, goodness instead of depravity. Partly this was for moral reasons; he was a theological optimist who believed in salvation. But he was also a pragmatist: he knew that most people respond better to encouragement than to harsh criticism.

The single most important reason for the failure of the Republicans and conservative intellectuals is that both groups have lost their faith in the American people. In the 1980s Reagan converted the right, traditionally the party of pessimism, into an optimistic movement. So perhaps it is not surprising that once Reagan left, the GOP and the conservative leaders reverted to their old familiar ways. If the Republicans fail to learn Reagan's lesson, they will soon lose their congressional majority and once again become a minority party and a marginal political movement.

There is no point in pining for "another Ronald Reagan." Great leaders don't come along very often, and in many ways Reagan was an American original. He isn't returning and there will never be another quite like him. But the truth is, we don't need another Reagan. Rather, we simply need to ask in every situation that arises, What would Reagan have done? As a national and world leader, Reagan succeeded where countless self-styled wise men have failed because he had a vision for America, he was not afraid to act, and he believed in the good sense and decency of the American people. In a democratic society, the extraordinary success of this in many ways quite ordinary man gives us the best reason for hope.

Notes

Prologue

1. John Burns, "Graham Offers Positive View of Religion in Soviet," *New York Times,* May 13, 1982.

2. Seweryn Bialer and Joan Afferica, "Reagan and Russia," *Foreign Affairs* (Winter 1982–1983): 263.

3. Cited by Peter Schweizer, *Victory* (New York: Atlantic Monthly Press, 1994), p. xiv.

4. John Kenneth Galbraith, "A Visit to Russia," *New Yorker,* September 3, 1984.

5. Paul Samuelson and William Nordhaus, *Economics* (New York: McGraw-Hill, 1985), pp. 775–776.

6. James Reston, "The New Hatchet Man," *New York Times,* June 19, 1985, p. A23.

7. Cited by Arnold Beichman, "On Getting It All Wrong," *Freedom Review* (July–August 1992): 6.

8. Strobe Talbott, "Playing for the Future," *Time,* April 18, 1983; Strobe Talbott, "The Case Against Star Wars Weapons," *Time,* May 7, 1984.

9. Stephen Cohen, "Sovieticus," *Nation,* April 9, 1983.

10. Ibid.

11. Arthur Schlesinger, Jr., "Some Lessons from the Cold War," in Michael Hogan, ed., *The End of the Cold War: Its Meaning and Implications* (Cambridge: Cambridge University Press, 1992), p. 57.

12. Ronald Reagan, speech at the University of Notre Dame, May 17, 1981.

13. Ronald Reagan, speech to annual convention of the National Association of Evangelicals, Orlando, Florida, March 8, 1983.

14. Ronald Reagan, speech to the British Parliament, London, June 8, 1982.

15. Ronald Reagan, speech at the Brandenburg Gate, West Berlin, June 12, 1987.

Chapter 1: Why Reagan Gets No Respect

1. Edmund Morris, "Official Biographer Puzzled by Reagan," *Miller Center Report* 6 (Winter 1990): 3.

2. Donald Regan, *For the Record: From Wall Street to Washington* (San Diego: Harcourt Brace Jovanovich, 1988), p. 371.

3. Lou Cannon, *President Reagan: The Role of a Lifetime* (New York: Simon & Schuster, 1991), p. 229.

4. Ibid.

5. Maureen Reagan, *First Father, First Daughter: A Memoir* (Boston: Little, Brown, 1989), p. 402.

6. Nancy Reagan with William Novak, *My Turn: The Memoirs of Nancy Reagan* (New York: Random House, 1989), p. 106.

7. George Shultz, *Turmoil and Triumph: My Years as Secretary of State* (New York: Charles Scribner, 1993), p. 1134.

8. Richard Nixon, *Real Peace* (New York, 1983), pp. 14, 23.

9. Richard Nixon, statement at Ronald Reagan Library opening ceremony, Simi Valley, California, November 4, 1991.

10. Steven Roberts, "Reagan's Final Rating Is Best of Any President Since '40s," *New York Times,* January 18, 1989.

11. James Tobin, "Reaganomics in Retrospect," in B. B. Kymlicka and Jeane Matthews, eds., *The Reagan Revolution?* (Chicago: Dorsey Press, 1988), p. 93.

12. Arthur Schlesinger, Jr., "The Ultimate Approval Rating," *New York Times Magazine,* December 15, 1996.

13. In a poll of 719 historians and political scientists, Reagan ranked twenty-sixth among all U.S. presidents, below Jimmy Carter, George Bush, and Bill Clinton. Among the terms scholars used to describe Reagan were "a con man" and "a popular sleepy head." William Ridings, Jr., and Stuart McIver, *Rating the Presidents* (Secaucus, N.J.: Carol Publishing, 1997), pp. xi, 267. See also Robert Murray and Tim Blessing, *Greatness in the White House: Rating the Presidents from George Washington Through Ronald Reagan* (University Park: Pennsylvania State University Press, 1994), pp. 81–89.

14. Adam Meyerson, "Mr. Kaplan, Tear Down This Wall," *Policy Review* (Fall 1993): 4.

15. Haynes Johnson, *Sleepwalking Through History: America in the Reagan Years* (New York: W. W. Norton, 1991), p. 13.

16. Barbara Ehrenreich, *The Worst Years of Our Lives: Irreverent Notes from a Decade of Greed* (New York: HarperCollins, 1991).

17. "Man of the Decade," *Time,* January 1, 1990.

18. James Perry, "For the Democrats, Pam's Is the Place for the Elite to Meet," *Wall Street Journal*, October 8, 1981.

19. Michael Kinsley, *Curse of the Giant Muffins: And Other Washington Maladies* (New York: Summit Books, 1987), p. 89.

20. Robert Wright, "Legacy: What Legacy?" *New Republic*, January 9, 16, 1989, p. 6.

21. Frances FitzGerald, "How Reagan Failed," *Rolling Stone*, February 25, 1988, p. 47.

22. Nicholas Von Hoffman, "Contra Reaganum," *Harper's* (May 1982): 35.

23. Cited by Bob Schieffer and Gary Paul Gates, *The Acting President* (New York: E. P. Dutton, 1989), p. 175.

24. Mark Green and Gail MacColl, *Reagan's Reign of Error* (New York: Pantheon, 1987).

25. Peggy Noonan, *What I Saw at the Revolution: A Political Life in the Reagan Era* (New York: Random House, 1990), p. 160.

26. Carl Bernstein, "Reagan at Reel II," *New Republic*, February 4, 1985, p. 25.

27. Jane Mayer and Doyle McManus, *Landslide: The Unmaking of the President, 1984–1988* (Boston: Houghton Mifflin, 1988), p. 27.

28. Anthony Lewis, "There's No There There," *New York Times*, February 20, 1983.

29. Gail Sheehy, "Reality? Just Say No," *New Republic*, March 30, 1987, p. 18.

30. "How Reagan Stays Out of Touch," *Time*, December 8, 1986, p. 34.

31. Jimmy Carter, *Keeping Faith: Memoirs of a President* (New York: Bantam Books, 1982), pp. 577–578.

32. Lou Cannon, *Reagan* (New York: G. P. Putnam, 1982), p. 20.

33. Michael Mandelbaum and Strobe Talbott, *Reagan and Gorbachev* (New York: Vintage Books, 1987), p. 125; Michael Paul Rogin, *Ronald Reagan, the Movie, and Other Episodes in Political Demonology* (Berkeley: University of California Press, 1987).

34. Schieffer and Gates, *The Acting President*, p. 382.

35. Anthony Lewis, "Teflon in the Stars," *New York Times*, May 12, 1988.

36. Garry Wills, "What Happened?" *Time*, March 9, 1987, pp. 40–41.

37. James Nathan Miller, "Ronald Reagan and the Techniques of Deception," *Atlantic Monthly* (February 1984): 68.

38. Johnson, *Sleepwalking Through History*.

39. Sidney Blumenthal, *Our Long National Daydream: A Political Pageant of the Reagan Era* (New York: Harper & Row, 1988).

40. David Stockman, *The Triumph of Politics: How the Reagan Revolution Failed* (New York: Harper & Row, 1986), p. 354.

41. Michael Deaver with Mickey Herskowitz, *Behind the Scenes* (New York: William Morrow, 1987).

42. *New York Times*, November 16, 1986; see also Regan, *For the Record*.

43. Robert Bartley, *The Seven Fat Years: And How to Do It Again* (New York: Free Press, 1995); "The Real Reagan Record," special issue of *National Review*, August 31, 1992; "Ten Years That Shook the World," *Policy Review* (Summer 1987).

44. "The American Presidency Survey," Intercollegiate Studies Institute, Wilmington, Delaware, 1997.

45. "What Conservatives Think of Reagan," *Policy Review* (Winter 1984): 14–19.

46. Brian Lamb, interview with Edmund Morris, C-Span, July 1, 1996.

47. Robert Barro, "A Gentleman's B-minus for Bush on Economics," *Wall Street Journal,* September 30, 1992.

48. Ronald Reagan, Farewell Address to the Nation, January 11, 1989.

Chapter 2: The Education of an Actor

1. Cited by Jack Kemp, *An American Renaissance* (New York: Harper & Row, 1979), p. 97.

2. President Carter introduced these themes in his inaugural address of 1977 and returned to them during his nationally televised "malaise" address of July 15, 1979. Jimmy Carter, Address to the Nation on Energy and National Goals, July 15, 1979; see also Jimmy Carter, *Keeping Faith: Memoirs of a President* (New York: Bantam Books, 1982), p. 21.

3. Hedley Donovan, *Roosevelt to Reagan: A Reporter's Encounters with Nine Presidents* (New York: Harper & Row, 1985), p. 277.

4. Mark Hertsgaard, *On Bended Knee: The Press and the Reagan Presidency* (New York: Farrar, Straus & Giroux, 1988), pp. 99–100.

5. John Osborne, "Preferring Jimmy," *New Republic,* June 14, 1980.

6. Richard Reeves, "Why Reagan Won't Make It," *Esquire,* May 8, 1979.

7. *Nation,* November 1, 1980.

8. Robert Lekachman, *Greed Is Not Enough* (New York: Pantheon, 1982), p. 180.

9. Eric Schmertz, Natalie Datlof, and Alexej Ugrinsky, eds. *President Reagan and the World* (Westport, Conn.: Greenwood Press, 1997), p. 450.

10. Ronald Reagan, remarks during the dedication of the Ronald Reagan Presidential Library, Simi Valley, California, November 4, 1991.

11. Ronald Reagan and Richard Hubler, *Where's the Rest of Me?* (New York: Dell, 1965), p. 22.

12. Maureen Reagan, *First Father, First Daughter: A Memoir* (Boston: Little, Brown, 1989), pp. 18, 31.

13. Gail Sheehy, "Reality? Just Say No," *New Republic,* March 30, 1987, p. 17.

14. Haynes Johnson, *Sleepwalking Through History: America in the Reagan Years* (New York: Norton, 1991), p. 43.

15. Garry Wills, *Reagan's America: Innocents at Home* (New York: Penguin, 1988), p. 111.

16. Ronald Reagan, *An American Life* (New York: Simon & Schuster, 1990), pp. 21–22.

17. George Will, "How Reagan Changed America," *Newsweek,* January 9, 1989.

18. Jerry Griswold, "Young Reagan's Reading," *New York Times Book Review,* August 30, 1981.

19. Ronald Reagan, remarks at the annual National Prayer Breakfast, February 4, 1982.

20. Mark Shields, "President Reagan's Wide World of Sports," *Inside Sports,* March 31, 1981.

21. Ronald Reagan, commencement address, Eureka College, May 8, 1982; Ronald Reagan, remarks at Eureka College, February 6, 1984.

22. Reagan and Hubler, *Where's the Rest of Me?* p. 54.

23. Reagan, *An American Life,* pp. 76–81.

24. *Los Angeles Times,* October 6, 1966.

25. Cited by Edmund (Pat) Brown and Bill Brown, *Reagan: The Political Chameleon* (New York: Praeger, 1976), p. 67.

26. Ronald Reagan, remarks to the National Chamber Foundation, November 17, 1988.

27. Reagan, *An American Life,* p. 637.

28. Laurence Barrett, *Gambling with History: Ronald Reagan in the White House* (Garden City, N.Y.: Doubleday, 1983), p. 306.

29. Lou Cannon, *President Reagan: The Role of a Lifetime* (New York: Simon & Schuster, 1991), pp. 283–284.

30. Wills, *Reagan's America,* pp. 252–257.

31. Ibid, pp. 285–286.

32. Lou Cannon, *Reagan* (New York: G. P. Putnam's Sons, 1982), p. 63.

33. Ibid., p. 64.

34. Nancy Reagan with William Novak, *My Turn: The Memoirs of Nancy Reagan* (New York: Random House, 1989), p. 111.

35. Jane Mayer and Doyle McManus, *Landslide: The Unmaking of the President, 1984–1988* (Boston: Houghton Mifflin, 1988), p. 8.

36. Rowland Evans and Robert Novak, *The Reagan Revolution* (New York: Dutton, 1981), p. 26.

37. Ronald Reagan, Remarks to Ohio Veterans Organizations, October 4, 1982; Remarks to State Chairpersons of the White House Conference on Small Business, August 15, 1986; Remarks to the National Alliance of Business, September 14, 1987; Remarks to the Future Farmers of America, July 28, 1988.

38. Ronnie Dugger, *On Reagan: The Man and His Presidency* (New York: McGraw-Hill, 1983), p. 298.

39. Michael Deaver with Mickey Herskowitz, *Behind the Scenes* (New York: Morrow, 1987), p. 75.

Chapter 3: Mr. Reagan Goes to Washington

1. Ronald Reagan, national television address, October 27, 1964.

2. Ibid.

3. Richard Bergholz, "Reagan Adamant on Not Moving Toward Center," *Los Angeles Times,* September 30, 1979.

4. Ronald Reagan with Richard Hubler, *Where's the Rest of Me?* (New York: Dell, 1965), p. 160.

5. Nancy Reagan with William Novak, *My Turn: The Memoirs of Nancy Reagan* (New York: Random House, 1989), p. 129.

6. Franklin Roosevelt, "Second Annual Message," January 4, 1935, in *The State of the Union Messages of Presidents* (New York: Chelsea House and Robert Hector Publishers, 1966), vol. 3.

7. Ronald Reagan, *An American Life* (New York: Simon & Schuster, 1990), p. 316.

8. Edmund (Pat) Brown and Bill Brown, *Reagan: The Political Chameleon* (New York: Praeger, 1976), p. 11.

9. *Los Angeles Times,* June 17, 1966.

10. Reagan, *An American Life,* p. 150.

11. TRB, "Reagan for President?" *New Republic,* July 2, 1966.

12. Ronald Reagan, inaugural address as governor, January 3, 1967.

13. Michael Deaver with Mickey Herskowitz, *Behind the Scenes* (New York: William Morrow, 1987), p. 66.

14. William Pemberton, *Exit with Honor: The Life and Presidency of Ronald Reagan* (New York: M.E. Sharpe, 1997), p. 76.

15. Peter Hannaford, *The Reagans: A Political Portrait* (New York: Coward-McCann, 1983), p. 19.

16. Lou Cannon, *President Reagan: The Role of a Lifetime* (New York: Simon & Schuster, 1991), p. 156.

17. *Los Angeles Times,* January 7, 1970.

18. Cited by Helene von Damm, *Sincerely, Ronald Reagan* (New York: Berkley Books, 1980), p. 91.

19. Ibid., pp. 93–94.

20. Reagan with Novak, *My Turn,* pp. 140–141.

21. Ibid., p. 145.

22. Cannon, *President Reagan,* pp. 95–96.

23. See, e.g., William Rusher, *The Rise of the Right* (New York: William Morrow, 1984).

24. Whittaker Chambers, *Witness* (Washington, D.C.: Regnery Publishing, 1980 [first published in 1952]), p. 8.

25. Cited by Ronnie Dugger, *On Reagan: The Man and His Presidency* (New York: McGraw-Hill, 1983), p. 352.

26. Lyn Nofziger, *Nofziger* (Washington, D.C.: Regnery Gateway, 1992), p. 74.

27. Lou Cannon, *Reagan* (New York: Putnam's, 1982), pp. 213, 216, 219.

28. Dugger, *On Reagan,* p. 273.

29. Michael Reagan with Joe Hyams, *On the Outside Looking In* (New York: Zebra Books, 1988), p. 153.

30. Jude Wanniski, *The Way the World Works* (Morristown, N.J.: Polyconomics, 1989).

31. These themes are articulated in a speech that Reagan gave to Republican audiences as early as 1978. See Hannaford, *The Reagans,* pp. 179–180.

32. Jimmy Carter, *Keeping Faith: Memoirs of a President* (New York: Bantam, 1982), p. 542; Tip O'Neill with William Novak, *Man of the House: The Life and Political Memoirs of Tip O'Neill* (New York: Random House, 1987), p. 337.

33. Mark Green and Gail MacColl, *Reagan's Reign of Error* (New York: Pantheon Books, 1987), p. 83.

34. Peter Bourne, *Jimmy Carter: A Comprehensive Biography from Plains to Post-Presidency* (New York: Scribners, 1997), pp. 311, 393.

35. Cited by Gerald Gardner, *All the Presidents' Wits* (New York: William Morrow, 1986), p. 59.

Chapter 4: A Walk on the Supply Side

1. Michael Deaver with Mickey Herskowitz, *Behind the Scenes* (New York: William Morrow, 1987), pp. 98–99.

2. Robert Kaiser, "Epic Political Struggle Looms," *Washington Post,* February 8, 1981.

3. Cited by Bob Schieffer and Gary Paul Gates, *The Acting President* (New York: Dutton, 1989), pp. 95–96.

4. Ronnie Dugger, *On Reagan: The Man and His Presidency* (New York: McGraw-Hill, 1983), p. xiii.

5. Donella Meadows, Dennis Meadows, Jorgen Randers, and William Behrens, *The Limits to Growth* (New York: Universe Books, 1972).

6. Robert Reich, "Ideologies of Survival," *New Republic,* September 20–27, 1982, p. 32.

7. Deaver and Herskowitz, *Behind the Scenes,* p. 212.

8. Ronald Reagan, *An American Life* (New York: Simon & Schuster, 1990), p. 250.

9. U.S. Bureau of the Census, *Statistical Abstract of the United States* (Washington, D.C.: Government Printing Office, 1990), p. 45.

10. "Past Due! The Bill for Consumer Debt Arrives," *Business Week,* December 10, 1990, p. 204.

11. Benjamin Friedman, *Day of Reckoning: The Consequences of American Economic Policy Under Reagan and After* (New York: Random House, 1988), p. 24.

12. Paul Krugman, *The Age of Diminished Expectations: U.S. Economic Policy in the 1990s* (Cambridge: MIT Press, 1990), p. 23.

13. Haynes Johnson, *Sleepwalking Through History: America in the Reagan Years* (New York: Norton, 1991), p. 194.

14. Michael Schaller, *Reckoning with Reagan: America and Its President in the 1980s* (New York: Oxford University Press, 1992), p. 76.

15. "What Conservatives Think of Ronald Reagan," *Policy Review* (Winter 1984); 14.

16. William Niskanen, *Reaganomics: An Insider's Account of the Policies and People* (New York: Oxford University Press, 1988), p. 3.

17. Fred Smith, "Learning the Washington Game," in Robert Rector and Michael Sanera, eds., *Steering the Elephant: How Washington Works* (New York: Universe Books, 1987), p. 39.

18. Fred Barnes, "Nap Master Ronnie," *New Republic,* January 9–16, 1989, p. 17.

19. David Frum, *Dead Right* (New York: Basic Books, 1994).

20. David Stockman, *The Triumph of Politics: How the Reagan Revolution Failed* (New York: Harper & Row, 1986), pp. 8, 11.

21. William Greider, *The Education of David Stockman and Other Americans* (New York: Dutton, 1982).

22. Nancy Reagan with William Novak, *My Turn: The Memoirs of Nancy Reagan* (New York: Random House, 1989), p. 61.

23. Ronald Reagan, Inaugural Address, January 20, 1981.

24. For verification of this statistic, see Office of Management and Budget, *The Budget for Fiscal Year 1998,* Washington, D.C., 1997, Historical Table 3.1, pp. 44–46.

25. Bureau of the Census, *Statistical Abstract of the United States,* Washington, D.C., 1995, pp. 336, 356.

26. Lawrence Lindsey, "Was the Defense Build-Up A Good Investment?" Working Paper, American Enterprise Institute, Washington, D.C., 1997.

27. Stockman, *The Triumph of Politics,* pp. 7, 391, 394.

28. Suzy Platt, ed. *Respectfully Quoted* (Washington, D.C.: Congressional Research Service, Library of Congress, 1989), p. 337.

29. Cited by Kenneth Thompson, ed, *Leadership in the Reagan Presidency* (Lanham, Md.: University Press of America, 1993), 2:6.

30. Tip O'Neill with William Novak, *Man of the House: The Life and Political Memoirs of Speaker Tip O'Neill* (New York: Random House, 1987), pp. 343, 349.

31. Daniel Patrick Moynihan, *Came the Revolution: Argument in the Reagan Era* (New York: Harcourt Brace Jovanovich, 1988), pp. 19, 26.

32. Dugger, *On Reagan,* p. 218.

33. Robert Reich, "Ideologies of Survival," pp. 32–33.

34. Lou Cannon, *President Reagan: The Role of a Lifetime* (New York: Simon & Schuster, 1991), p. 130.

35. "Goodbye Balanced Budget," *Newsweek,* November 16, 1981, p. 32.

36. Walter Isaacson, "Yeas 238, Nays 195," *Time,* August 10, 1981.

37. Herbert Stein, *Presidential Economics: The Making of Economic Policy from Roosevelt to Clinton* (Washington, D.C.: AEI Press, 1994), p. 235.

38. Cannon, *President Reagan,* pp. 264–265.

39. Kevin Phillips, "Post-Conservative America," *New York Review of Books,* May 13, 1982.

40. "The Failing Presidency," *New York Times,* January 9, 1983.

41. Lester Thurow, "Reagan's Self-Deceit," *New York Review of Books,* October 7, 1982, p. 8.

42. Cannon, *President Reagan,* p. 266.

43. Sam Donaldson, *Hold On, Mr. President!* (New York: Random House, 1987), p. 121.

Chapter 5: They Don't Call It Reaganomics Anymore

1. Measured in 1987 dollars, the gross domestic product rose from $3,776 billion in 1980 to $4,838 billion in 1989. U.S. Bureau of the Census, *Statistical Abstract of the United States,* Washington, D.C., 1995, p. 451.

2. Bureau of the Census, *Money Income of Households, Families and Persons* (Washington, D.C.: Government Printing Office, 1990), p. 202.

3. Robert Bartley, *The Seven Fat Years: And How to Do It Again* (New York: Free Press, 1995); Edwin Rubenstein, *Right Data* (New York: National Review, 1994), p. 36.

4. Robert Dallek, *Ronald Reagan: The Politics of Symbolism* (Cambridge: Harvard University Press, 1984), p. 120.

5. A survey of forty-two leading economists produced a "consensus" that "Reagan's proposed tax cuts are excessive and would be likely to further fuel inflation." See Hedrick Smith, Adam Clymer, Leonard Silk, Robert Lindsey, and Richard Burt, *Reagan the Man, the President* (New York: Macmillan, 1980), p. 63. Similarly *Business Week* reported "widespread skepticism among economists and other opinion makers" who insisted that Reagan's economic program would "worsen inflation rather than cure it." *Business Week,* December 1, 1980.

6. Kevin Phillips, *The Politics of Rich and Poor* (New York: Random House, 1990), pp. xvi, xviii.

7. Robert Reich, "As the World Turns: U.S. Income Inequality Keeps on Rising," *New Republic,* May 1, 1989; Donald Barlett and James Steele, *America: What Went Wrong?* (Kansas City: Andrews and McMeel, 1992).

8. Sam Donaldson, *Hold On, Mr. President* (New York: Random House, 1987), p. 120.

9. U.S. Bureau of the Census, *Statistical Abstract of the United States,* Washington, D.C., 1995, p. 480.

10. Rubenstein, *Right Data,* p. 146.

11. U.S. Bureau of the Census, *Statistical Abstract of the United States,* Washington, D.C., 1995, pp. 481, 483.

12. U.S. Bureau of the Census, *Statistical Abstract of the United States,* Washington, D.C., 1995, p. 474.

13. Rubenstein, *Right Data,* p. 26.

14. Phillips, *The Politics of Rich and Poor,* p. 4.

15. John Adams, "If I Really Were a Rich Man," *Newsweek,* October 1, 1984, p. 14.

16. Larry Lindsey, *The Growth Experiment* (New York: Basic Books, 1990), p. 83; Richard McKenzie, *What Went Right in the 1980s* (San Francisco: Pacific Research Institute, 1994), pp. 276–277.

17. See, e.g., Daniel Patrick Moynihan, *Came the Revolution: Argument in the Reagan Era* (New York: Harcourt Brace Jovanovich, 1988), p. 25; Peter Levy, *Encyclopedia of the Reagan-Bush Years* (Westport, Conn.: Greenwood Press, 1996), p. 56.

18. Paul Craig Roberts, "What Everyone 'Knows' About Reaganomics," *Commentary* (February 1991).

19. "The Demographics of Giving," *American Enterprise* (September–October 1991): 101; McKenzie, *What Went Right in the 1980s*, pp. 59–60, 63.

20. Ronald Reagan, remarks to the National Catholic Education Association, Chicago, April 15, 1982.

21. Ronald Reagan, Inaugural Address, January 20, 1981.

22. Robert Reich, "As the World Turns," p. 23.

23. U.S. Bureau of the Census, *Statistical Abstract of the United States* (Washington, D.C.: Government Printing Office, 1995), p. 766.

24. See, e.g., Robert Reich, *The Next American Frontier* (New York: Times Books, 1983); Barry Bluestone and Bennett Harrison, *The Deindustrialization of America* (New York: Basic Books, 1982); Bennett Harrison and Barry Bluestone, *The Great U-Turn* (New York: Basic Books, 1988).

25. Ronald Reagan, remarks at a luncheon for Representative Connie Mack, Miami, June 29, 1988.

26. Ronald Reagan, radio address to the nation on international free trade, November 20, 1982.

27. Morton Kondracke, "Reagan's IQ," *New Republic*, May 24, 1982, p. 10.

28. Donald Regan, *For the Record* (San Diego: Harcourt Brace Jovanovich, 1988), pp. 207–208, 212–213.

29. Jeremy Greenwood, *The Third Industrial Revolution* (Washington, D.C.: AEI Press, 1997).

30. U.S. Bureau of the Census, *Statistical Abstract of the United States*, Washington, D.C., 1990, pp. 571, 759, 764.

31. George Gilder, *Recapturing the Spirit of Enterprise* (San Francisco: Institute for Contemporary Studies Press, 1992), p. 39.

32. "At the very least, government deficits of such unprecedented magnitude threaten to boost interest rates, reignite inflation, and hinder growth." *Time*, March 5, 1984.

33. Milton Friedman, "Why the Twin Deficits Are a Blessing," *Wall Street Journal*, December 14, 1988.

34. Moynihan, *Came the Revolution*, p. 154; Suzanne Garment, "Liberal Openers: Mr. Frank Comes to Washington," *Wall Street Journal*, February 27, 1981.

35. Budget of the United States Government, Historical Tables, Fiscal Year 1993, Table 1.3, p. 17.

Chapter 6: Confronting the Evil Empire

1. R. W. Apple, Jr., "Gorbachev Urges Major Changes In the World's System of Alliances," *New York Times*, June 5, 1990, pp. A1, A16.

2. Martin Malia, "The Yeltsin Revolution," *New Republic*, February 10, 1992.

3. Zbigniew Brzezinski, "The Cold War and Its Aftermath," *Foreign Affairs* (Fall 1992): 34.

4. George Kennan, "The GOP Won the Cold War? Ridiculous," *New York Times*, October 28, 1992; Strobe Talbott, "Rethinking the Red Menace," *Time*, January 1, 1990; Raymond Garthoff, "Why Did the Cold War Arise, and Why Did It End?" *Diplomatic History* 16, no. 2 (Spring 1992): 127–129.

5. Statement by Henry Kissinger, video commemoration of Ronald Reagan, Republican National Convention, San Diego, 1996.

6. Lou Cannon, *President Reagan: The Role of a Lifetime* (New York: Simon & Schuster, 1991), p. 282.

7. "Sizing Up the Kremlin," *Washington Post*, February 1, 1981.

8. Mark Hertsgaard, *On Bended Knee: The Press and the Reagan Presidency* (New York: Farrar Straus & Giroux, 1988), p. 134.

9. Ronald Reagan, remarks at the Annual Convention of the National Association of Evangelicals, Orlando, Florida, March 8, 1983.

10. Václav Havel, "Words on Words," *New York Review of Books*, January 18, 1990, p. 58.

11. Anthony Lewis, "Onward Christian Soldiers," *New York Times*, March 10, 1983.

12. Anthony Lewis, "What Reagan Wrought," *New York Times*, June 21, 1984.

13. Barbara Tuchman, "The Alternative to Arms Control," *New York Times Magazine*, April 18, 1982.

14. Whittaker Chambers, statement before the House Un-American Activities Committee, August 3, 1948.

15. Jean-François Revel, *How Democracies Perish* (New York: HarperCollins, 1985); Jean-François Revel, "Can the Democracies Survive?" *Commentary* (June 1984): 27.

16. Ronald Reagan, *An American Life* (New York: Simon & Schuster, 1990), p. 267.

17. Ronald Reagan, speech to Eureka College commencement, Eureka, Illinois, May 9, 1982.

18. Ronald Reagan, speech to the British Parliament, London, June 8, 1982.

19. Ibid.

20. Vladimir Bukovsky, "The Peace Movement and the Soviet Union," *Commentary*, May 1982.

21. Jonathan Schell, *The Fate of the Earth* (New York: Alfred Knopf, 1982).

22. Carl Sagan and Richard Turco, *A Path Where No Man Thought: Nuclear Winter and the End of the Arms Race* (New York: Random House, 1990); Russell Seitz, "In from the Cold: Nuclear Winter Melts Down," *The National Interest*, Fall 1986.

23. Douglas Hand, "An Antinuclear Crusader Confronts the Ultimate Medical Issue," *Life* (June 1982): 21.

24. McGeorge Bundy, George Kennan, Robert McNamara, and Gerard Smith, "Nuclear Weapons and the Atlantic Alliance," *Foreign Affairs* (Spring 1982).

25. Fox Butterfield, "Anatomy of a Protest," *New York Times*, July 11, 1982.

26. Ronald Reagan, address to the nation, March 23, 1983.

27. Alexander Haig, *Caveat: Realism, Reagan and Foreign Policy* (New York: Macmillan 1984), p. 222.

28. Strobe Talbott, "Playing for the Future," *Time,* April 18, 1983; see also Strobe Talbott, *Deadly Gambits* (New York: Alfred Knopf, 1984).

29. Haig, *Caveat,* p. 229.

30. Jay Winik, *On the Brink* (New York: Simon & Schuster, 1996), p. 203.

31. Steven Weisman, "Reagan Calls Nuclear Freeze Dangerous," *New York Times,* April 1, 1983, p. A8.

32. Reagan, *An American Life,* p. 566.

33. *New York Times,* September 3, 1983.

Chapter 7: Making the World Safe for Democracy

1. Jeane Kirkpatrick, "Dictatorships and Double Standards," *Commentary* (November 1979); Jeane Kirkpatrick, *Dictatorships and Double Standards* (New York: Simon & Schuster, 1982), pp. 32, 134.

2. See, e.g., Hodding Carter, *The Reagan Years* (New York: George Braziller, 1988), pp. 7, 85; Ronnie Dugger, *On Reagan: The Man and His Presidency* (New York: McGraw-Hill, 1983), p. 374.

3. Ronald Reagan, speech to the Irish Parliament, Dublin, June 4, 1984.

4. Ronald Reagan, State of the Union address, February 6, 1985.

5. Carl Bernstein, "The Holy Alliance," *Time,* February 24, 1992.

6. Haynes Johnson, *Sleepwalking Through History: America in the Reagan Years* (New York: Norton, 1991), p. 472.

7. *New York Times,* October 30, 1983.

8. Ronald Reagan, remarks to troops at Camp Liberty Bell, South Korea, November 13, 1983.

9. Jane Mayer and Doyle McManus, *Landslide: The Unmaking of the President, 1984–1988* (Boston: Houghton Mifflin, 1988), pp. 67–68.

10. Paul Seabury and Walter McDougall, eds., *The Grenada Papers* (San Francisco: Institute for Contemporary Studies Press, 1984).

11. Lou Cannon, *President Reagan: The Role of a Lifetime* (New York: Simon & Schuster, 1991), p. 448.

12. Shirley Christian, *Nicaragua: Revolution in the Family* (New York: Random House, 1985).

13. Ronald Reagan, Remarks to the Captive Nations Week Conference, Los Angeles, July 15, 1991.

14. Abraham Lincoln, speech on the Mexican-American War, January 12, 1848.

15. Ronald Reagan, televised address to the nation on Central America, May 9, 1984.

16. John Barry, *The Ambition and the Power* (New York: Penguin, 1990), pp. 500–503; Edwin Meese, *With Reagan* (Washington, D.C.: Regnery, 1992), pp. 238–240.

17. Paul Hollander, *Political Pilgrims* (Lanham, Md.: University Press of America, 1990).

18. Adam Wolfson, "The Good, the Bad and the Ugly," *Policy Review,* Summer 1985, p. 64.

19. Claudia Dreifus, "Daniel Ortega: Playboy Interview," *Playboy* (September 1983).

20. Paul Hollander, "Political Tourism in Cuba and Nicaragua," *Society* (May–June 1986): 37.

21. Peter Rodman, *More Precious Than Peace: The Cold War and the Struggle for the Third World* (New York: Charles Scribner, 1994), p. 415.

22. Dinesh D'Souza, "Missionaries Without a Mission," *Chief Executive* (May 1990): 8.

23. Ronald Reagan, speech to the British Parliament, June 8, 1982.

24. Ronald Reagan, *An American Life* (New York: Simon & Schuster, 1990), pp. 363–365; George Shultz, *Turmoil and Triumph: My Years as Secretary of State* (New York: Scribner's Sons, 1993), pp. 634–636; Larry Speakes, *Speaking Out: The Reagan Presidency from Inside the White House* (New York: Charles Scribner, 1988), p. 209.

25. Cited by Thomas Carothers, *In the Name of Democracy: U.S. Policy Toward Latin America in the Reagan Years* (Berkeley: University of California Press, 1991), p. 156.

26. Samuel Huntington, *The Third Wave: Democratization in the Late Twentieth Century* (Norman: University of Oklahoma Press, 1991), pp. 22–25.

27. Ibid., pp. 21, 25.

28. Daniel Patrick Moynihan, "The American Experiment," *Public Interest* (Fall 1975): 6–7.

29. Cited by John Morton Blum, *The Progressive Presidents* (New York: Norton, 1980), p. 94.

Chapter 8: And the Wall Came Tumbling Down

1. "Defrosting the Old Order," *New Perspectives Quarterly* (Winter 1996): 18; see also Margaret Thatcher, *The Downing Street Years* (New York: HarperCollins, 1993), p. 463.

2. Alexander Bessmertnykh, "A Retrospective on the End of the Cold War," remarks at Princeton University conference, February 23, 1993; see also Peter Schweizer, *Victory* (New York: Atlantic Monthly Press, 1994), p. xi.

3. Peter Hannaford, *Recollections of Reagan* (New York: William Morrow, 1997), pp. 168–170.

4. Martin Anderson, *Revolution* (New York: Harcourt Brace Jovanovich, 1988), pp. 80–83.

5. William Broad, *Teller's War* (New York: Simon & Schuster, 1992), pp. 122–125; Lou Cannon, *President Reagan: The Role of a Lifetime* (New York: Simon & Schuster, 1991), p. 327.

6. George Shultz, *Turmoil and Triumph: My Years as Secretary of State* (New York: Charles Scribner, 1993), p. 250.

7. Charles Mohr, "Scientists Dubious over Missile Plan," *New York Times,* March 25, 1983.

8. Strobe Talbott, "The Case Against Star Wars Weapons," *Time,* May 7, 1984.

9. *New York Times,* March 27, 1983.

10. Michael Mandelbaum and Strobe Talbott, *Reagan and Gorbachev* (New York: Vintage Books, 1987), p. 136.

11. Union of Concerned Scientists, *The Fallacy of Star Wars* (New York: Vintage Books, 1984), pp. 5, 175.

12. Ronald Reagan, Second Inaugural Address, January 21, 1985; Ronald Reagan, address to the nation, March 23, 1983.

13. Anatoly Dobrynin, *In Confidence* (New York: Times Books, 1995), p. 528.

14. *Izvestiya,* October 17, 1986.

15. Andrei Gromyko, *Memoirs* (Garden City, N.Y.: Doubleday, 1989), p. 307.

16. Strobe Talbott, "Grand Compromise: SDI Could End the Arms Control Stalemate," *Time,* June 23, 1986.

17. Cited by Schweizer, *Victory,* p. 198.

18. "An Interview with Gorbachev," *Time,* September 9, 1985.

19. Mikhail Gorbachev, *Perestroika: New Thinking for Our Country and the World* (New York: Harper & Row, 1987), pp. 10, 25, 72, 128; Mandelbaum and Talbott, *Reagan and Gorbachev,* p. 75; Robert Kaiser, "Gorbachev: Triumph and Failure," *Foreign Affairs* (Spring 1991): 163.

20. Mary McGrory, "A Smashing Performance," *Washington Post,* December 8, 1988.

21. Gail Sheehy, *The Man Who Changed the World: The Lives of Mikhail S. Gorbachev* (New York: HarperCollins, 1990), pp. 162, 180.

22. "The Gorbachev Touch," *Time,* January 1, 1990.

23. Zbigniew Brzezinski, "The Cold War and Its Aftermath," *Foreign Affairs* (Fall 1992): 46.

24. Don Oberdorfer, *The Turn: From the Cold War to a New Era* (New York: Poseidon Press, 1991), p. 23.

25. Charles Krauthammer, "The Week Washington Lost Its Head," *New Republic,* January 4–11, 1988, p. 19.

26. William F. Buckley, Jr., "So Long, Evil Empire," *National Review,* July 8, 1988.

27. George Will, "How Reagan Changed America," *Newsweek,* January 9, 1989.

28. Winston Churchill, *Thoughts and Adventures* (London, 1932), p. 39.

29. Ronald Reagan, *An American Life* (New York: Simon & Schuster, 1990), p. 639.

30. Mandelbaum and Talbott, *Reagan and Gorbachev,* p. 44.

31. Tip O'Neill with William Novak, *Man of the House* (New York: Random House, 1987), p. 295.

32. Oberdorfer, *The Turn,* pp. 258–259.

33. Reagan, *An American Life,* pp. 14–15, 637.

34. Lou Cannon, "Reagan-Gorbachev Summit Talks Collapse as Deadlock on SDI Wipes Out Other Gains," *Washington Post,* October 13, 1986, p. A1.

35. "Sunk by Star Wars," *Time,* October 20, 1986.

36. Lou Cannon, *President Reagan: The Role of a Lifetime* (New York: Simon & Schuster, 1991), p. 770.

37. Tom Bethell, "Ducks and Bees," *American Spectator* (February 1985): 11.

38. Hedrick Smith, "The Right Against Reagan," *New York Times,* January 17, 1988.

39. Peter Robinson, "Tearing Down That Wall," *Weekly Standard,* June 23, 1997, p. 10.

40. Oberdorfer, *The Turn,* p. 355.

41. Ibid., p. 431.

42. Peter Rodman, *More Precious Than Peace: The Cold War and the Struggle for the Third World* (New York: Charles Scribner, 1994), p. 290.

43. Henry Kissinger, *Diplomacy* (New York: Simon & Schuster, 1994), p. 764.

44. Cited by Richard Ned Lebow and Janice Gross Stein, "Reagan and the Russians," *Atlantic Monthly* (February 1994): 35.

Chapter 9: The Man Behind the Mask

1. Michael Deaver with Mickey Herskowitz, *Behind the Scenes* (New York: William Morrow, 1987), p. 143.

2. Frederick Ryan, ed., *Ronald Reagan: The Great Communicator* (San Francisco: HarperCollins, 1995), p. 96.

3. Jane Mayer and Doyle McManus, *Landslide: The Unmaking of the President, 1984–1988* (Boston: Houghton Mifflin, 1988), p. 26. Similarly Michael Schaller includes "an afternoon nap" as part of Reagan's daily schedule. Michael Schaller, *Reckoning with Reagan: America and Its President in the 1980s* (New York: Oxford University Press, 1992), p. 57.

4. Larry Speakes, *Speaking Out: The Reagan Presidency from Inside the White House* (New York: Charles Scribner, 1988), p. 115.

5. Donald Regan, *For the Record* (New York: Harcourt Brace Jovanovich, 1988), p. 272.

6. Deaver with Herskowitz, *Behind the Scenes,* pp. 101–102.

7. Laurence Barrett, *Gambling with History: Ronald Reagan in the White House* (Garden City, N.Y.: Doubleday, 1983), p. 124.

8. David Shribman, "Plan to Bolster Social Security Gains in Senate," *New York Times,* March 23, 1983.

9. Cited by Gerald Gardner, *All the Presidents' Wits* (New York: William Morrow, 1986), p. 33.

10. Caspar Weinberger, *Fighting for Peace: Seven Critical Years in the Pentagon* (New York: Warner Books, 1990), p. 33.

11. Ronnie Dugger, *On Reagan: The Man and His Presidency* (New York: McGraw-Hill, 1983), p. 264.

12. Ibid.

13. Ronald Reagan, *Abortion and the Conscience of the Nation* (Nashville, Tenn.: Thomas Nelson, 1984).

14. Julie Johnson, "Reagan Vows to Continue Battle on Abortion," *New York Times,* January 14, 1989; "Reagan Says Ending Abortion Will Mean U.S. Is 'Civilized,'" *New York Times,* January 16, 1989.

15. Lou Cannon, *President Reagan: The Role of a Lifetime* (New York: Simon & Schuster, 1991), pp. 288–289.

16. Helene Von Damm, *Sincerely, Ronald Reagan* (New York: Berkley Books, 1980), p. 89.

17. Ronald Reagan, *An American Life* (New York: Simon & Schuster, 1990), p. 352.

18. Marlin Fitzwater, *Call the Briefing!* (New York: Times Books, 1995), p. 151.

19. Geoffrey Smith, *Reagan and Thatcher* (New York: W. W. Norton, 1991), pp. 26, 245.

20. Speakes, *Speaking Out,* p. 104.

21. Helene Von Damm, *At Reagan's Side* (Garden City, N.Y.: Doubleday, 1989).

22. This incident is recounted by Peggy Noonan in a lecture on the character of Ronald Reagan. Robert Wilson, ed., *Character Above All: Ten Presidents from FDR to George Bush* (New York: Simon & Schuster, 1995), pp. 219–221.

23. Nancy Reagan with William Novak, *My Turn: The Memoirs of Nancy Reagan* (New York: Random House, 1989), p. 108.

24. Lou Cannon, *Reagan* (New York: G. P. Putnam's Sons, 1982), p. 406.

25. Ed Rollins with Tom DeFrank, *Bare Knuckles and Back Rooms: My Life in American Politics* (New York: Broadway Books, 1996), p. 96.

26. Reagan, *An American Life,* p. 131.

27. Regan, *For the Record,* p. 9.

28. Cannon, *President Reagan,* p. 173.

29. William Bennett, *The De-Valuing of America: The Fight for Our Culture and Our Children* (New York: Summit Books, 1992), p. 246.

30. Reagan, *An American Life,* p. 123.

31. Patti Davis, *The Way I See It: An Autobiography* (New York: G. P. Putnam, 1992), p. 271.

32. Cited by Doug McClelland, *Hollywood on Ronald Reagan* (Winchester, Mass.: Faber and Faber, 1983), p. 184.

33. George Shultz, *Turmoil and Triumph: My Years as Secretary of State* (New York: Charles Scribner, 1993), p. 484.

34. Jane Mayer and Doyle McManus, *Landslide: The Unmaking of the President, 1984–1988* (Boston: Houghton Mifflin, 1988), p. 366.

35. Rollins with DeFrank, *Bare Knuckles and Back Rooms,* p. 97.

36. Michael Reagan, *On the Outside Looking In* (New York: Zebra Books, 1988), p. 60.

37. Davis, *The Way I See It,* pp. 130, 136, 205.

38. Maureen Reagan, *First Father, First Daughter* (Boston: Little, Brown, 1989), p. 42.

39. Reagan, *On the Outside Looking In,* p. 105.

40. Ibid., pp. 122–123.

41. Davis, *The Way I See It,* p. 203.

42. Reagan, *On the Outside Looking In,* pp. 157–158.

Chapter 10: Spirit of a Leader

1. "Mitterand and Duras on Reagan's America," *Harper's,* August 1986, p. 12.

2. William Berman, *America's Right Turn: From Nixon to Bush* (Baltimore: Johns Hopkins University Press, 1994), p. 143.

3. Ronald Reagan, Remarks to the United States Negotiating Team for the Nuclear and Space Arms Negotiations with the Soviet Union, March 8, 1985.

4. Pete Hamill, "The Looking Glass War," *Village Voice,* April 29, 1986.

5. Alexander Cockburn, "Reagan Tosses Aside Reason in His Bullying of Libya," *Wall Street Journal,* April 17, 1986.

6. Lou Cannon, *President Reagan: The Role of a Lifetime* (New York: Simon & Schuster, 1991), p. 654.

7. Ronald Reagan, Remarks at Bergen-Belsen, May 6, 1985.

8. Remarks of President Reagan to Regional Editors, White House, April 18, 1985; interview by Representatives of Foreign Radio and Television, White House, April 29, 1985.

9. Ronald Reagan, Remarks at Bitburg Air Force Base, May 5, 1985.

10. Sidney Blumenthal, *Our Long National Daydream: A Political Pageant of the Reagan Era* (New York: Harper & Row, 1988), p. 8.

11. For a published account, see Robert Denton, *The Primetime Presidency of Ronald Reagan* (New York: Praeger, 1988), p. 70.

12. Sam Donaldson, *Hold On, Mr. President!* (New York: Random House, 1987), p. 114.

13. Colin Powell with Joseph Persico, *My American Journey* (New York: Random House, 1995), p. 298.

14. Alexander Haig, *Caveat: Realism, Reagan and Foreign Policy* (New York: Macmillan, 1984), p. 85.

15. Ann Reilly Dowd, "What Managers Can Learn from President Reagan," *Fortune,* September 15, 1986.

16. James Baker with Thomas DeFrank, *The Politics of Diplomacy: Revolution, War and Peace* (New York: G. P. Putnam's Sons, 1995), p. 26.

17. Max Kampelman, *Entering New Worlds: The Memoirs of a Private Man in Public Life* (New York: HarperCollins, 1991), p. 339.

18. Powell with Persico, *My American Journey,* p. 304.

19. Martin Anderson, *Revolution* (New York: Harcourt Brace Jovanovich, 1988), p. 295.

20. Lawrence Walsh, *Firewall: The Iran-Contra Conspiracy and Cover Up* (New York: Norton, 1997).

21. Marlin Fitzwater, *Call the Briefing!* (New York: Times Books, 1995), pp. 116–117.

22. Michael Kinsley, *Curse of the Giant Muffins* (New York: Summit Books, 1987), p. 90.

23. Fred Barnes, "The End," *New Republic,* December 22, 1986, p. 10.

24. Richard Reeves, *The Reagan Detour* (New York: Simon & Schuster, 1985), p. 10.

25. Ronald Reagan, *An American Life* (New York: Simon & Schuster, 1990), p. 247.

26. Kenneth Thompson, ed., *Leadership in the Reagan Presidency* (Lanham, Md.: University Press of America, 1993), pp. 90–91.

27. David Gergen, "Ronald Reagan's Most Important Legacy," *U.S. News & World Report,* January 9, 1989, p. 28.

28. Halford Ryan, ed., *U.S. Presidents as Orators* (Westport, Conn.: Greenwood Press, 1995), pp. 330–331.

29. Ronald Reagan, Farewell Address to the Nation, January 11, 1989.

30. Cannon, *President Reagan,* p. 484.

31. Frank Freidel, *Franklin D. Roosevelt: A Rendezvous with Destiny* (Boston: Little, Brown, 1990), p. 207.

32. Paul Allen Beck, "Incomplete Realignment," in Charles Jones, ed., *The Reagan Legacy: Promise and Performance* (Chatham, N.J.: Chatham House, 1988), p. 168.

Index

PUYALLUP PUBLIC LIBRARY